To Louise
with all the best wishes
Monika
5/3/2014 Durham

OCCUPY MANAGEMENT!

It can be said that our times are characterized both by the omnipresence of organizations and by the destabilization of organized social life, caused by the erosion of its structural and moral foundations such as long-term employment, social trust or an actual observance of the proclaimed codes of ethics. At the same time there is huge and growing potential for organized change due to the amount of students and graduates of different types of management studies and programmes all over the world.

The role of the state may become atrophied and corporations seem all too eager to seize ever more power while renouncing responsibility towards the environment and the employees, but a huge and unprecedented number of people from all walks of life, all social classes and all countries now have the qualifications to take over the responsibility for social organizations.

The objective of *Occupy Management!: Inspirations and ideas for self-organization and self-management* is to make it evident to the student why and how he or she can manage without becoming part of corporate power structures. Aimed at postgraduate students studying organizational and management theory as well as social entrepreneurship, this book is not a simple repetition of essential knowledge in these areas, but a redirection of such knowledge towards self-management and self-organization.

Monika Kostera is Professor Ordinaria and Chair in Management at the University of Warsaw. She is the author, co-author and editor of 31 books in Polish and English; and of numerous scientific articles. Her current research interests include organizational archetypes, self-management and organizational ethnography.

OCCUPY MANAGEMENT!

Inspirations and ideas for self-organization and self-management

Monika Kostera

Routledge
Taylor & Francis Group

LONDON AND NEW YORK

First published 2014
by Routledge
2 Park Square, Milton Park, Abingdon, Oxon OX14 4RN

and by Routledge
711 Third Avenue, New York, NY 10017

Routledge is an imprint of the Taylor & Francis Group, an informa business

© 2014 Monika Kostera

The right of Monika Kostera to be identified as author of this work has been asserted by her in accordance with sections 77 and 78 of the Copyright, Designs and Patents Act 1988.

Trademark notice: Product or corporate names may be trademarks or registered trademarks, and are used only for identification and explanation without intent to infringe.

Every effort has been made to contact copyright holders for their permission to reprint material in this book. The publishers would be grateful to hear from any copyright holder who is not here acknowledged and will undertake to rectify any errors or omissions in future editions of this book.

British Library Cataloguing in Publication Data
A catalogue record for this book is available from the British Library

Library of Congress Cataloging in Publication Data
Kostera, Monika
Occupy management! : inspirations and ideas for self-organization and self-management / Monika Kostera.
   pages cm
   Includes bibliographical references and index.
   1. Management. 2. Organizational sociology. 3. Organizational behavior. I. Title.
   HD31.K625 2014
   658–dc23
                                                  2013028649

ISBN: 978-0-415-70305-5 (hbk)
ISBN: 978-0-203-79503-3 (ebk)

Typeset in Bembo
by Wearset Ltd, Boldon, Tyne and Wear

Printed and bound in Great Britain by
TJ International Ltd, Padstow, Cornwall

To the memory of my grandfather Jan Stolarczyk (1913–1982), skilled grinder, ardent reader and thinker, and beautiful human being, who lived a life of compassion and freedom, even under the difficult circumstances provided by the times he lived in.

CONTENTS

ACKNOWLEDGEMENTS

I would like to thank my friends and colleagues who have in many ways helped and inspired me to write this book. First and foremost, I am infinitely grateful to Piotr Korzeniecki and Jadwiga Dziekan-Michalik, who encouraged me to break the genre barrier. Roman Batko deserves a special acknowledgement for his support, friendship and intellectual courage, which gave me the confidence to try my steps on this new and not very familiar path. Inga Grześczak was an inexhaustible source of knowledge for the historical fragments. I would not have been able to find my way around the classics without her. I am also grateful to the anonymous reviewers who gave me really helpful advice, which I have used extensively. A special thanks for reading and commenting on fragments of the manuscript are directed to: Roman Batko, Zygmunt Bauman, Barbara Czarniawska, Jerzy Kociatkiewicz, Mateusz Janiszewski, Linda Williamson and Michał Zawadzki. Finally and especially, thank you Jerzy Kociatkiewicz, my husband, for everything.

IMAGE ACKNOWLEDGEMENTS

All images by Monika Kostera except:
Image A (p. v), by family friend/workmate;
Images N (p. 186) and O (p. 204), by Jerzy Kociatkiewicz.

INTRODUCTION

'The social affections', says the economist, 'are accidental and disturbing elements in human nature; but avarice and the desire of progress are constant elements. Let us eliminate the inconstants, and, considering the human being as a merely covetous machine, examine by what laws of labour, purchase, and sale, the greatest accumulative result is obtainable. Those laws once determined, it will be for each individual afterwards to introduce as much of the disturbing affectionate elements as he chooses, and to determine for himself the result of the new conditions supposed.' ...

> Observe, I neither impugn nor doubt the conclusion of science if its terms are
> accepted. I am simply uninterested in them, as I should be in a science of
> gymnastics which assumed that men had no skeletons.
>
> *(Ruskin, 2012, pp. 2–3)*

The era we have just left behind us, one which Zygmunt Bauman (2000) calls solid
modernity, and which those of us who are over 40 years old still remember quite
well, was all about faith. My generation grew up to believe in many things, and
most of all – the future. The future we believed in would turn out well for the
whole of humanity, and, hopefully, for each of us, because of three fundamental
ideas: technological progress, democracy and science. When I was little, I watched
the first landing on the Moon on TV. I was allowed to stay up unusually late, as
were most of my friends from kindergarten. Small wonder: this was indeed 'one
small step for man, one giant leap for mankind', something our parents knew we
would remember for the rest of our lives. We all played astronauts, of course, and
we believed we would spend our summer holidays of the future on the Moon,
jumping around, just like Neil Armstrong, dressed in cosmically cool suits.

That particular dream did not come true, but so many other incredible things
became possible: travelling by air is now accessible to almost everyone in the
developed countries; the once so expensive flight between Warsaw and London
can now be bought cheaper than the same trip by train – which, by the way, is in
itself another wonder. It has become possible to travel by railways all the way from
Warsaw to London, including the bit under the Channel. We move around more
than ever before, not always to our greatest satisfaction: it is now expected of many
of us to be 'mobile', to be ready to displace ourselves without making a fuss; a
meeting in Norwich one day, a lecture in Helsinki another ... I know many families living and working in different cities, even in different countries, not because
they want to be separated, but because it is possible, and – thus – taken for granted
by employers.

Other means of communication have also become fantastically easy and fast; the
internet especially has altered our lives so irrevocably that people born in the 1980s
and later are often unable to imagine a life without it. Neither can I, even though
I have lived in an internet-less world for quite a part of my life, depending for
information and communication on physical movement, telephones, the wired sort
and the post office services. Just think how brilliant the net is! Such stuff as science
fiction is made of: it has made it possible for so many to access culture and information; to instantly exchange messages, for free; for some of us, to get a social life.
Once I had to carry dozens of books in my suitcase, making my back less than
happy, every time I went abroad. With my country suffering from a lack of relevant
literature in my discipline, I became my own librarian. Since the rise of the internet
era, with on-line bookshops and antiquarians, I do not need to punish my spine any
longer. Neither do I have to spend long hours waiting in queues at the post office.
All I need for my work is accessible from my home; well, almost; of course my

empirical work and most of the teaching still demands physical movement and actual face to face conversations. Less contact-dependent matters can be arranged over the phone, and, to use it, I do not need to sit in a dusty corner of the room any longer; since the spread of the mobile telephony throughout the world people can talk when and where they choose. Which they do.

I am not so sure if that particular instance of technological progress pleases me too much; I think the world was a better place without the necessity of listening in to others' private conversations in all areas of public space. When I was little a person who was talking aloud in the street was, clearly, mentally ill. Nowadays she is probably negotiating a sound business deal with a partner, perhaps shouting out his replies in a train carriage to Chelmsford.

Apart from the internet and mobile there are so many more things which many of us cannot do without or would consider their absences to make our lives more restricted: first, Walkmans, then increasingly miniaturized mp3-players, and nowadays, even more convenient combined carriers, such as iPhones and tablets. And computers, of course, which have grown smaller and more powerful: my current laptop, bought over five years ago, has a hard drive capacity 150 times larger than that of my computer from 1993, and I am not a technophile. Neither now nor then did I possess the best or the largest of the thinking machines. I can lift as many as 40 of my old hard drives with the small finger of my hand, because that is more or less the capacity of my microSD card. Cars have not grown much faster, as we thought they would when I was a teen-ager, but they have become somewhat safer and cleaner. Not everyone has a private jet in the garage, but many people have enormous flat screen TVs in their living rooms. Yes, our faith in technological progress has delivered results.

We also believed in democracy. This was particularly true of the Western countries. In Sweden, where I went to secondary school, most museums and many history lessons were based on the simple but beautiful moral: once people were poor and oppressed, now the conditions have improved for many; in the future they will get better for even more people. More and more countries will become democratic, because democracy is so much better, and it is, therefore, an irresistible force. It cannot be stopped.

People in the oppressed countries, like my own country of origin, Poland, then located behind the so called Iron Curtain, and forced into a system without fully free elections, and with censorship and limitations to human rights, often took to the streets to protest and chose to suffer many hardships for the sake of democracy. In developed countries people demonstrated to acquire even more rights and to curtail all kinds of injustice and repression. It was just a matter of time until equality became the obvious choice for all of humankind.

To a degree, this dream came true, even if just for a short while. In 1989, miraculously, the Berlin Wall fell, free elections were held in countries throughout the former Eastern Bloc, people acquired many freedoms and rights such as freedom of faith, political views and movement. We could now travel without the lengthy and complicated formalities necessary under the old system – and even the inhabit-ants of countries such as Romania where it was much more difficult to get a passport than in Poland could now venture out into the world. We were looking forward to the abolishment of visas and restrictions which an imminent admittance to the EU would bring. But many soon realized that some of the old rights have been irrevocably lost, such as the right to life-long free education, the right to work...

The current global disillusionment with politics and the massive loss of public engagement is often seen as a failure of, or at least people's loss of faith in, democracy.[1] As I write these words extreme parties acquire surprisingly large shares of the votes in old democracies, people who are perceived as unserious or even present themselves as such gain seats in the parliament; many voters declare that they will not vote at all, or vote 'none of the above'; voices of distrust and contempt for politicians fill the media throughout Europe, the Americas, Australia ... And even though some of the old dictatorships have fallen, new ones arise. It seems we are not approaching the democratic Shangri-La after all.

Finally, we believed in science. It would save us from all evil, answer all of our reasonable questions and solve all of our problems, including the problems we ourselves, the human race, are causing. Science was the only reliable and rational faith, and soon religion would become obsolete and forgotten. When I attended the eighth grade of elementary school in Poland, my lovely teacher of Polish, Ms Jadwiga Dziekan-Michalik, asked us to write an essay: *The year 2000 and myself.* This was a wonderful topic! Most pupils came up with bright futures for themselves: astronaut, writer, film director, but, most of all, we all imagined the future to be happy and constructive, all thanks to science.

First of all, there would be no illnesses. There would be an easy and accessible cure for cancer, of course. And no one would die of hunger; poverty would be history. We would travel in time, back and forth; instead of learning history from books, schoolchildren would make field trips backwards. All conflicts would be resolved scientifically by computers, making wars a barbaric archaism. As for myself, I believed everyone would be a writer, actor or painter, as everything else would pretty much run itself and robots would perform all the tough work.

Well, science did, since, deliver quite a few interesting and life enhancing propositions, such as new fascinating theories of the Big Bang and even of what came before, a better knowledge of how the ecosystem works and promising research in medicine, such as stem-cells, but we have come nowhere near the visions contained in those essays. We know more about the world but we still do not know how to fix it. Now as then, we turn to religion for the big questions, science having by far not been able to replace it in that role. And sadly, both science and technology are having their vast share in causing pollution, impoverishment and maybe even imminent destruction of the planet.

Solid modernity had, apart from its faith and at times reckless optimism, a huge and dramatic shadow side. It was an era when brutal and deadly dictatorships were born and for many years thrived, such as Nazism and Stalinism. People were incarcerated, tortured and murdered if they showed dissent or were suspected of it by the dictator's paranoid and intrusive intelligence services. Millions of people lost their lives in two catastrophic world wars, and, in the second, most of the victims were completely vulnerable civilians, just because they were of the 'wrong' nationality, as defined by the Nazis. Zygmunt Bauman (1991) has described, in his *Modernity and the Holocaust*, the systemic nature of this modern mass murder: it was made possible and effective due to the way society was organized and managed. Solid modernity developed the technologies, as well as a management culture, which turned 'just following orders' into a viable replacement for moral judgement, turning people, who would perhaps otherwise have been peaceful clerks, into mass murderers, on an unprecedented scale. It was the core aspects of solid modernity that constituted this sinister shadow. As Burkard Sievers (2000) persuasively demonstrated, the war mentality was far from limited to the actual wars, it pervaded organizations during times of peace, management sharing many of its symbolic roots with the army, and being based on an ideal of competition and aggression.

That shadow side and the constant threat it posed made many people rather pleased to see solid modernity go. However, the new era, which Zygmunt Bauman (2000) called liquid modernity, also has its – not insignificant – problems. We have lost some of the things which have for centuries been an important part of the human condition. First of all, we have forsaken the future. As Bauman (ibid.) argued, our times are characterized by increasingly high uncertainty, constant, ever accelerating change and a dissipation of stable structures, making relationships fluid, unstable and insecure. Long-term commitments such as life-long partnerships and permanent employment have ceased to be the norm and instead become oddities, choices made by certain individuals who for one reason or another do not mind taking unreasonable risks. How can a person take upon him- or herself a long-term obligation, when social trust has become an empty slogan, and not even sufficiently popular to be of much use in the ever inflatable rhetoric of contemporary politics? Alienation has become the core of contemporary life; solidarity and cooperation becoming redundant and increasingly unlikely. Strong and stable bonds between people which would diminish the impermanence that underpins all contemporary organizations and relationships are not encouraged. The impermanence is essential, not transient, as many people still seem to believe, because it supports one of the fundamental dogmas of the dominant neo-liberal creed – that of individual choice. Individuals are thought of as completely free agents following the demands and the flows of the Market, wherever the most rational path takes them. Getting rooted, committed to another or to anything, is not profitable as it causes resistance, it slows us down, makes our choices not fully rational, our responses to the economic forces not sufficiently instantaneous.

Second, we have relinquished the past. Richard Sennett (1998) showed how this is due to a loss of balance, caused by the dogma of so called flexibility. This word is nowadays used in a way very much unlike its original meaning, which implied a temporary change of shape and return to the original form. Currently no return is expected or desired; change is ever present and occurs in a strange temporal continuum, made up of a never ending series of 'presents'. Core identities, shapes and structures are thrown, together with stability, into the wastebasket of what is impossible, unprofitable, plainly wrong. Without history, organizations become amoebas, devoid of shape and identity. All sense of responsibility vanishes: corporations keep the power, but 'outsource' responsibility to faceless forces such as 'the market', or 'the team'. It does not mean that organizations have become structure-less – there is a structure in place, only it has become opaque and dim. It makes it hard to protest against the system, which has grown amorphous and abstract, resembling more a figment of imagination than anything concrete and real. At the same time people are urged to 'think positively'; negative ideas can be seen as symptoms of an individual's, not the system's, weakness; indeed, of his or her mental ill health. Without a past there are no visible structures to act upon. Also, there are no obligations: the current state cannot be compared to any state's precedent. Even the managers have no sense of lasting obligation toward their organizations (Sennett, 2006).

Finally, we have renounced mystery. Instead, we have become hyper-rational. George Ritzer (1996) has portrayed contemporary society as subjected to a process he calls McDonaldization, which through efficiency, quantification, predictability and control aims to turn all of society's activities and forms into a fully rational system, modelled on the fast food chain. Everything is managed in the name of efficiency: people, space, time, things; management colonizes all aspects of human life and continues to take over new domains. Quantification and financialization are now imperatives, regardless of whether they are useful or not, if they indeed make sense or not; all aspects of human activity are subject to measurement and counting (Martin, 2002). People are using the language of finance to account for things that would have been unthinkable to connect with such a language only 30 years ago: the desire to have children, the choice of an education, the wish to take care of one's elderly parents. Predictability is achieved through ever more perfect standardization. Abstract and impersonal standards, such as best practices and routines, define how everything should be done (Ritzer, 1996). Control makes the activities even more impersonal; it is carried out by and built into technology, devoid of professional or moral judgement. All aspects of such organizations are seen as resources: things, people and knowledge. The hyper-rational organization is like a totalitarian state: smooth and self-referring, but monstrous (Ritzer, 1996). Everything not fitting into its shape is relegated into non-existence, in particular all that cannot be accounted for on these terms is regarded as irrational and therefore prohibited (Denhardt, 1981). Mystery has been abolished.

This situation causes enormous human suffering, a loss of sense of meaning, solidarity, closeness, perhaps even humanity itself (Bauman, 2000; Sennett, 2006). At the same time, the system does not even deliver what it promises: instead of rationality and economic growth it produces growing social problems, global poverty, increasing injustice (Bauman, 2011) and worsening economic crises (Chang, 2008). The system, even though apparently monolithic and lacking an alternative, seems to be intrinsically flawed. It does not create new solutions, only further and more insolvable problems, produced in search of a way out of the former ones. These are compelling signs of the system having lost its ability to regenerate itself; *autopoiesis* (Maturana and Varela, 1980) goes on an automatic pilot, and therefore no changes occur, even such that the system's survival depends on. Regarded in the terms of a dynamic living system, as Kenneth Boulding (1981) depicted complex social organization, it does not seem to be alive, rather, it appears dead. This state of things Zygmunt Bauman (2012) called, after Antonio Gramsci, times of *interregnum*. The term originally meant an era in between monarchs: after the death of one sovereign, yet before the enthronement of a new one. Applied to contemporary society, it refers to a situation like the one I have just sketched: the phase in between operational systems that would be able to offer political, economic and cultural frames for human civilization to function and develop in a sustainable relationship with the planetary ecosystem.

> Times of interregnum are ... times of uncertainty, and while raising many questions, three of them seem particularly pertinent to address at a time when rulers no longer *can* rule and the ruled no longer *wish* to be ruled: institutional disparity, the future of migrants and the endurability of the planet.
>
> *(Bauman, 2012, p. 51)*

Institutional disparity refers to the divorce between power and politics and the consequent disempowerment of the nation state. Power has been removed from the level of the institutions of state and turned global, whereas politics has remained local, and unable to influence what is really going on. Important issues are increasingly handled by powers beyond political control, such as corporations, banks and global NGOs.

Migration is another key issue of contemporary times: while capital is allowed to flow increasingly freely across borders, human migration, so much needed from a planetary point of view, is strongly restricted. Instead, labour is outsourced to places where it is cheap, thus enhancing injustice and inequality, and causing problems both in the poor countries, home of the sweatshops, and in the wealthy, suffering from unemployment. At the same time, the population of the developed parts of the world is ageing and diminishing. Finally, the planet itself is being put at serious risk by the current dynamics of human civilization. Apart from the alarming pollution, there are also questions of the growing social tensions triggered by the increasing inequality between the rich and the poor (Bauman, 2012).

These problematic areas are growing with no sustainable cure in sight; what is proposed in its stead, or rather, dressed as a way towards a cure, is management and entrepreneurship. People are proposed to engage in 'social entrepreneurship' as a solution to the political problems (Dees, 2001); the unemployed are recommended to become entrepreneurs to create jobs and save the region (Singer, 1999); ecopreneurship and sustainable management are said to provide a way out of the ecosystemic imbalance (Bennett, 1991). Management and its language have infiltrated every aspect of human life, and the popularity of management education of various kinds seems to be constantly beating its own records.

When I was first admitted to a kind of management education, a joint programme with the Department of Education at the University of Lund in the early 1980s, it was still considered something of a niche educational project, aimed at those who would work as managers and administrators, perhaps because they were to inherit a business, or were in some other way dedicated to a career strictly within public administration or industrial management. I ended up as a student of this programme by complete accident; it would never have occurred to me, as to most of my classmates and friends, to elect such a path of studies. Indeed, these were the times when young people dreamed of studying the humanities, maybe sociology or psychology, perhaps technical subjects. Consequently, our entire group consisted of no more than 30 people.

Some years afterwards I became a student of management at the University of Warsaw, again by coincidence rather than by any conscious choice on my side, and the entire number of students, including daytime and evening ones, did not surpass a thousand. Nowadays, several of my colleagues teach individual courses with a thousand students registered. The numbers of people studying management have grown exponentially since I first became in touch with the subject. Today millions of people attend some kind of management education each year just in the United States, and the participants come from all walks of life and professions, from business managers and entrepreneurs, through to nurses, teachers, journalists, to artists and clerics (Hatch *et al.*, 2005). The percentages are similar all over the globe, in all developed and most developing countries.

This poses, in itself, a problem, because of the intrusion and colonization: management has become a – dubious – part of the human condition; as well as because of the massification of education, mainly, albeit not exclusively, connected to the management programmes. It is impossible to even dream of a teacher–student relationship based on trust and mutual respect in classes of several hundred usually completely anonymous people. Students, who once used to be the driving force of all social change, on the first lines whenever and wherever there were demonstrations, social movements, revolts, now constitute a passive and rather bewildered crowd, burdened with a future of possible and even likely unemployment and huge debts that successfully put a dulling curb on even the most idealistic youthful enthusiasm.[2] Not all even enjoy studying very much; they come to attend university courses because they were led to believe that they have otherwise only themselves to blame for the prospective lack of employment. Academics, from having been the conscience of the societies, courageously pioneering causes of human rights, democracy and equality, exercising their academic freedoms to serve higher social causes, have turned into rational and cautious managers, considering their fragile and highly fluid careers and insecure conditions of work and life before making any pronouncements beyond the strict area of their technical competence. Life is managed, management is life.

However, at the same time there is a huge and growing potential for organized change due to this gigantic amount of staff, students and graduates of different types of management studies and programmes all over the world. The role of the state may have become atrophied and corporations are all too eager to seize ever more power while renouncing responsibility towards the environment and the employees, but a huge and unprecedented number of very different people, from all social classes and countries, now have the qualifications to take over the responsibility for social organizations and push them towards the global level, to collectively retrieve the power that has accrued there.[3] Such people: social and ethical activists, cooperative organizers, employees and other ordinary people are more and more often educated in management and organization. Self-management and self-organization are, in fact, already a growing phenomenon, quite naturally offering a viable alternative to the inhumane and corrupted shape that work has taken in the modern world (Sennett, 2012). It is starting to become a massive global movement, worldwide in its scope. What we need at this point for global self-management to materialize are, I believe, three things: imagination, courage and a revision of the knowledge we already possess with this specific goal in mind. This text proposes to be used in the last function, for readers equipped with the two former capabilities.

This book is an advanced academic (postgraduate) textbook, aimed at students with existing knowledge of management and organization theory, or to be used for purposes of self-study, preferably in collective settings such as study circles and book collectives. It is not a simple repetition of essential knowledge in these areas, but offers a synthesis written with a specific aim in mind – namely, a redirection of such knowledge towards self-management and self-organization. The fundamental blocks that the book is based on are familiar perhaps worldwide to all graduates of basic management courses and much of what it says is a reference to that already acquired knowledge. However, the managerialist and corporationist ideology is absent from this text and, instead, the objective is to make it evident to the student why and how he or she can manage without becoming part of corporate power structures. The project this book invites the reader to undertake is based upon finding new, workable solutions to an old problem that has refused resolution before. In other words, the book proposes to recycle and reclaim already existing knowledge in ways that may work for novel purposes.

The introductory chapter outlines the context of the book, why and how to read it for the purposes of self-management and self-organization. Thinking in terms of the global ecosystem and the ecology of management (inspired by Bateson, 1972) is the fundamental worldview that this book is based on. Not pretending to be objective or unbiased, the book is instead unabashedly political both in aim and in contents. However, it does not support a mainstream or traditional political stance, rather, it encourages the reader to work together with others to change the world, using not violence but insight, imagination and practical action. The book contains resources for the recycling and reclaiming of ideas and models from a standard management education. With the corporate ideology removed, these ideas and models are presented here with explicit intention to be used in self-management and self-organization.

The new era needs a reflection on the state of the world, what modernity has given us and what it has deprived us of. The thrust of social activity during the whole modern era, including its liquid stage, was directed at the pursuing of comfort and wellbeing, conceived of in material terms. Managers managed for the rest of us – and received excellent financial compensation for their efforts. In solid modernity, these efforts often brought perceptible results; nowadays, the results are more often than not seen as disappointing by popular and specialist commentators alike, but the financial gains of managers are as great (if not greater) than before. In the future, self-managing organizations, cooperatives and other non-corporate endeavours we will engage in, will not be based on the same logic or propelled by the same kind of forces. What hired managers did for huge financial rewards, we will now have to do 'for free'. Not financial, but other kinds of gain will have to become the driving force of society. Perhaps it is time to return to the reflections of John Ruskin (2012) who proposed a broader view of profit and worth, not limited to finance, but including such values as happiness, inspiration, creativity, good work, etc. Such is, broadly, the contents of this book: not financial organizational values, but much broader ones, transposed onto the discourse on organizational realities from classical philosophy, from the humanities and from everyday life.

The book's aim of recycling known ideas, not through repetition but as a basis for new insights, drives its structure, presented here but described in more detail further on, in the introduction. The book is organized in four main parts, based on the classical management functions proposed by Henri Fayol (1949): planning, organizing, motivating and controlling. These parts are broken down into three chapters each, taking up some key aspects of the function, selected from a broad tradition of reflection around the main theme. In other words, the functions are considered as broader humanistic archetypes.

The key aspects associated with them are considered for their use not just in organization studies but in a much broader tradition derived from the humanities. For example, planning, in accordance with such a tradition, is linked to the following three key abilities: imagination, intuition and inspiration. I have been striving to create an appellative structure of the text based on indeterminacy, of the kind that Wolfgang Iser (1970) calls for: multilayered, leaving many empty spaces for the reader to fill with his or her reading, engaging the reader to experience and explore. The language and concepts I am using belong to the area of the humanities, not strictly associated with the discourse of management, which, especially in the last decades, relied on a terminology not directly related to the sphere of human experience. My intention is, on the one hand, to return to the language of the early authors, which I regard as much more vibrant and suitable for the aims I have in mind with this book, and, on the other, to reconnect the discourses of management and the humanities – a link without which there is, in my opinion, no sustainable future for the former (Kostera, 2012). The method that served me to select and order topics for this book is borrowed from Inga Grześczak's (2012) notion of textual nomadism, which she derived from Johan Huizinga's ideas of intellectual wandering.

> Every letter of the alphabet is a point of departure, from which we can start out in any direction and wander wherever our feet and eyes take us. It is impossible to ever exhaust all the possibilities of travel, but, indeed, it does not matter at all. What gives pleasure is the wandering itself.
>
> (Grześczak, 2012, p. 7)

The text offers points of departure for such an exploration of ideas, with the structure serving as an inspiring pretext to undertake such an endeavour, opening up – not closing down, the field of inquiry. Instead of alphabetic order I have opted for the classical four functions divided in three aspects each, presented in the form of alliterations. This is my homage to traditional management writing, where such alliterations are the main poetic device. The subchapters contain theoretical musings, as well as examples, from empirical organizations, as well as from art and fiction. Each chapter ends with questions to reflect on, which can serve as further possible departure points.

The book is, then, nothing more than a guide in a well known terrain, but showing it from a side that perhaps has been previously hidden from view. We all know the terms, the models, the theories. What I propose are some new interesting ideas about how to use them, coming from authors and thinkers, as well as glimpses of inspiration from art and life, not directly linked to these ideas but allowing to see beyond the more obvious layers of culture and practice, to peek into the entirely novel, original areas of own creative activity that is fully the reader's to make happen. The stories I am telling, the images, sounds and tastes I present, are not illustrations or case studies helping to learn the theory, like in most management textbooks, but doors into the imaginative space which is for the reader to explore and to use.

Let us manage ourselves out of the crisis – we all know how to do it – it is time to reclaim our knowledge, not in the interest of corporations, banks, the few rich of the world, but on our own terms, in ways that would, at last, put an end to the sterile and inhibited era of systemic interregnum and pave a way into a ecologically, economically and humanely sustainable future.

Occupy management!

Notes

1

> Our 'interregnum' is marked by a dismantling and discrediting of the institutions that used to service the processes of forming and integrating public visions, programmes and projects. Having been subjected to processes of thorough deregulation, fragmentation and privatization, together with The Rest of the social fabric of human cohabitation, such institutions remain stripped of a large trustworthiness, with only a vague chance of recovering them.
>
> *(Bauman and Donskis, 2013, p. 82)*

2

> Students who acquire large debts putting themselves through school are unlikely to think about changing society. When you trap people in a system of debt, they can't afford the time to think. Tuition fee increases are a disciplinary technique, and, by the time students graduate, they are not only loaded with debt, but have also internalized the disciplinarian culture.
>
> *(Chomsky, 2011)*

3 Even if the boom for business education has been but a bubble, about to burst, it has brought an endurable learning. It failed to deliver what it promised: skills, jobs and a guaranteed 'return on investment' in education for the students; it gave them the one thing that university education actually does – knowledge.

PART I
Planning

Introducing the 3 I's: imagination, inspiration and intuition

The management function traditionally known as planning means, in non-mainstream settings, having a sustainable and original vision of the endeavour. *What is to be done?* The idea or project needs to be novel, interesting, engaging for its inventor and important for other people and the environment. In order to be able to come up with such an idea, three fundamental faculties are needed: imagination, inspiration and intuition.

- *Imagination* helps to open the mind and to create.
- *Inspiration* is necessary to access higher mind function and feelings.
- *Intuition* makes it possible to come into contact with various aspects of the environment.

1

IMAGINATION

Under the tree
a shadow-map
He said: the cross
marks the treasure[1]

Imagination is the capacity to connect existing elements into something new, that has not yet been conceived. It is an activity that involves the whole person: whereas much of it is undertaken by the mind, also the feelings, the soul and the body are involved, although not always to the same extent. For example, spatial imagination, or the ability to think creatively in terms of space, involves principally the mind and the body, but it may also engage the soul, as does James Turrell's art (see Chapter 5, Section 3), and feelings, for example feelings of liberation and elation as many designers of bridges affirm. Imagination actively works in an imaginative space, one outside of the physical or socially constructed spaces in which people spend most of their adult lives. It may engage with the intersubjective spaces, by using non-sensory elements taken from them. It may also lead to the creation of a representation of the imagined in the intersubjective spaces, in the form of a work of art, an invention, text, music, product, design, choreography, etc. Imaginative thinking may also result in the discovery of new elements or characteristics within the intersubjective spaces, by a radical re-interpretation of them, leading to a new view of how they work, or by the lifting out of certain of their aspects and reconnecting them in imaginative space and realizing some hitherto unknown qualities or patterns. Imagination does not rely primarily on sensory experience, although it often may refer to it. For example, imaginative dancing can be an imaginative activity, undertaken foremost by the embodied aspect of the person; the body creates images that are non-visual and the movements and kinetics may then follow these images. This can of course include mental and emotional activity, and that of the soul, if the dance is providing inspiration (see Chapter 2). Such imaginative dancing, as any creative activity, may take place in the imaginative space only; it does not have to be realized within the intersubjective spaces. Similarly, imagining how it would feel to be in another person's shoes is mainly based on emotions but does not relate directly to any of the surroundings of the one who is imagining it. However, it may lead to compassion and the acting on it, for example, by helping that person or joining her in her everyday work. Imagining may be spontaneous, as in dreaming, or intentional, as in the performance of a storyteller in front of an audience. It can be lucid, when the person knows that he or she is imagining, or unaware, when the boundaries between the imagined and intersubjective spaces are blurred, for example in a state of ecstasy or intoxication. It can also be both at the same time, as in play, or roleplaying games,[2] when the subjects purposefully act on the imagined sphere in the intersubjective ones, and intentionally blur the boundaries between them, but only during the play or the game.

Imagination lifts out the person from the sensory context, the intersubjective spaces, and into a different if often not unrelated one, thus offering another perspective on or insight in matters of life, be it great or small. So Vincent Van Gogh was able to see that the stars were not all white, Albert Einstein could realize that time is relative, and the craftsman knows how to make the surface of the frying pan completely smooth and resilient at the same time. Imaginative activity is an experience, as much as sensory activity can be, but it is less obviously straightforward to share. In order to become that, it has to be transferred into elements of the intersubjective spaces, realized by the creation of sensory representations.

Imagination is, perhaps, the force that drives humanity to reach out for more than is currently the realistic path to take.

1.1 A short history of imagination

Aristotle[3] (1987) thinks of imagination as a definite ability, that makes it possible for the mind to create images, which, to him, include dreams, visual thought and memory. Imagination creates images where there is no perception and thus can sometimes be false. It is to him a capacity common for humans and some animals, an inherent part of every thinking process. However, not all thinkers appreciate the role of imagination. Notably, Plato[4] (2007) believes it is a faculty of a lower order, as it refers to what is not true: shadows and reflections. Jean Jacques Rousseau[5] (2007) does not have a high regard of it, either, although for different reasons:

> The world of reality has its bounds, the world of imagination is boundless; as we cannot enlarge the one, let us restrict the other; for all the sufferings which really make us miserable arise from the difference between the real and the imaginary.
>
> *(p. 43)*

Immanuel Kant[6] (2008) is slightly more positive and considers it

> a blind but indispensable function of the soul, without which we should have no cognition whatever, but of the working of which we are seldom even conscious.
>
> *(p. 78)*

Imagination, according to Kant, is an unrefined but necessary quality of the mind that enables connecting reproduced experiences into a whole, as well as linking ways of understanding and perception into schemes and based on that drawing conclusions and making generalizations. Adam Smith[7] is even more optimistic about the role of imagination – according to him, imagination is what makes the philosopher capable of seeing connections between things seemingly mundane; in other words, it is what makes a philosopher.

The thinker who perhaps most famously celebrates the role of imagination is Albert Einstein:[8]

> [I]magination ... is more important than knowledge. Knowledge is limited. Imagination encircles the world.
>
> *(Einstein, 1929, as quoted in Taylor, 2002)*

In an interview with the poet and journalist George Sylvester Viereck the great scientist explains that imagination and inspiration indeed play a crucial role in his work – it oftentimes happened that he did not know something but intuited the direction for thinking and exploring it. He also sees in himself an artistic soul, enabling him to draw on imagination (Taylor, 2002).

1.2 Reflection 1

Imagination enlightens, empowers and makes it possible to make sense. C. Wright Mills (1959) coined the term 'sociological imagination', a vital faculty that enables the individual to raise above his or her social reality. It makes everyday life cease to seem obvious and the only possible way that things can be. Thanks to it, the person acquires the capacity to see the connections between what is individual and what is historic. For most people, everyday experiences do not teach how to solve problems of a broader systemic nature, that surpass the world of the human being and his or her closest others such as family, friends and workplace colleagues. Sociological imagination makes it possible to take that step and learn; to link one's own life stories with the place one occupies in society and history. Thanks to it we can view our life situation from a distance, perhaps not to take things as personally as usually, perhaps to brave what we thought of as solid frontiers defining what is possible to achieve. It is so because social facts are rooted in systems and social structures rather than in the individual. Usually they indeed are out of reach for the human being and form the fabric of fate. However, if seen from a perspective offered by imagination, they turn out to be parts of a broader context that can be influenced when regarded that way. In that sense, imagination is, then, what links individuals and groups, societies, it is the stuff that collective experience is made of – the kind of experience that makes it possible to influence what is normally unreachable, to cross boundaries. It also helps to see the difference between what is collective and what is individual and to focus attention on the one or the other dimension. It gives us the experience of moral sense and thus can serve as a kind of internal compass, even in a world where everything changes perpetually, where people are unable to navigate according to their values, a world that from Mills' times has accelerated even more and accelerates still, reaching the state that Bauman (2000) labels *liquid*. Sociological imagination is, then, an ability that has vital individual, cultural, sociological and political consequences.

This is also true about the way we conceive of the world of organizing and organizations. Andrzej Koźmiński (1982) proposes a notion similar to Mills' sociological imagination which he calls economic imagination. It refers to the dimension of business and enables people to transcend the apparent economic impossibilities – something he witnessed in Poland, then stricken with a severe systemic crisis, in the final decade before the fall of the Berlin Wall. After the martial law was introduced in the country by General Jaruzelski in December 1981, its enterprises were taken over by new management, quite often with a military background and all the former attempts at modernizing and liberalizing the economy were overturned (see, e.g. Kelemen and Kostera, 2002). Nonetheless, even without much in the way of resources, and often having to operate in the grey sphere of the economy, Polish entrepreneurs from that era managed to make a living. This remarkable ability to make something out of nothing did strike Koźmiński as something beyond standard management technique. Similarly, I (Kostera, 1996) present the idea of organizational imagination as one crucial for the understanding of the decade of early East

European transformation. Many people were able to transcend the boundaries of their everyday organizational lives and regard the structures they were part of from a perspective. Thanks to this a sudden carnival of organizational creativity took place in Poland during that time, which alas soon became limited by the constraints of the new rapidly crystallizing system. Raza Mir and Ali Mir (2002) depict organizational imagination as linking theory and practice – a feature of socially engaged science. The crossing of boundaries does not only apply to an intellectual activity consisting of distancing oneself from the studied situation but also to the blurring of the boundaries between theory and practice itself. According to the authors, organizational imagination is a state of mind enabling the organizational participants, researchers and consultants to envisage organizations as controllable.

Gareth Morgan (1993) believes that imagination enables people to deal with organizational change. Without it, people are bound to repeat the same routines and mistakes regardless of the problems that accrue. According to Karl Weick (2001) imagination is crucial for everyday sense-making in organizations, which is a key step within the process of organizing itself; organizing is a process continuously structured by sense-making. No imagination, then – no organization. Gibson Burrell (1997) can think of instances of such a lack within organizations, however, it is then an instance of linearity, mentally dead organizations. Linearity kills, as he repeatedly points out in his book, *Pandemonium.* Zygmunt Bauman (2011) shares the opinion that something dies when imagination is absent – the current moral deficit is due to a deficit of imagination. Without it, the human being can only look for technical solutions; there is no place for the crossing of one's world and opening up for the consequences that the solutions may have for others. Without imagination, Bauman says, there is no empathy.

A failure of organizational imagination can also have catastrophic consequences. Karl Weick (2005) gives the examples of the failure of imagination described in the 9/11 Commission Report and the Columbia Accident Investigation Board. A great deal of these disasters was in fact due to an inability of the responsible organizations to engage in real processes of imagination. Instead, many contemporary organizations prefer to rely on acts of fancy, or a kind of linear thinking, consisting of the reconfiguring of remembered experience. Imagination is something else altogether – it is the ability to create something completely novel, beyond linear sequencing.

> [P]rimary imagination is about the formation of meaningful images that are associable, then secondary imagination is about an associating principle that reorders, fuses, and moves these associables around, which enables them 'to form around and encrust any new object or experience with which they have an affinity.... From an internal fund, ideas and feelings rush to surround any object that presents itself to the mind' (ibid., 201). 'Surround' is a key word in this description because it signifies that the associating principles involve more than simply assembling discrete episodes, steps, and objects. Secondary imagination gathers experiences and images into 'more comprehensive schemata' (ibid., 14). The products of secondary imagination are like original

> paintings whose images have no visible joints or seams and no suggestion that they were assembled from multiple constituent parts. Such seams are, however, visible in the products of fancy.
>
> *(Weick, 2005, p. 428)*

When people engage in acts of fancy, they produce associations of adjacency, or sets of formerly existing elements put together into a new whole, such as the image of Pegasus – a winged horse. Imagination is based on compound associations of simultaneity, in other words, 'imagination gives form to unknown things' (Weick, 2006, p. 447). While fancy only modifies, imagination shapes and modifies. It works with wholes rather than assembles and associates elements with each other. Another interesting fact about imagination is that the ideas that arise from it grow exponentially. The power of imagination is actively self-renewing itself – the more of it there is, the more it is used.

I have proposed a method for the exploration of the imaginative space (Kostera, 2006), which another author, an alternative management consultant, turned into a consulting tool (Nilson, 2009). It consists in the collection of fictive stories created by the interlocutors. The researcher asks the interviewees to compose stories on a given subject or to finish a story that begins with a sentence provided by the researcher. The authors themselves decide how the story is going to develop. The researcher collects and puts together the stories, interprets them, and seeks to find what they reveal about the cultural context of organizing. The consulting version aims at preparing a map of an organization's creative potential. The process of collecting material is just like the narrative collage as research method, but Henrietta Nilson developed the method to include music and art. The stories, pieces of music and drawings can inspire each other and build upon each other, showing the organized aspects of the imaginative space. The principles for narrative collage differ depending on the situation. The process always begins with interviewees creating stories and ends with several layers of textual reading and analysis, or, in the case of consulting, mapping an organization's imagination.

1.3 Sounds, images, dreams

When I first heard Led Zeppelin's *Kashmir* (1975) at my friend Basia's place, my soul woke up. It did that somewhat prematurely, I was just 12, but it is indeed as Rumi says, when you hear music, the soul shivers with recognition; times and places unknown to the eyes of the body suddenly come back to life. This is what happened to me then; as if with a sudden start, I found myself right there, in Basia's rather chaotic room, with its sweetish smell, her dog performing the doggy twist in front of me, and the warm September sun flowing in through the window, open wide toward a green inner yard. I remember it all so clearly as if an alarm clock had gone off and I had opened my eyes, immediately wide awake with a photographic gaze. 'I am a traveller of both time and space', Robert Plant sings, and the listener is indeed moved towards memories he or she was not aware of having, outside of the area of rational experience, and in some original, unreachable inner spaces that can perhaps only be reached by the power of imagination. There are echoes of an ancient past, dating back to the times when the *Upanishads* were told for the first time, a direct connection between now and then is forged and the listener looks right into it, as if they were his or her childhood memories, only darker, more diffuse and more tawny in colour. The song plays on tones that invoke such impossible images, by the slowly interweaving haunting riff of the guitar, tuned in an alternative way, associated with Eastern music, and the vocal themes; by the elemental rhythms of the percussion, and the musical threads sometimes as if out of sync, as at times the instruments are using different rhythmic patterns. It all sounds as if they were interlocking, pausing and changing places. The vocal is prayer like, slightly plaintive and it, too, reminds of Eastern singing styles. When the song begins to fade out, the calling out to the listener becomes more distinct: 'let me take you there'. I did not understand the words, as I was not used to listening to songs in English then, nor, indeed to any rock songs at all, I just learned that the title of this piece was *Kashmir*, which I knew was somewhere in India. I started to study English more intensively in order to understand this, and other, songs, but it was not until much later that I learned that none of the group's members had actually been to Kashmir at the time that the song was recorded. They, as much as I, addressed a space beyond their immediate reality. In Robert Plant's own words it was

> an amazing piece of music to write to, and an incredible challenge for me. Because of the time signature, the whole deal of the song is ... not grandiose, but powerful. It required some kind of epithet, or abstract lyrical setting about the whole idea of life being an adventure and being a series of illuminated moments. But everything is not what you see. It was quite a task, because I couldn't sing it. It was like the song was bigger than me.
>
> *(Open Culture, 2013)*

Goodbye, See You Tomorrow (Morgenstern, 1960) is the debut of the renowned Polish film director, Janusz Morgenstern, one of the precursors of the so called Polish cinema of moral unrest, a philosophically orientated genre. It tells the story of a student, Jacek, who confesses that his motto in life is: 'dream as a driving force'. At a rehearsal of his amateur student theatre troupe, he meets and falls in love with Marguerite, the daughter of a French diplomat. She lives elsewhere and is only visiting Poland for the holidays, but she knows some basic Polish. She loves theatre, just as he does, and this common passion immediately brings them together. They take off for an imaginative journey of the post war city of Gdańsk. Jacek recognizes her as the personification of his dream and starts dreaming up a whole world for her, one which they can share, touching everything that surrounds them with a theatrical magic. He speaks to her in long dramatic cadences, invoking rhythms and images, and even though she does not understand most of what he is saying, she seems to hear it, anyway. She is not an audience but another theatre, speaking through silence; and soon enough, she gets to love him, too. They walk around, they ride a horse carriage, run along the windy Baltic beach, hide from the rain at a bus stop, and together they create a better time, a better place, where there has been no war and where they will not have to part. The streets and the houses, areas ravaged by the war and turned into ruins, all turns into a peaceful yet dramatic stage; an inner beauty of the city is revealed through Jacek's and Marguerite's imaginative presence. Two scenes in particular focus the whole narrative around them. In one, the shadows of the protagonists, displayed on the wall of a building, appear to be animated all by themselves, independently of their owners, as if performing their own theatrical play. In the second one, Jacek, immersed in darkness, uses two lit cigarettes as puppets in a miniature performance. The film is a tale of an inner journey of two people and a city, unlimited and endless, even though in real time it only lasts a few hours. When night falls Jacek pronounces the eponymous 'Goodbye, see you tomorrow', even though they both know that she is going away and he will not be able to see her. But they do not run away together, maybe because they lack the courage, or maybe because they by now want to believe that their world is there to stay. When Jacek comes back to her house the next morning, she is gone, together with her family; only the things remain, carried out into the yard by a stranger, possibly someone employed for the removal. Jacek keeps looking for her among the anonymous objects, he looks lost, out of place among the solid, expensive looking items that speak of the transience and precariousness of life. And yet the viewer realizes that something has, indeed, changed; the protagonists have succeeded in altering reality, imagined something into being. The film itself, most certainly, is such a something. It is based on a real story, as written down by Zbyszek Cybulski, the actor playing the role of Jacek, who never ceased to hope that his dreamy tomorrow, one day, would come.

1.4 Reflection 2

Management of organizations is a process that depends on imagination. Gareth Morgan (1993) believes that imagination is the only ability that enables people to manage in rapidly changing environments. It is something we all as humans have, but it needs to be cared for, developed and cherished. He proposes ways to train imagination such as mind games or brainstorms. The challenge is, however, to learn to be creative and imaginative together with other people. Karl Weick (1998) suggests that jazz improvisation is a good way of thinking of how collective imagination in action works. People engaged in processes of organizing and managing also need to use an active imagination, constantly analyse what themselves and others are doing, and make decisions – not a priori, as the normative textbooks would have it, but while they are immersed in the process. Quite often this happens based on how they feel about one or the other course of action, and not because of a rational analysis they have made of the situation. A real managerial talent is about such non-linear, simultaneous imaginative action, just like with jazz musicians. They may try many motifs but only one proves to be a success, and both this process of trials and the successful find are part and parcel of good jazz music – and good managerial work. The latter also needs to embrace learning and here, once again, imagination is irreplaceable. Karl Weick (2002) speaks of the need for a disciplined imagination, working in a non-linear and complex way, for the development of learning process in organizations. This process cannot be programmed or be solely dependent on rational thinking, and it embraces remembering, forgetting, asking questions, pursuing values, collecting facts and setting goals. Imagination helps to maintain a dynamics that makes it possible for knowledge to accrue – and for managerial wisdom to emerge. Rather than a linear growth of 'things known', it gives shape to visions and entices to embark on paths to seek and explore new ideas. Old dogmas are forsaken and abandoned; the seeker travels light.

Another important point for the seeker-manager is to understand that imagination and rationality both belong in managerial work (Kociatkiewicz and Kostera, 2012a). Together with a co-author I use the fictional character of the famous Victorian detective, Sherlock Holmes, to demonstrate the importance of a non-linear rationality in managerial work. Normative textbooks present management processes, and especially decision making, in a highly reductionist fashion. If the world were shaped like that, managers would spend their working days calculating, comparing and editing graphs. However, the empirically based literature we have studied shows that managers, even if they usually try to be as rational as possible, do not work in a linear way. Their rationality is more complex and has an extra dimension, just like the rationality of Sherlock Holmes – imagination. Holmes plays the violin, he enjoys music, he jumps to conclusions based on limited or improbable material, he has an ability to put together facts and ideas that would not occur to someone else. Such an extended rationality is usually necessary in a manager's work as well. It enables decisions to be made while keeping a sense of the changing environment and, generally, staying in touch with ideas and people. Imagination can be, first and foremost, used for invention and innovation. Imaginative thinking may help to deal with change in constructive ways while at the same time help the social actors to experience their work and environment as meaningful (Magala, 2009). It is important to think in non-linear ways in managerial work, especially when facing complex or mutable situations (Butler, 2010). The method called lateral thinking relies on an ability to disregard from experience, one's assumptions about how the world works, a courage to ask questions, even if they seem 'strange', and especially a creative mindset, the ability to be imaginative. In addition to these characteristics, lateral thinking includes rational logic and reasoning. A talented manager knows how to rely on all of them, letting them work in synergy.

So, all in all, imagination is vital and very valuable indeed, and it can be used as a perfectly renewable resource in management and entrepreneurship, connecting available ideas that have been around at least since antiquity with novel impulses and forms (Kostera, 2012).

However, imagination has also a dark side. Management can use it for selfish purposes, harmful for others. It can employ a morbid and unempathic kind of imagination, focused on greed and personal success, that gives birth to crime and abuse. Some organizations seem to be very imaginative indeed; however, they lack a conscience that would hold them back from engaging in reckless and destructive activities. These organizations resemble psychopaths in their lack of empathy (Boddy, 2011). In recent years, there have been many examples of dramatic collapses of enterprises, resulting in massive losses of employment and damage to whole regions and their infrastructures, often revealing stories of colossal mismanagement and harmful activities that had been going on for years. However, in the wake of these events, the managers seem to be able to keep their heads cool and to use their imagination to try to explain away the facts, as if they were some kind of silly blaming game.

> They present themselves as glibly unbothered by the chaos around them, unconcerned about those who have lost their jobs, savings and investments, and lacking any regrets about what they have done. They cheerfully lie about their involvement in events, are very persuasive in blaming others for what has happened and have no doubts about their own continued worth and value. They are happy to walk away from the economic disaster that they have managed to bring about, with huge payoffs and with new roles advising governments how to prevent such economic disasters.
>
> *(Boddy, 2011, p. 1)*

Such people often make a good impression and are, especially in our times, often promoted to managerial positions, because they seem to embody all that is regarded as skilful management. This happens because they are masters of manipulation, while, at the same time, they lack empathy. Their impact on people and organizations is highly destructive, including several areas such as motivation, job satisfaction, conflict and bullying in the workplace and organizational results. They lack an emotional connection with other people and their imagination has reins unconstrained by any consideration of a moral or compassionate nature. Organizations nowadays seem to encourage such thinking, associating it with success and leadership skills (Babiak and Hare, 2006), creation of wealth (Boddy, 2010), or a spirit of entrepreneurship (Linsley and Shrives, 2009). Some companies use imaginative hypocrisy in order to avoid taxation while simultaneously they legitimize themselves via codes and ethical statements (Sikka, 2010). On the one hand, they spin talented and convincing tales of responsible conduct, and on the other, they engage in almost boundless displays of inventive accountancy practices, such as tax evasion. These two very different worlds are linked effortlessly in one very contemporary corporate talent – imaginative hypocrisy. Its dark power stems from a lack of consideration for the human side of organizing:

> Money and power seem to have developed their own logic and have become indifferent to human concerns about producing a just, equitable and open society.
>
> *(Sikka, 2010, p. 166)*

1.5 Stories from organizations

> Imagine a bunch of kids from kindergarten, each with one of those annoying
> drums that aunties and uncles insist on giving their little nephews and nieces
> for Christmas. So they sit there and make a hell of a racket. Now, imagine a
> new kid who comes in and says, hey, let's make a computer. And he makes
> them sit like this [he draws a circular shape on the blackboard], and tells each
> to tap their drum in a given sequence, like this [he adds numbers to the
> sketch]. And, there! We have a computer. It works![9]

I can easily imagine Wojtek as this new kid who comes to kindergarten and
makes the kids play something like this. Not a computer, though, they barely
existed when he was small. I have invited Wojtek as guest lecturer to teach my
students how computers work. The year is 1990 and the computer is for many still
a mystery machine; a hostile one (I recall one of my students of that time saying that
computers were like Fenrir, the big demonic wolf of Norse mythology who
devours the Sun on Ragnarök). Wojtek is a freelance consultant and he makes his
living helping organizations to set up their first IT systems; sometimes he is asked
to order equipment as well as put it all together; and sometimes, like in the case of
a large government institution, to 'perform a technology check'. Much to his
amusement, the latter turns out to be a collection of computers safely locked away
in a big safe. He tells me how he took them all out, made sure that they were in
working order, and was then asked to put them back in the closet again. After
having signed all the provided papers, he tried to explain that stuff sitting unused in
a closet hardly can be described as 'technology'. Things, yes, machines, maybe, but
technology is something that works together with people. The clerk looked at him
as if he were from another planet.

But he seems at home in the classroom. He is a spirited lecturer and the students
like him very much. They later tell me that they actually were able to understand
how computers work, thanks to him, they could imagine them as something they
knew already and build an own understanding on that. I ask Wojtek whether he
would consider working as a teacher.

'Nah', he says, 'not now, I'd like to work more with computers now, they
develop so fast, it's great fun.'

I ask him if that means working for a corporation. He shakes his head vehe-
mently, no, never, he would never be able to be owned, pretending to be somebody else, dressing in a suit. But he does not tell me, then, that he will start his own
firm. Perhaps he does not know yet. This happens five years later. Wojtek invites
several of his friends from the University of Warsaw, from mathematics and management, and they continue working together, creating one of the most groundbreaking organizations in Poland, IT Dragon, developing original and customized
IT solutions for business. Their motto is: 'sensibly, elegantly, creatively and reliably'
(IT Dragon, 2013). Their clients range from small firms to giant global corporations. The Dragons offer a variety of IT solutions, in most business areas, from

email to complicated financial services. They also provide consulting services, such as audit and maintenance of IT systems, systems analyses and various IT optimizations. Success is not an unusual story in Poland's transformation economy; I have encountered many stories of growth and fame. IT Dragon is different because it has preserved its original mood of imaginative freedom. Power dressed displays of status would be as out of place here as a UFO parked in the middle of the company's lawn, indeed, much more. On second thoughts, this is exactly where a UFO would land, one of those alien ships visiting the Earth in Szymon Rogiński's photos (2009; Chapter 3, Section 3). I pay the Dragons a visit one sunny autumn afternoon of 2004. The firm is located in a villa in one of Warsaw's green inner neighbourhoods, rather inconspicuous for an HQ of a well known company. But it is such a cosy place to work, the receptionist explains to me, as she leads me to the common kitchen. I sit there for a while and chat with three persons, two women and one man, who call themselves 'the cat people': they take care of some stray cats who come to get fed and cuddled by them every day. They tell me that the kitchen is a place where quite a few of the employees hang around to socialize, drink tea, play games.

'But if you want to see the most popular social space you have to go to the cellar, there's a ping pong table there, that's a really much loved place.'

Before I go to take a look at the table, I stroll around the office spaces, a mishmash of work stations and computers spread around two floors, each distinctly different, chaotic. There is a pervasive soft hum, in some places ascending to a rumble, like onboard a big ferry boat in motion across the Baltic sea. The whole place smells faintly of electricity, this must have been one of the things that enchanted Nicola Tesla so much. Or maybe it is the smell of heated metal and plastic fusing together in a robotic cooking extravaganza? I see people working in the most unlikely spaces, such as the mezzanine floor between staircases. An employee I ask later says that the occupant of that space insists on keeping it, as 'he likes to have a good view of things'. Some rooms are populated by people sitting by the computers. They do not seem to communicate with each other but some look up at me, smiling but not encouraging me to talk with them. I have been talking with some earlier; I wave and continue my tour – I have learned from my interlocutors how they abhor being disturbed when they think and I do not want to be one of these annoying disturbers. One of them, Paweł, explained to me that they need to concentrate very hard, especially when they work with something new. Often they do something else in the background, play computer games ('non-immersive ones'), listen to music (in fact, most of the people here wear headphones), even perhaps communicate via the computer. But the actual face to face exchange is what may break their concentration and they resent outsiders who do not understand or respect that. That is one of the reasons why many of the Dragons choose to come to work here, even if they could easily work from home; nobody checks on their attendance – as long as they do their job, everything is fine.

'That, and the ping pong room of course', Paweł adds.

So, to the ping pong room. It is, indeed, interesting, even if at that time, completely empty of people. It is dominated by a large table, surrounded by some free space. However, the space by the walls is all but empty: apart from some chairs and a sofa, it contains all sorts of things, such as cartons full of papers, computer parts, a pile of used looking tyres. Adjacent to this room there is an unremarkable looking door, without a plaque or any kind of sign saying that this is, in fact, the office of the President of the firm. I enter, after having knocked and heard a 'come in'. We shake hands: Wojtek looks just like he used to, dressed in jeans and a sweater. With a look of genuine joy on his face, he brushes off some papers from a chair and makes a sign for me to sit down. I do so and take in the room. Albert Einstein purportedly said that if a messy desk indicates a messy mind, then what, indeed, does an empty desk point to? This is not one of such desks. Not one of such rooms, either. The chaos of the space is happy, unabashed, uninhibited. The omnipresent piles of papers seem to be held in place only by some own mysterious gravity force; computer parts, arranged as if in a number of installations; books, caught in mid-flight, huddling together. In the corner there is a sink, complete with all the adherent plumbing.

'Does it work?', I wonder.

'Sure. This room was converted from a bathroom.'

There is no window but the room is bright enough, with artificial lighting reminding me of sci-fi movies from the 1970s. I think that this is art, all this is somehow art. The room reminds me of some rooms of painters and sculptors that I have seen, and envied, painfully; only the paint, the plaster, the chisels and easels are missing, and, instead, you get all these apparently mundane objects, taken separately so pristinely utilitarian and yet, assembled together, animated by something as mysterious as are these traditional tools of the imaginative trades.

> IT Dragon is a team of talent: it brings together people filled with a passion, dedication and competence to use the possibilities created by new technologies.
>
> *(IT Dragon, 2013)*

1.6 Questions to reflect on

1. Write a story beginning with the lines: *Happy New Year 2030! With the words still ringing in my ears, and somewhat tired after the party, I entered my office. It was still dark . . .*

2. Who did you want to become when you went to secondary school? Did you have dreams about your future occupation? How do they relate to what you actually are doing? Write down the dreams. Are you happy with how you are realizing them? Think about how they can be made to happen now, with what you have achieved, learned and with the resources you have. Write a plan.

3. Write a letter to yourself from the age of 16. Try to be as empathic as possible, do not preach or play the all-knowing adult. Tell your younger self the story of your life since you were 16 in a way that he or she would find the most engaging and interesting. Embellish when you feel like it, but do not lie.

4. Think of something you would really want to achieve, something global and big like world peace, or local and small, like a neighbourhood book cafe. Imagine an organization that would deal with such a goal. Describe it, prepare an action plan.

Notes

1 All the poems cited at the beginning of chapters come from Kostera (2013).
2

> Roleplaying games are an activity, related somewhat to theatre, in which a group of people (called the players) creates and roleplays characters in a world created by one other participant, called the Game Master, who describes the results of their actions and the actions of everything and everybody else in this created world. They are 'a peculiar kind of activity, a state of mind that totally absorbs the player's attention and transports him/her into the dimension of his/her own imagination. By leaving all the restrictions of the outside world behind s/he gains an ability to act in ways free from any restrictions, at least theoretically' (Jasiński and Kociatkiewicz, 1996). This, coupled with their social aspect, parallels the socially constructed reality (Berger and Luckmann, 1966/1983) that usually surrounds us.
>
> *(Kociatkiewicz, 2000, p. 71)*

3 384 BC–322 BC, Ancient Greece.
4 424/423 BC–348/347 BC, Ancient Greece.
5 1712–1778, Geneva and France.
6 1724–1804, Prussia.
7 1723–1790, Scotland.
8 1879–1955, Germany and USA.
9 Based on recollections, notes (field visit 2004), and the website of Wojtek's firm IT Dragon (not real name).

2

INSPIRATION

Ode to my Muse
Sing for me, Muse
I will follow you
I am following you
like love, like sleep
like a sudden gasp of nausea
I want to sit near you
up on a hill
In the plentiful garden
The wind shall pass through
but you are not in it

a fire shall burst through
but you are not in it
You are
shadow and ash
Speak to me;
not
with the breath,
the word,
not with avowal,
but with the waves,
the tightened embrace
just as we fall
– We are falling –
The spirit is sucked into
the lung
You, Muse,
right at the centre

Inspiration means touching the higher feelings and higher needs of a person. Perhaps it is so that inspiration connects us with some primeval aspect of ourselves and others, within a domain not conscious in ordinary states of mind but available during meditation, trance or lucid dreaming. Through inspiration we become beautiful, if beauty is the reflection of the life force within us. We can be inspired by other people or by encounters with art, architecture, nature, qualities of light and shadow, etc., and we can inspire others. In most religious traditions there is a belief that some people can be inspired by higher powers: by God, angels or saints. For example, one of the central ideas in Christianity is that the Bible was inspired by God; supernatural influence rendered the writing of human authors completely true and reliable. The scripture was received as a revelation; while most theologians would not claim that it was dictated to the humans word by word, they would propose that God had been guiding their thoughts and their hand to express what He had intended, more or less literally. Ancient cultures believed in a kind of divine inspiration of artists and visionaries; supernatural beings such as the Muses in Greek and Roman tradition supported their creative processes, although, usually, the effects of such creativity were seen as the fruit of the human beings' talent and work, and not considered to be divine as such, with the exception of oracles, such as Delphi, intuitively verbalizing prophecies and visions sent by Apollo (see Chapter 3, Section 1). In more recent times the faith in a divine source of inspiration of creativity is usually less common, instead, the artist is seen as someone with an ability to get in touch with higher faculties, get in the mood, through a state of grace, hard work, or both, and unlock the power to produce imaginative work. But inspiration is not only about art, it is also about the stimulation of a person to do good, act compassionately, be a better human being. It means the awakening of a desire to act on these aspects of the human psyche, to follow the impulses deriving from needs such as that of developing selfless relationships, of justice, or of creating something new and original, and reflecting ideas acquired from excursions into the imaginative space.

Some people have a gift to inspire others, to reach out to their higher selves and touch their creative and compassionate feelings in such a way that they become moved to act on them and realize them. People with this ability are often to be found in religious vocations, but not exclusively; they also work as pedagogues, social and political activists, socially engaged artists or journalists, etc. If they are to be regarded as genuinely inspirational, they must act in good faith, with a sincere intention to reach out to others' higher aspects and to selflessly help them in doing whatever is good and true for them. Otherwise, attempts at persuasion and mobilization of other people are rather to be seen as the establishing of power or manipulation. Inspiring others means to work selflessly for them and not to realize one's own aims through them.

There also exist dark inspirations, when people are compelled to use their higher faculties to act in ways that are harmful to others, for example when they use their faith in order to condemn others, when they are persuaded that a vice is indeed a virtue, or a triviality an aim worth living and dying for. These are examples of the misuse of higher and creative faculties, leading typically to a more or less permanent damage of such faculties: loss of faith, trust, sincerity, disillusionment with the world.

2.1 A short history of inspiration

According to ancient Greek mythology, inspiration was brought to humans from the sphere of the divine. The divinities in charge of it were, in particular, Apollo and the Muses. Hesiod[1] names the original nine daughters of Zeus – the Muses – in *Theogony* (1914a) and speaks of the gift they bestow on human beings:

> whomsoever of heaven-nourished princes the daughters of great Zeus honour, and behold him at his birth, they pour sweet dew upon his tongue, and from his lips flow gracious words.... And when he passes through a gathering, they greet him as a god with gentle reverence, and he is conspicuous amongst the assembled: such is the holy gift of the Muses to men. For it is through the Muses and far-shooting Apollo that there are singers and harpers upon the earth.

The inspired poet is able to rise above his sad and limited condition; he or she is a servant of the Muses, who are able to turn his or her attention away from the limitations and into the holy flow of artistic expression. Isidorus of Seville[2] (2006) contends that the Muses are named from a Greek word signifying 'seeking', because it was through them that the singer sought inspiration. He explains that the Muses, being daughters of Zeus and Mnemosyne, goddess of memory, demand that the products of inspiration are written down and memorized in some form, otherwise these works perish.

For romantic poets, such as Ralph Waldo Emerson[3] (2012) inspiration is a pure and divine force, it is 'God's wine' (p. 300). It can be shared and has the power to enlighten others:

> If the imagination intoxicates the poet, it is not inactive in other men. The
> metamorphosis excites in the beholder an emotion of joy. The use of symbols
> has a certain power of emancipation and exhilaration for all men.
>
> *(Emerson, 2012, p. 300)*

Inspiration as something both shared and individual is also embraced in the Jungian
idea of archetypes. Carl Gustav Jung[4] (1990) speaks of a collective unconscious, a
spiritual domain connecting all humanity. This space contains archetypes, empty
slots, ready to accommodate images, characters or plots important to culture and
individual development. Archetypes activate imagination, motivate and inspire;
they can be understood as pathways connecting human beings to something larger
than ourselves.

2.2 Reflection 1

I believe that archetypes, be they brought down to us by the Muses, or merely by
human cultures, hold an enormous power to inspire us, also when we manage and
organize (Kostera, 2012). I shall return to them later, but first I would like to show
how different ideas retrieved from culture, new and old, even if brought together
apparently arbitrarily, inspire to undertake a journey into experience and culture –
including the cultural context of organizing – a kind of intellectual wandering
which in itself brings joy and a taste of the detail which preserves the memory and
makes a whole new understanding or image emerge. For inspiration does not have
to be only grand ecstasy and peak experience. It can be a journey from symbol to
symbol, from detail to detail (Grześczak, 2012).

Neither is inspiration something uniquely reserved for poets and mystics. It can
be experienced by most people, in many creative and mundane workplaces. Mihály
Csíkszentmihályi (1990) describes a state of mind he calls flow, which makes a
person completely immerse him- or herself in what he or she is doing, and feel at
one with it. The state of flow means that one achieves complete focus on the
present moment, forgets about one's ego, or does not pay it the usual attention.
Instead one becomes highly aware of the task at hand – an almost meditative state,
accompanied by a strong sense of connection with what one is doing and feelings
of profound happiness. There is a deep contact between the actor and the act, a
oneness which make it possible to correct any mistakes the moment they appear.
Neither the ego, nor rules, standards or regulations get in the way. The necessary
conditions for this state of mind to occur are: intense concentration, sufficient and
adequate abilities and the possibility of exerting self-control. The last one will be
the subject of another chapter (Chapter 10), but the first two are closely linked to
the ability to receive inspiration. Concentration on the performed task and acute
awareness of the present moment are a precondition to achieve a state of simultaneous openness and control over the present moment. Actual abilities to perform the
task, such as sufficient sense of colour and technique for the painter, handiness and
competence to work with appropriate tools and materials for the carpenter, etc., are

necessary to connect with the rhythm of the performed task instead of on the mere technicalities. Too high or too developed abilities are not favourable for the state of flow, just as the lack of important abilities is – they should be perfectly matched with the difficulty and the nature of the task. Csíkszentmihályi observes that flow can both be an individual and a collective experience. An organization for collective flow is what the author calls good business (Csíkszentmihályi, 2003), whether it refers to an enterprise or a theatrical troupe. The doings of such a collective cannot be written down to a simple goal, such as profit, growth or market success. A 'good business' is about bringing happiness to people – the participants and workers, and the audiences, readers and clients. Joy can and should be shared, then it multiplies itself and becomes a transformative power. Businesses that only focus on money, gain and success are, regardless of the effects of their dealings, 'bad businesses'. Self-centred and greedy organizations, no matter how acclaimed and celebrated, are not sustainable, as much in the ecological as in the human sense. Resources are depleted, people burn out. However, a good business is based on a principle of inexhaustible energy generation, a kind of human *perpetuum mobile* – the more flow you produce, the more likely it is to reproduce itself and to be experienced by the user and client. It is true that a meal lovingly prepared is enjoyed by more consumers, the owners of Warsaw's VegeMiasto (Chapter 11, Section 5) proclaim. Bands playing in a club succeeded each other: a band technically skilled and focused on their self-image were replaced onstage by a band completely immersed in the music they were playing, a trio from Kraków calling themselves UDA (Chapter 2, Section 3). The audience immediately 'caught' their flow, even the people sitting and drinking at the bar, mostly clubbers presumably not having come for the concert at all. Happiness inspires happiness and Csíkszentmihályi (2003) emphasizes that it is the role of the manager to start this good circle. If there is someone among the employees who has a tendency to like his or her work, to experience flow, he or she should be promoted and cherished, as this employee is a tremendous resource: flow rubs off. He or she will share the state of working mind with others, if given any chance at all, and so it may become a collective experience.

Another idea for creating an inspiring work environment is Pierre Guillet de Monthoux's (2004) art firm. It is based on the assumption that organization and management are a kind of art. Art can inspire managers to look for new ideas for technologies, products and structures. It does not do that through a normative, textbook like enumeration of 'should' and recipes for success, but by 'rubbing off' its inspiring qualities, just by being there. It may also help to provide a dictionary and terminology for management ideas, and especially aspects of organization that are absent from mainstream discourses, such as beauty, ugliness, kitsch, enlightenment, etc. All human actions have an aesthetic dimension and it provides for much of the sustaining success of an enterprise:

> We are not able to understand management without the understanding of art. We will not grasp economic development without an aesthetic perspective.
> *(Guillet de Monthoux, 1993, p. 1)*

Management should strive for beauty. Even if the zeitgeist makes it impossible to discuss it in such terms explicitly in the popular sphere, the experience is still there. People – individuals, but also groups and classes – have different tastes but it is often, in the end, the sense that something is beautiful, according to that sense, that compels people to buy something. This applies to products as much as to services, and the sense of beauty is one of the major constituents of one of the central ideas of contemporary management – the brand (Hatch and Schultz, 2008). Branding is a creative practice, not only aimed at attracting consumers but ultimately concerned with the supporting of a sustainable identity which harmonizes cultural expression with impressions made upon the environment. Guillet de Monthoux (1993) claims that managers can learn the skills necessary to engage in these important practices by visiting art galleries and museums. Management is a 'journey in aesthetic space' (ibid., p. 4), a breaking away from what is everyday and mundane towards something that is possible.

What inspires managers and organizers does not have to be visual or even 'high' art. It can be ordinary albeit gripping stories (Gabriel, 2000). Stories are

> narratives with simple but resonant plots and characters, involving narrative skills, entailing risk, and aiming to entertain, persuade and win over [the listeners].
>
> *(Ibid., p. 22)*

There are four main types of narrative in organizations: comic, tragic, epic and romantic (ibid.). They differ as to the main character type, emotions they evoke, and typical plot. In a comic story the main character is a fool or deserving victim. Misfortunes or punishments that he or she encounters are well deserved. The listener feels superior to the protagonist and this feeling may be tinged with contempt. In a tragic tale the character has not earned their fate; he or she is a noble victim. The reader is empathic, the story invokes sorrow or righteous anger. The tragedy and the comedy both end with the protagonist's failure, but while the ending of the comic story can be seen as happy because it teaches a lesson and restores equilibrium, the ending of the tragic story brings fear and sorrow. The epic is different: the hero achieves victory and success. The listener feels admiration, respect, an uplifting joy, but the plot may also invoke envy. Finally, the romantic story shows the triumph of feelings. The protagonist deserves love and, despite adversities, is able to unite with his or her beloved or companion. The story awakens empathy and love in the audience, as well as gratitude. Good managers are also good storytellers and they are often known to be able to dramatize their visions so that they become compelling for the co-workers and stakeholders. The book *Three Faces of Leadership*, based on material from interviews with successful CEOs published by *Harvard Business Review*, promises inspiration to the business leader offered by these illustrious examples.

> The aesthetic perspective on leadership this book presents features clear and accessible explanations of aesthetic philosophy applied to key aesthetic

concepts including creativity, imagination, courage, virtue, inspiration, faith and ethics. It presents techniques for developing aesthetic sensibilities and the associated capacities of storytelling, dramatizing and mythmaking that express these sensibilities and communicate them to others. Finally it links aesthetic leadership practices to several important and perennial themes of business education and the development of human potential: organizational culture, change, vision, values and identity.

(Hatch et al., 2005, p. viii)

2.3 Sounds, images, dreams

It is ferociously cold outside and with each new guest a gust of freezing air flows into the dimly lit room.[5] One of the many clubs in Warsaw city: a haphazard collection of vintage furniture that had seen kinder days, colours that are both hip and sad, making the darkish interior look cheaply mysterious, a decor turning the rooms into a kind of postmodern spatial limbo. It is rather dark in the three rooms and people huddle by the tables or sit close to the two bars, more generously lit up. In the largest room a band is playing some kind of jazzy music. They are technically skilled and they visibly try to impress the audience with their solos, fashionable clothes and charming smiles. The saxophone is fighting for supremacy with the drums, the small space is filled up with sounds, energy and attempts at allure. But the aura is fractured; groups and individuals seem to be suspended in their own moods. People come and go; some sit and talk, someone tries to dance but gives up; in a few minutes somebody else repeats a similar attempt, and then, again, another one.... The people sitting closest to the scene clap their hands after each number, but their clapping is drowned by the sonic vigour of the band. Hands, mouths, limbs move chaotically against the uniform background. Then the music stops and nothing seems to change, except a few people leaving the room. Another band enters the scene, a young band from Kraków calling themselves UDA. Immediately, they start playing. Immediately, everything seems to shift. It is as if we were transported into a different cosmos just like that, without the time for being surprised. They play less loud but the music fills up all the space, it has flow, it *is* flow. The musicians step into it at once; after a few tones they are both intensely present and not quite here. Sometimes they hold eye contact with the audience, especially the singer, which seems to be absolutely personal, but at the same time they do not try to tell us anything or to make us notice them, like them. They stay powerfully connected to each other and as if forgetful of everything else, yet there is a compelling feeling is of being included, drawn into their music. The effect on the audience is immediate and dramatic. People stop their conversations, some move closer to the stage, some begin to dance. Many people start coming in from the other rooms and once inside, they do not leave. The bitter winter evening, Warsaw city, Friday city centre drunks – everything has stayed behind, as has my own usual insecurity and feelings of being out of place among the crowd. The music is a kind of psychedelic inward journey, not unlike late 1960s music such as Yes, Emerson Lake and

Palmer or Pink Floyd, but original and with a strong personal tone. Members of the audience are behaving as if they were following the call in a number of different ways: some dance, some sway, sitting on their chair, some clap their hands energetically. I see one man who closes his eyes and slowly moves his head from one side to the other, a woman who is drinking copiously and shouting with the band in more or less appropriate moments. I write four poems about a variety of things, among them about the creation of the world.

John Ruskin[6] was an art critic and social activist from the Victorian era with an intense awareness of the associations between art and society. Among his many initiatives, the Guild St George is one that is perhaps best known in Sheffield, the city where I am living in as I write these words. It was a community with an aim to create opportunities for people who wanted to lead a life outside of the increasingly dark industrial cities in the area. The guild bought land and supported rural handicraft, which it still does today. However, its best known venture became the Ruskin Collection which has recently been refurbished and is now hosted by Sheffield's beautiful, airy Millennium Galleries (Museums Sheffield, 2013). Ruskin was deeply moved by the poverty and bleakness of the industrial cities, and wanted to share with their inhabitants what he had seen, to give them hope and an idea of what the world may be. So he assembled a huge collection of items: sketches, architectural drawings, paintings, originals and copies, shells, minerals and many other beautiful objects. They originated from different parts of the world, from England to Japan; and from different epochs, from antiquity to contemporary times. In this way, he shared what he considered his true wealth: 'life, including all its powers of love, of joy and of admiration' (Ruskin, 2012, p. 156). They were to serve as tools of education but most of all they were intended as inspiration. Among other objects, the visitor to the Gallery can admire the work of Jacopo Tintoretto, in contemporary copy by Angelo Alessandri, an example of sublime Venetian art, representing Adam and Eve in Paradise. They are praying, at peace, their heads inclined towards each other. They are surrounded by a crowd of enraptured saints and angels, held up in the air by an otherworldly force. An experience of a different kind is offered by the sketch of the Arch from the Facade of San Michele, in Lucca, Italy, a plate from Ruskin's book *The Seven Lamps of Architecture* (1849, as quoted in Museums Sheffield, 2013). He describes there what he considered the most important principles of architecture: sacrifice, truth, power, beauty, life, memory and obedience. The detail represented on the plate shows columns decorated with images of animals, plants and fantastic creatures – a hunting scene; with shadows and light emphasizing the simplicity and, at the same time, vivacity of the shapes. In itself, this is an object of profound beauty, but also a key to imagining what the whole building can be like. *Study of a Mollusc* shows the beauty of a creature of the sea. It is an illustration from one of Edward Donovan's books on natural history. The creature is painted in arm ochre, and its shell is thorny, like the fruit of a mysterious underwater chestnut. The *Study of Stained Glass, Clerestory Window, Chartres Cathedral* by the contemporary British artist Frank Randal depicts the story of Mary

Magdalene encountering the serene risen Christ: she kneels before him, frightened but also overwhelmed with happiness to see him, yet unable to touch him. The image is known as *Noli me Tangere*, do not touch me. These are just a few examples of the cornucopia of very diverse, powerful and evocative images and objects, each of them as if opening a tiny window towards an infinitely interesting world, waiting not just to welcome visitors, discoverers and adventurers, but also inviting them to take an active part in the celebration of beauty and creativity.

2.4 Reflection 2

Managers, unlike poets and artists, do not have a Muse of their own. Therefore, as we have seen in Reflection 1, they are advised to learn from these traditionally creative groups. Another way to inspire management and organization is to seek the guidance of archetypes to look for an own Muse. Carl Gustav Jung (1990) believed that all important ideas originate in the archetypes, which are like river-beds in the collective unconscious of humanity, waiting for contents to fill them. Some archetypes are connected to the development of the person and mark the path of individuation. Others are linked to characters: social roles, animals, divinities. Finally, there are archetypes referring to stories. In my book, *Organizations and Archetypes* (Kostera, 2012), I present 12 archetypes that have a bearing on organizations and processes of organizing, chosen from all these categories: Self, Shadow, Anima/Animus, Persona, Sage, King, Adventurer, Trickster, Eternal Child, Gaia, Cosmogony and Soteriology. My perspective is not rooted in psychology but rather in organization theory where I look for archetypical tales, or stories containing archetypical elements. Stories more commonly known to include archetypical tales are myths, sagas, legends, fairy tales, traditional ballads, etc. However, in my study of scientific articles, books and tales from field research of organizations, I have found an abundance of such tales. For example, organizations are quite often pre-sented as superpersons (Czarniawska, 1997) and much effort is being put into a quest to define and describe organizational identity (for review see Hatch and Schultz, 2002). This interest originated in a need to make organizations account-able, but is now, perhaps first and foremost, concerned about the possibility of the creation of persuasive organizational brands on the one hand, and the perseverance of collective sense of belonging and togetherness (Hatch and Schultz, 2008). The quest for identity has also its dark side: some organizations strive to define the iden-tities of their participants in minute detail, they set out to control all aspects of their life (e.g. Coser, 1974). But organizations can learn and, by doing this, they can shred oppressive identities, they can become enlightened and allow people to be free and cooperate more on their own terms (e.g. Argyris and Schön, 1978). Theo-ries and studies referring to these issues often use the archetypes of the Self in various roles: subject, plot, setting, morale, etc. Another archetype with much relevance for management is the King. It is very multifaceted, its role ranging from anointed leader, healer and redeemer of his or her[7] people – but also tyrant, despot, enslaving people and waging bloody wars. Organizational leaders are said to be symbolic characters in charge of controlling fate and people often expect them to have special causative powers (Czarniawska-Joerges and Wolff, 1991). However, if they take these expectations too literally and begin to think of themselves as more than human, they risk losing their humanity and become monsters, tyrants devoid of empathy. More about the light and dark sides of leadership will be presented in Chapter 7 (especially Section 4). Let me just say here that the archetypical tale has a penchant for certain characteristic plots. The tyrant king is either defeated and overthrown or becomes enlightened and frees his people and himself. So is the path of leadership also depicted in organizational theory (e.g. Cunliffe and Eriksen, 2011; Kets de Vries, 2009). Another archetype that I would like to briefly introduce here is the Adventurer. This is a typical story-archetype, one of the classical kinds of story, which Joseph Campbell (1993) described as *The Hero with a Thousand Faces*, a plot and character present in many myths and legends. The hero leaves his or her village and sets off into the unknown, visits places and meets a variety of characters, and is subjected to tests. He or she is often helped by supernatural characters and receive from them gifts, be they artifacts or pieces of wisdom. Then they go home and bring these gifts with them to share with their fellow villagers. In organization theory the role of the Adventurer is often ascribed to the entrepreneur: a passionate and restless figure, sometimes obsessed by his or her drive to create new organizational forms, push the boundaries a little bit further, discover new ideas, products, markets, or set right some social wrongs, raise the awareness of some political cause (e.g. Johannisson, 2005). Some entrepreneurs and managers display the darker traits of an adventurer – they are troublemakers, reckless risk-takers (e.g. Boddy, 2006). They seem to lack empathy with others and are easily bored; the only thing that makes them feel alive is playing with risk, the higher the better, without consideration of the consequences. But their satisfaction, or rather, thrill, is only temporary; even if they succeed, they do not settle down but go back for more. Their and their companies' end is often dramatic and tragic. These and other archetypes offer a learning based on inspiration (Kostera, 2012). Instead of textbook like fashionable advice, recipes for success and streamlined solutions, they do not promise an instant fix and they do not seduce with visions of achievements if some simple formula are implemented and some best practices imitated. But neither are they complicated theories suitable for researchers but not for practitioners. They can be spoken of in theoretical language but they are easy to translate into practical inspirational stories, images, presentations or action. They motivate to look for new innovative solutions to problems, to open doors that one never thought were possible to open, to invent new ideas and things, not to shy in front of the unknown. Archetypes also always come with a warning as to their darker side. They are never just tools, they are much more compelling and untamed to be treated as such. And indeed, it is worth remembering that people and organizations are often driven by dark images and passions, such as described for each of the archetypes in my book, but nowadays perhaps most notoriously – by greed. Enormous resources are invested in creating and supporting brands but what is considered 'avoidable costs' are cut, meaning, for example, that production is outsourced to poorer countries, where vulnerable workforce is employed for starvation-level wages in sweatshops (see, e.g. Klein, 2000). There seem to be no limits to what some corporations can do in order to withhold the money that they owe to the public domain, and no 'saving' seems too insignificant to make (Sikka, 2010). Indeed, greed is one of the central features of contemporary organizational and managerial life (Wang and Murnighan, 2011). Major religions condemn it, for example Buddhism sees it as a harmful attachment and in Christianity it counts among the cardinal sins. Nonetheless, greed is often seen as the main driving force in capitalism and in more recent years it has been glorified as illustrated by the famous film quote from *Wall Street*, when Gordon Gecko proclaims: 'Greed is good. Greed is right. Greed works.' In fact, many managers are nowadays inspired almost exclusively by greed when making decisions, all other considerations and values coming at best second. And yet, this is not a simple atavistic drive but, as any inspiration:

> greed [is] a sophisticated social phenomenon that often involves a set of internal battles: e.g. the self versus others; cognitions versus emotions; and hot versus warm emotions. The decision to succumb or to resist greed seems to be a product of these internal battles.
>
> *(Wang and Murnighan, 2011, p. 304)*

And, indeed as any inspirational force, greed is contagious, corrupting populations of organizations and managers (ibid.). There is convincing evidence that education contributes to the spreading of this inspiration, through economic related courses and success stories (Wang *et al.*, 2013).

2.5 Stories from organizations

We are sitting on the train, one of the 'big trains' that go to Stockholm. We are students at the University of Lund, and we meet on the train almost every morning this frosty autumn, as the days grow shorter, and the trees are slowly turning inwards. These are the days from before the mauve commuter trains and most of the trains that take us from Malmö to Lund continue further, hundreds of kilometres northwards, to places I have never seen, like Hässleholm, Göteborg, or even further, to Stockholm. Up north, there is a place where the ruffled cliffs begin, and the air grows cold, colder than here, but kinder, more honest, the colours are clearer, and everything is astonishing, my childhood still remains there, a little washed out, but still there.

'Oh, if we only could just go on, stay on this train, go to Stockholm...', I suddenly say.

'Yeah! That would be so cool! Instead of sitting and listening to these boring lectures...', Lars energetically agrees.

'We could go to Moderna Museet, it's free, and then to a pub in the evening', Sigge proposes and everybody starts dreaming, as the fields, cottages and willow trees flick by in the thick grey haze outside the car window. Then we arrive at Lund station and as we all leave the train, I notice that one of us is missing. I turn back. I see Ronny's smiling face in the window, him waving to me.

I was lucky to have known him. He was the only one who really did not mind when I came out as a foreigner in the second year of studies (yes, I could pass as Swedish with my only slightly ambiguous name, blonde hair and native accent), maybe he even thought the better of me for it, while the other friends I had just dispersed. He never used the word impossible, he was tall and quite dark, which was maybe unusual for a Swedish person from the Stockholm area, and he always looked as if his sight was directed at some distant point at the horizon. Sometimes he would look straight at you, and his face would warm up with a smile. He became a legend of the Swedish social entrepreneurship, a human rights and peace activist. He died suddenly in 2010.

Ronny liked the studies. I wondered why; I was terribly depressed after the inaugural lecture which was about organizing, organization theory, infinitely uninspiring things. All the classes: management, pedagogy, statistics, did not improve my mood in any way. Sociology was nice, but why suffer all the rest, I had no clue. This is not what I had wanted to do with my life. I reapplied to psychology and got accepted. I started to study at both programmes, and was for one semester running between buildings and classes, trying to make the schedules work together, and failing. I was talking with the others, with Ronny; he told me how our programme, a combination of pedagogy and management, then not the popular topic it is today at all, but rather an education for rich kids who wanted to become managers (never! never in my life would I have dreamed of this; I ended up here by sheer accident), could help us to learn to do things we really wanted to do, but which did not exist, not yet. Things that did not match any profession, interest area or walk of life. Completely new things. The academic year came to an end. I was tired, studying at two programmes simultaneously and working. I needed to choose. So I stayed with the management programme. I did that. I regretted my decision on and off for most of my later life, until now. Now I can see what he meant, because I realized that I just have been doing that. I am creating something new, something that did not exist and no educational programme could have foreseen. Did management theory help me, did it teach me how to do it? No, it did not. But it inspired me.

As it inspired Ronny. After finishing his studies, he sold everything he had; it was not much, mainly his motorbike; and he went to China. When he came back, he started to work with different peace initiatives. It was the mid-1980s, and the media were full of images of aggressive youths, rebels without a conscience, revolting against responsibility and against the necessity to have a good life. These youths were dangerous and indolent; there was no need for society to care for them. The winds of individualism as the divine driving force of the free market religion were already blowing hard. Homelessness suddenly became a vice. Unemployment turned out to be sloth. The press depicted youth gangs, some foreign, some 'just' from 'bad' areas of the cities, armed with chains and knives. Ronny did not understand any of this. So he decided to do something, give those kids a place where they could do something fun together. For, why would young people turn evil all of a sudden? Kids were kids, they wanted to have something fun to do. Such as making music, or why not learning? Learning was fun, as was reading or skating. He believed in a good life and he believed in learning and growing. He generously shared this faith with others: family, friends, strangers. He began working with organizations that supported such initiatives, he got engaged in the peace movement, fighting against the weapons industry and the hypocrisy of established world politics, which was pronouncing messages of peace but being driven by the profits and power that the arms industry brought to governments, even such a seemingly peaceful one as in Sweden. He also took part in the activity of organizations working for free education at different levels, for young people and for adults; he helped to set up the Glocal People's University, the aim of which was to be a source of knowledge and inspiration to all, be it with a practical purpose such as filling in educational gaps in order to be admitted to a 'real' university, to get a job, or with a completely impractical one, such as to find out whether the Romans visited Scandinavia at all, or why π is such an interesting number. All the time he carried in him a burning idea of his own, a dream to create an organization that would offer a peaceful space for young people to develop and grow. He did not have much, but he never considered that an obstacle. Instead, he went around various authorities, asking them what was needed to make such an organization happen. They told him: it's a lovely idea, you know, but it demands some serious resources, things such as capital, business plan, land, a source of income. He made a note of everything, nodded and continued his quest. He never hesitated when he heard about money, he never regarded it as anything more serious than just a means to an end; the new faith that was elevating money to a kind of free market god, a supernatural value above all the other values, never got to him. So he just put it down as one more thing to get on his list. Now he knew what was needed. That was a start. He then went on, to further authorities, asking them, in turn, how to get capital? land? steady income for the organization? Whatever he heard from them, he committed to his list of assets, as something already acquired, which was worth much more than the things on the list: knowledge. Because everything can be done and every problem can be solved, when we know what it is and where to look, he told me later. Take, for example, a business plan. It is very complicated and when we were students, it was not part of the curriculum. But we did study management, right? So that one was, indeed, quite easy to get. He went to Lund and asked one of his former teachers for help, which was readily offered. The teacher asked his students to propose a business plan for such an organization as a class project. He chose the best one, improved it and filled in the gaps together with Ronny; they signed it with the students' and their own names and that was it. As for the money, he learned which grants could be applied for. Again, an old teacher from Lund helped him to put together an application. Everything was falling into place for Ronny. And then one day we were contacted by a group of young people who were struggling for a place to skate. Together they created Bryggeriet, a place converted from an old brewery to contain first an indoor skatepark, then also a photography studio and finally an own school (Bryggeriet, 2010). Ronny was asked to become its boss and he agreed, but he always claimed that he was not doing anything special, it was the young people themselves who had done it all, and who continued to create a Bryggeriet for fun and peace. But they all knew then, as they do now, that working with Ronny made a difference. In a tribute to Ronny his co-organizers say:

> Ronny's engagement and driving force was, and still is a huge inspiration for all that have been working at Bryggeriet and we have all lost a fantastic friend, mentor and role model. We are so incredibly happy and grateful for all our time together, everything we have learned and will continue to spread round the world in a true Ronny Hallberg-spirit. In Ronny's world there seemed to be no obstacles at all, only possibilities and he was our expert in finding those possibilities and making them reality.
>
> *(Ronny Hallberg, 2010)*

2.6 Questions to reflect on

1. Think of a film, piece of music, book or work of art that has particularly moved you. Describe it in as much detail as you can, take good time to remember the feelings you had when looking at it, listening to it or reading it. What did you learn from it?
2. Think of an organization that you admire but are not part of: social, such as Médicins Sans Frontières; cultural, such as the Arts and Crafts Movement; or economic, such as Suma. Why is it inspiring to you? Write an essay; imagine yourself joining it and describe your role in it, what do you do?
3. Look out through the window where you are sitting right now. Take in the view very carefully, try to be aware of every detail. What time of day or night is it? Which time of the year? Is it light or dark? What do you see? Write a short poem.

Notes

1 Between 750 and 650 BC, Ancient Greece.
2 c.560–636, Spain.
3 1803–1882, USA.
4 1875–1961, Switzerland.
5 Notes from my book of everyday ethnography. The name of the band is real.
6 1819–1900, UK.
7 The King is not a gendered archetype, it can be embodied by both a man and a woman (the Queen is a different role and archetype altogether). See Kociatkiewicz and Kostera (2012b).

3

INTUITION

The snow is falling
the swallows are silent now
and the voice is stilled

Intuition is an ability to think extra-rationally and gain insight from signals in the environment that are not a result of rational processes. In modern times, due to the cult of linear rationality, it has not been highly regarded, even though it is necessary in many walks of life and occupations. It is often referred to as 'gut feeling': entrepreneurs, doctors and artists have often admitted to using it, as a kind of instant recognition of the situation at hand, which would otherwise have demanded prolonged decision making and assembling of data. Even though it is not seen as scientific or indeed legitimate in many contexts, it is usually accepted as a way of dealing with complex and ambiguous situations by professionals. Quite often, intuition has been gendered as 'feminine intuition', a quality of the presumably less rational gender, based on characteristics such as sensitivity and emotionality. Women were said to possess it and be able to produce conjectures based on illogical assumptions, which has been, in modernity, regarded as a less than reasonable way of thinking, but sometimes resulting in mysteriously accurate conclusions. Traditionally intuition has been connected to spiritual faculties, and looked up to as a faculty to gain esoteric knowledge without the use of earthly reasoning, but perhaps through the contact with higher beings and supernatural realms.

The working of intuition can be based on sensory inputs, making connections between impressions without logical reasoning, letting them form an idea to be absorbed by the soul or imaginative faculties rather than by the rational mind. Often non-intentional or unconscious impressions, such as facial cues or body language, are intuitively linked into valid and enlightening ideas and observations. Space contains an abundance of such signals, left by others as aesthetic imprints or in the more immaterial form of spatial memory. They can be intuitively grasped and processed in order to gain a deeper understanding of the culture of a place, the people inhabiting it and its history.

Intuition may, alternatively, consist of non-sensory thinking, by making contact with spiritual or imaginative spaces and aligning different experiences made in these spaces. Certain kinds of so called extrasensory perceptions may be regarded as intuitive in this sense, such as telepathic long distance experiences, where no sensory impression is possible, or the prediction of future events by oracles or prophets. Also spiritual experiences, such as interactions with angels or saints, are based on intuitive communication.

Intuition may offer insights about people and things present in the intersubjective spaces, for example, a hunch about the feelings of a person towards another, or about the intentions behind an action. This may lead to astoundingly correct understandings but just as often to misinterpretations and prejudices. In our culture the use of intuition is rarely subject to discipline and fine-tuning; it is thrown into a black box with other irrational faculties, and small wonder that something entirely different is often taken for it, such as projections, distortions and anxieties. With training it is possible to see boundaries to what can be intuited and what not, but most people never try to develop this faculty beyond a very rough inexpert form, which makes it quite unreliable.

Intuitive thinking can also be used to gain insight about the future, about things existing in spiritual and imaginative spaces and their relationship to physical space, etc. It is based on personal experiences made in these spaces and the ability to see how they relate to other experiences. It may reach as far as identification with the object and transcending the ego and by that gaining a knowledge that surpasses the conceptual and relative.

It is often believed that aesthetic sensitivity and competence helps to develop intuitive faculties, as well as an aptitude for introspection. The scope of inner experience is as rich as that of extroverted sensations, and with discipline and perseverance, it can be developed into a capacity for acquiring detailed and truthful realizations, concerning not just the state of things and events but their meaning.

3.1 A short history of intuition

According to Immanuel Kant[1] (2008), intuitions are conscious representations, distinct from sensation. For example, 'space and time are only forms of sensible intuition, and hence are only conditions of the existence of things as phenomena', or they are ideal constructs, depending on the subjective workings of the mind. Henri Bergson[2] (2002) holds that intuition is a faculty of knowing, an experience that allows us to experience the world as an interconnected whole. His view is not unlike what Joseph Campbell[3] with Bill Moyers (1988) describe as the shamanic experience, a way some people in hunter societies were able to access directly a shared knowledge, not just belonging to human communities but to the world as a whole. They usually accessed that domain in trance, drug induced or meditative, in order to share with the others. In ancient Greek society the role of sharer of wisdom was played most notably by the Pythia. The oracle operated at the temple of Apollo in Delphi since the eighth century BC, although originally the site was dedicated to Gaia, the primordial goddess of the Earth. It was famous for giving ambiguous albeit strikingly accurate answers to those seeking its wisdom, among which were kings, warriors and philosophers (Kempiński, 2001). The last of Pythia's pronouncements made in 393 AD to the emperor Theodosius I concerned herself:

> Tell the king; the fair wrought house has fallen.
> No shelter has Apollo, nor sacred laurel leaves;
> The fountains are now silent; the voice is stilled.
> It is finished.
>
> *(Broad, 2007, p. 71)*

The Oracle was knowledgeable because she had a special gift, enhanced by the trance-inducing drugs. The idea of a prophetic or intuitive gift brings us to Carl Gustav Jung's[4] (1992) psychological types. Jung discerned four main functions of consciousness: sensation and intuition, which are perceiving functions, and thinking and feeling – judging functions. In addition he also proposed that there are two attitude types: extroversion and introversion. A combination of these functions gives eight psychological types, of which two are intuitive, which means they act not on the basis of rational analysis but on direct perception. Intuition is, to Jung, a kind of perception from the collective unconscious, beginning as an inward journey to bring out ideas and visions not necessarily accessible within the material reality.

3.2 Reflection 1

Intuition has been something of a taboo among management scientists in the last century, although not necessarily among practitioners (Akinci and Sadler-Smith, 2012; Isaack, 1978). However, old masters such as Chester Barnard (1966) recognize the importance of intuition for the good manager. According to him, it is exactly as important as logical reasoning and a good manager should develop his or her intuitional abilities. Thomas Isaack (1978) is among the rare researchers of his era who actively advocates for the reincorporation of intuition into management education. He emphasizes its unique advantages:

> Through intuition, a pattern is presented as a complete whole without our being able to explain how it was arrived at. It can grasp the meaning, significance, or structure of a problem without explicit reliance on analytical apparatus. Intuition is not limited by conventional time since it has no boundaries of duration. Intuition can synthesize disparate ideas, achieving serendipity as it senses combinations which did not appear to be related in the past.
>
> *(Isaack, 1978, p. 919)*

Intuition and intellect work very well together and complement each other: the latter prepares logical lines of thought and sets of a structure, and the former makes sudden insights and creative solutions possible (ibid.). Outstanding decision makers know how to use both qualities (Mintzberg, 1976). Cinla Akinci and Eugene Sadler-Smith (2012) chart the intuition research of the last 80 years, contrasting the profusion of studies in related disciplines and the paucity of such studies in management studies during much of that period. However, this is changing fast; especially during the last decades there has been much promising work on the topic, ranging from learning, through decision making to entrepreneurial processes. This advance has resulted in a rich and diverse body of knowledge, potentially very inspiring for future researchers. The authors conclude by listing four recommendations for future research: a more careful conceptual framing, a cross-disciplinary integration, more methodological rigour and attention to levels of analyses issues.

And yet, intuition is ever present in all instances of the practice of organizing. One author who has not explicitly used the term 'intuition' as his topic of interest but whose writings have undoubtedly thrown some light on intuitive aspects of the processes of organizing is Karl Weick. He points out that organization works very much like jazz music (1989). Choices are made during, rather than before, action, quite often because one or the other direction seems appropriate to the actors. They often feel it is a good idea – but do not have a precise vision of goals and results. However, after the fact they may rationalize their choices by explaining them in terms of plans, goals and results and show how they made the decision in purely rational terms. That kind of ex ante rationalization is very usual in the practice of management (Weick, 1979). Yet real managerial talent reveals itself in non-linear, simultaneous action. A good manager finds the right ideas and actions through trial and error, much like the jazz musician. He or she fails more often than succeeds, but once in a while finds a motif that works for him or her and knows how to develop it and how to propose it to others to be collectively built up. This mode of collective action is like jazz improvisation and talented managers use all of their faculties not only to take part in the collective processes but also to have a grasp over it all – they have a responsibility for the organization (Weick, 1989). What we call managerial intuition may, then, well be likened to a musical ear and is a necessary ingredient in all everyday organizational and managerial activities.

One of the most acknowledged uses of intuition in management concerns decision making processes, where it is seen as a crucial and integral part of action and expertise (Klein and Weick, 2000; March, 1971; Simon, 1987). Erik Dane and Michael Pratt (2007) refer to research showing that intuition is vital in complex tasks, involving short time horizons, such as: planning, stock analysis, performance appraisal, strategic decision making and decision making in turbulent environments. Intuitions are defined as 'affectively charged judgments that arise through rapid, nonconscious, and holistic associations' (Dane and Pratt, 2007, p. 40, emphasis removed). The authors compare analytic and intuitive processes and conclude that intuition is highly beneficial in complex situations; they are able to make 'both fast and accurate decisions in organizations' (ibid., p. 50). Mindful managers are better tuned in to their environments and learn better to respond to them. Intuition is very useful in strategic thinking, understood as a subtle balance between passion and discipline (Obłój, 2010). On the one hand, the strategist has to find and actively invent a preferred path of development for the company. On the other, he or she should be able to respond to the environment. Strategy is an interplay of these two aspects, based on a few key and mutually complementary choices that will ensure that the organization succeeds (ibid.). Given the complexity and the hyperdynamism of contemporary environments, this is particularly important for strategic management (Hodgkinson *et al.*, 2009). More attention should be paid to the development to such qualities, in education, selection and rewarding of organizational decision makers. I will address education for intuition development in the Reflection 2 section.

Let us now give some more thought to the collective aspects of intuition. It is not just an issue of promoting the right abilities in individuals, but since

> strategic competence is a collective activity, [it is important to] consider the implications of our analysis for managing and leading teams, such that a requisite blend of individual cognitive competencies (both intuitive and analytical) and the development of shared understandings of intuitions (which are inherently subjective and experiential) might be achieved.
>
> *(Ibid., p. 278)*

The strategy making unit should be organized in such a way that an optimal blend of intuitive and analytically inclined individuals is achieved. Solely analytically oriented strategists are unable to face the challenges of a turbulent environment and the participation of just intuitive individuals poses a risk that decisions will be made without a complete understanding of the situation. Therefore a balanced composition is truly helpful. This is the task of the leader of the group. He or she should then be able to manage such a cognitively diverse group. The leader should be able to encourage people to express their intuitive ideas and then allow for a debate which involves rational analysis. In the process, he or she should manage conflict and not allow it to escalate which is rather common in such diverse groups. Intuitions are difficult or impossible to express in words. The leader has to facilitate communication in the strategy making unit by proposing some kind of sharing, for example, through metaphors. The leader then serves as a mediator and translator, transferring meaning between different individuals and taking care so that all are respectfully received by the others.

Organizational decision making is then a relatively established domain for the use of intuition. Much less explored in literature is the role that intuition plays in extraordinary organizational efforts, such as creativity. Viktor Dörfler and Fran Ackerman (2012) propose to further the understanding of creative intuition, which they regard as a kind of knowledge operating at high levels of expertise. They distinguish between intuitive judgement and intuitive insight. The first kind is needed for decision making, for example for thinking of alternatives and feeling a preference for one or a few of them, rather than others. This is a standard activity of managers and experts in organizations and so this type dominates in the literature. The second kind, or creative insight, is necessary in creative work, when people in organizations face ill-structured problems. The way of arriving at a solution to such problems is often unaccountable for in any kind of symbolic language, even though some people may be able to either express it metaphorically (or poetically), or, more, commonly in contemporary organizations, rationalize it ex post in the Weickian (1979) manner. This distinction is not exclusive: creative processes may contain both kinds of intuition (Dörfler and Ackerman, 2012).

Another increasingly important aspect of managerial work concerns projects. Project management is about organizing in order to reach a specific goal. It involves much novelty, a temporary structure and little routine. This kind of work is highly dependent on the ability to improvise and thus demands that managers are able to make decisions intuitively (Leybourne and Sadler-Smith, 2006). Rationality does not play a role in the capability to improvise. Research also reveals that customers express more satisfaction with the outcomes of the work of such managers. More experienced project managers tend to improvise more than less experienced ones. They act and feel more confident in the unstructured conditions of the project.

3.3 Sounds, images, dreams

Szymon Rogiński is a Polish artist and photographer of the post-transformational generation. The *UFO Project* (Rogiński, 2009) is a series of photographs taken in the Polish countryside, creating, with the use of natural and artificial light, the expectation of an unearthly presence. The photographer himself describes his work as being born out of a conversation with a friend.

> My work on this cycle was inspired by my friend and assistant – Grzegorz. His profound faith in the possibility of encountering a UFO during our night expeditions made me turn my camera lens towards the stars. I started to imagine such a thing landing somewhere in a Polish forest or field and this picture make me smile. With time I got involved in this and began to search for mysterious spots that, according to ufologists, may have been landing strips long ago.
>
> *(Rogiński, 2009)*

'Projekt UFO #12' depicts a flat field, seen slightly from above, the crops, which might be corn, not yet ripe, grown in symmetrical rows, dark green with a light ochre fizz on top. The light is dim, even if the sky is still intensely blue, but the mood in the picture is definitely that of falling dusk. In the middle of the field, that stretches itself to the horizon, there is an irregular spot of brightly white light. There is something unnatural about it, neither the sun nor the moon gives off light of this shade. There is also a suggestion that its source may be approaching. It is not an aura of foreboding or threat, it is entirely serene; if it is a UFO, it carries perhaps an extraterrestrial family on holiday excursion, or a group of students exploring ancient civilizations. In '#10' the mood is different: it is a longing, a lonely looking out, emphasized by the low purple light, the black silhouettes of the trees and in particular the strange rock shaped like a human face, looking up at the sky, as well as a lonely barren branch protruding from the right side of the picture. The presence of the Others is much more distant in this photograph, almost like an archaic imprint, left in the stones. '#17' is perhaps the best known of the set; it has been presented at several exhibitions and published in newspapers and magazines. It presents a rounded colonnade in the middle of a leaf-less forest, lit up with a strong white light emanating from within. The sky is very dark, turning toward midnight black in the upper corners, but a swarm of stars encircle the scene from above, looking as if they were swirling over the arcade. The architecture looks quite mysterious: the shape is vaguely antique but the material almost certainly concrete. On second look, the arches are too angular to be older than dating from the last century, but what could its function have been? Maybe attracting aliens. Another photo, '#02', depicts a trunk of a pine, lit up from behind by a white light, turning the surrounding night a cold blue but illuminating the ground in a rather warm, if somewhat eerie, shade of green and yellow. Small plants and straws of grass produce long and robust shadows. The atmosphere is festive, albeit not in a highbrow way, more like an imminent folksy fete, maybe the landing of the members of an extraterrestial stag party? The most striking aspect of these photos, and others of this series, is how they turn the attention of the onlooker into a readiness to embrace the unknown, to encounter the unusual. They access the mindset through the door of intuition, and we tune ourselves into a mood of watching something that, indeed, is not there in a realistic sense but which, nonetheless, makes a powerful presence. When our gaze is then turned to the everyday reality which surrounds us, we see it differently, the sense of wonder and expectation to meet the unknown lingers on for some time still.

The film *Dead Man* (1995) by the independent American film director Jim Jarmusch is a psychedelic Western, according to Jarmusch himself (Hawker, 2005), a label signalling transgression, and it certainly transcends boundaries of both genre and of narrative expectation. It tells the story set in the late nineteenth century, of a young accountant, significantly albeit coincidentally named William Blake, setting out to a frontier town, where he has been told a job is waiting for him. However, when he arrives at his destination, the job has been already taken by someone else and he is forced to leave. In a flurry of misunderstandings, he is shot at by a man who later turns out to be the son of his would-be employer, and he shoots him in turn. The father sends hired killers after Blake, who, exhausted and in a daze, manages to flee and is found by an Indian, calling himself Nobody. The latter happens to be a great admirer of William Blake, the poet, and believes Bill Blake the accountant to be his incarnation. Nobody tries but fails to remove the bullet which has planted itself close to Blake's heart. They then set out on a journey to the ocean where Blake's spirit can be properly sent further on his way ahead. Encountering adventures and strange characters, they finally reach the edge of the land, from where the dying Bill Blake is pushed out into the sea in a canoe, and he drifts away, while dazedly watching his companion being unexpectedly shot at and die on land. *Dead Man* is filmed entirely in black and white, with a haunting guitar soundtrack composed by Neil Young, and several references to William Blake's poetry, most notably recited by Nobody. Bill's journey towards death is an intense experience of learning; he learns from his Native companion for whom death is part of himself and not something separate from life, as it is for most ordinary white people. He also learns from William Blake, the visionary poet, who also understood the mystery of life and death to be an undividable journey. The viewer is included into this learning relationship, if we let intuition become the sense through which it is mediated as a profound wisdom that endures, as if gained by our own experience. This wisdom pertains to life and death as change, in the words of Peter Pelzer (2001), who contemplates the implications of *Dead Man* for management, about a 'world in transformation where change is happening, not managed' (ibid., p. 49).

3.4 Reflection 2

Entrepreneurship is an area rather famously connected with intuitive thinking and acting. This is not just a popularly held idea but it does, in fact, reflect the nature of entrepreneurial work (La Pira, 2011). Entrepreneurs do not mind ambiguity and uncertainty; they are happy to make decisions based on incomplete material, because they trust their intuitive thinking. They rely on a holistic approach to decision making and know how to use emotions to better discern what is going on in difficult and rapidly changing environments. They are also highly creative and believe that their intuition guides them to truly innovative solutions. They are risk-takers and do not obsess about always 'getting it right', they understand that gaining experience involves making mistakes. Again, intuition both helps them to orient themselves in risky situations and itself evolves and develops in time, with more experience containing both successes and failures (ibid.). Intuition is also quite often aimed by entrepreneurs at solving everyday problems and quickly coming up with reactions to what comes their way (Glinka and Gudkova, 2011). Srinivasan (2012) proposes the notion of innovative consciousness, a state of mind in which both imagination and intuition play a vital role.

> The flame of innovation is ignited when the innovative consciousness of people find an enabling organizational environment.
>
> *(Ibid., p. 135)*

There are three types of innovation: incremental improvement of qualities of the product related to economy and efficiency; evolutionary change consisting of developing the existing product or service; and completely new ideas. All of these types, but in particular the third and most revolutionary, are based on a kind of thinking that engages faculties beyond analytic and rational thinking. The key constituents of such thinking are: attitudes, the thinking process, development of imagination and intuition, and motivation. Attitudes supportive of innovation are open toward new things and ideas, curiosity, perseverance in looking for the unknown. The thinking process needs to be reorganized, away from focus on the routine and conventional. People have to be able to formulate goals and share them and their ideas with others. They should have the possibility to ask questions beginning with 'why' and to discuss possible answers to such questions, even the 'strangest' ones. Intuition and imagination are present in most of us, at the deeper levels of consciousness. It is not necessary to learn new ways of thinking but to encourage the development of an ability that is already there, perhaps suppressed by conventional education and curbed by many contemporary workplaces. M.S. Srinivasan (2012) suggests methods for the awakening of these modes of consciousness, such as Indian yoga or the use of non-linear problem solving techniques, including not only problem formulation and generation of alternatives, but also a state of mind, turning towards silence, aspiration for truth and goodness. Keeping the broader context in mind, such as the ecosystem, is important for the development of such innovative mindfulness. Finally, motivation is important, and not just by the use of monetary incentives, but also 'creating a culture which leads to an intrinsic joy in innovation is a deeper source of motivation' (ibid., p. 140). Creativity is not possible without freedom; people need an atmosphere of intellectual freedom to be persistently creative. Furthermore, creativity cannot be controlled and directed, for example towards customer satisfaction. Such innovations happen, but only within a climate allowing for many expressions of creativity, including such directed at the employees themselves, relaxation, free thinking. An innovative organization is, however, not an unstructured construct: there needs to be a system, albeit supportive and flexible, that provides a sense of security and order.

Not only entrepreneurs and innovators learn through intuition. All organizations benefit from a balanced approach to learning, based on both reflection and intuition (Korthagen, 2005). Eradicating the duality between the two makes it possible to eliminate the dichotomy of work and learning. Reflection and intuition working together create a setting for genuine perpetual development, not just of the individuals but of the collective as well. This is possible, because this balance enables to achieve awareness and thus gain a truly experienced vision of the situation within its context. In other words, such learning gives a deep satisfaction and encouragement to seek more experiences of this kind (ibid.), because it is closely linked with sense-making, that are fundamental components of all processes of organization (Weick, 1995). The same can be said about ethical considerations at work – people engaging in sense-making in uncertain conditions are relying on both analytic and intuitive thinking (Sonenshein, 2007).

> [I]ndividuals construct ethical issues from equivocal and uncertain environments, develop intuitive judgments about these constructions, and then explain and justify those reactions.
>
> *(Ibid., p. 1034)*

And yet, intuition is largely absent from management education programmes, despite being such an important part of managerial and entrepreneurial work, including decision making, creative work and ethical problems (Sadler-Smith and Burke, 2007).

> In an educational environment where opportunities do not exist to acquire experiences and test intuitive judgments, either directly or by proxy, students may suppress their intuitions, leaving their judgments untested and unrefined.
>
> *(Ibid., p. 245)*

Students are not encouraged to consider their intuitions carefully but, if they use them at all, rather tend to do so hastily and perhaps stealthily, which deteriorates and corrupts their intuitive capacity rather than helps them to refine it. Students should be taught that intuition is not a magical ability, present in some people, enabling them to see what is hidden to others. But nor is it a tricky ploy, adopted by some in order to deceive the gullible. Instead, it is a characteristic common to most people, enhanced with experience, that can be developed and perfected. Eugene Sadler-Smith and Lisa Burke (ibid.) propose several techniques for educational use. One of them is journalling, or writing down of intuitions before they are altered by the rational mind. Students can be encouraged to adopt their intuitive thinking to consider vague or ambiguous experiences. A subsequent analysis of these intuitions may prove very helpful in the process of developing a refined intuitive mind. Another technique consists of creating visual images. Students may be asked to depict the essence of something. This technique helps to learn to think in terms of wholes rather than analytically and to reflect on the relationship between different objects or ideas. The latter capacity can in particular be trained by the use of cognitive mapping, where students are asked to place arrows between images symbolizing different phenomena and things. It is, of course, very important that the students are given good feedback and that the teacher points out the pitfalls and biases that unskilled intuitive thinking (wild guessing or self-fulfilling prophecies) can have.

However, intuition also has a dark side. As leading force of action can easily mean a loss of boundaries, not only the ones between the possible and impossible, which enable innovative thinking, but also those that help us engage with the world, the protective boundaries of integrity and sense are necessary. Daniel Erics-son (2004) talks about the vices of entrepreneurship and intuitive organizing in terms of the blurring of boundaries, antropomorphization and festishization. Entre-preneurs ascribe human qualities to things they produce, put them in a position above themselves and so, in a sense, become slaves to them, while at the same time getting self-obsessed and egotistic.

> They become mirror-images, reflecting their beauty in the eyes of the market, letting themselves to be seduced by the seduced.... The market is enchanted by the entrepreneur's productive action, and it enchants them in turn. A feeling of invulnerability, perhaps even immortality, that emerges turns the gendered order and the feminine 'beauty' invites them to a dance and enables them to choose and pick among the cavaliers – but soon it brutally is turned back against themselves.
>
> *(Ibid., p. 103)*

3.5 Stories from organizations

Ewa is the Marketing Director at the Theatre.[5] She is one of the most intuitive people I have met, and, at the same time, she is a brilliant organizer. When she became the director at the Theatre, the marketing function was not doing very well: it fluctuated between a disdainful nothing at all and what is often believed to be the 'market bottom line' in Poland, or an attempt to sell at whatever cost it may be to the aesthetic sensibilities of the observers. Most of the people working at the Theatre formed a very tightly connected team, having known each other for decades, often having spent most of the time together, at work and otherwise. The team included first and foremost the actors, directors, all of them first class and many considered to be the Polish elite, technical personnel, such as light and sounds technicians, carpenters, wardrobe crew and many others, also, many of them, the top in their profession. There was also a group of cleaners, administrative person-nel, people employed at the box offices. Some had been working with the theatre for all of their lives and remembered the post war period, when it was being reconstructed or rather, built anew after its almost total destruction by the Nazis. They recalled the eccentric designer who came with the plans for the reconstruction and how he obsessed over every single detail of the decoration. He was then seen as obnoxious by many, but is now remembered with a reverence that is associated more with a cult of a local saint than an ex-co-worker. His passion for the project rubbed off; when it materialized it became a home at once. It was based on the original historic building but contained some new elements, in accordance with the credo of modernism and with the original ideas of the designer.

The people of the Theatre were very close; they saw both the building and themselves as something of a magical island, where the tempests of the times: Breshnev, central planning, Thatcherism, the Polish transformation, neoliberalism, simply did not have access. They were able to rise from the ashes of the Second World War and to survive all the madness of our recent history. They would not be swayed by any novelties now. That is why the marketing function, regarded as something alien and accidental, never did take root at the Theatre. Until Ewa's arrival.

She is anything but a stereotypical marketer. She is a quiet, empathic, reflective person. She listens, she looks her interlocutor in the eyes, never interrupts. A good ethnographer, one could say; and, no wonder, that is exactly what she has been doing for many years – listening to people of the Theatre, to artists, designers telling their stories. She has an aura that is somewhat otherworldly, but she is not turning away from this world. Dressed in a sober brown dress, she greets us in the marble clad lobby of the Theatre. Everything around us glitters and sparkles, I get starry-eyed; this is how it is meant to be, she says, the lobby is supposed to attract, even seduce. A visit to the Theatre has always been something of a celebration. She leads us through the muted corridors, red carpet beneath our feet, crystal lamps on the walls. I have learned from her lecture that these crystals are, together with the brass seat numbers, the things that are most likely to disappear from the Theatre. I have an urge to touch them, which I resist. We enter a small side staircase which Ewa presents to us as the 'gummy stairs'. They are indeed very inconspicuous and our steps are muted by the surface.

'They are only used by the employees.'

The stairs lead to a domain beyond the access or, indeed, imagination of the visitors. The red carpet and the crystals are gone, here the walls are grey and the floors made of the kind of industrial laminate all Poles remember from school. The corridors are narrow and winding, we pass some actors covered in white makeup, I feel suddenly shy; so this is it, the real thing, the Theatre from the inside. We enter a sound-proofed room, furniture from the 1960s lines the walls, I fall in love with the huge futurist clock, a comforting childhood ghost. When we pass through another corridor, Ewa shows us the cleaners' rooms. They are covered with colourful naive paintings of flowers, people and doodles that remind me of folklore from the Mazovia region.

'One of the cleaners does that, and the others have asked her to decorate their rooms, too.'

Ewa admiringly shows us the paintings; they radiate some kind of inner music of their author, a refreshing simplicity that nonetheless has a peculiar twist. The cleaners are not there; I feel like I am trespassing and even though I really liked looking at the rooms, I feel relieved when we continue our journey. We pass through the cafeteria, full of lively people, with a truly astounding view of the city ('look, look at the view we have!'), and into an even greyer domain, austere, with an aura of administrative space from the early 1970s, something I more intuit than actually remember. Ewa opens a heavy door: beyond is darkness, a warm, embracing obscurity. I look around: the walls have receded, so has the ceiling. We have to step carefully, as if the floor was about to recede, too. The space around us is humming with a silence that is suffused with some kind of mysterious energy. Ewa points to the ceiling and whispers:

'Look. Candelabra. Stage props.'

Indeed, these are the strangest candelabra I have ever seen: as if flattened, anamorphic, they make me think of the painting *The Ambassadors* by Hans Holbein, with the deformed skull extended on the floor by the feet of the two central figures. They are made this way so to give the impression of a vast hall or ballroom when looked upon from the audience. Here, in the darkness, among carton forests and silvery folds of tapestry hanging down from huge hangers, they look peaceful and slightly mischievous. The floor softly creaks under our feet. We enter a black space, illuminated by bright points of light, focused on the ancient sound systems. The men working there greet us briefly and bend anew over the console. I look up and I see the radiantly lit, festive audience. We are behind the stage.

The space of the Theatre, the humming darkness, the traces left by the people who have been using it all these years: this is what Ewa learns from, respectfully, silently, inhaling the knowledge with her intuition rather than disturbing anything with assertion and speech. She moves silently through the building, she does that almost every day, even when she is busy, even when there is a much shorter and more effective way to where she is heading. She absorbs the history but also the dreams, the longings of the place. And, of course, she listens to the people, to their drawings, their stories, sometimes to their rants and protests, especially in the beginning, when they did not trust her, believing that she was yet another intruder of the unwelcomed reality outside. And that she was not. They soon realized that and started to trust her, even though she never tried to persuade them or present herself to them as trustworthy and important. One day she proposed that an album be made as promotion campaign, dedicated to the designer of the post war reconstruction of the Theatre. This was greeted as a welcome, yes, perhaps a simply natural thing to be done by the others. She knew then that she has been accepted. She listens to the people, the building, and she speaks for them with the campaigns – is that not what marketing really is, if you pluck it free from managerialism and corporate belligerence? Recently she came up with another marketing idea – the floor on the main stage is being replaced after having served for 50 years. Instead of throwing the wooden floor boards away, she is turning them into memorial gifts. She has asked to cut them into small pieces and stamp with the Theatre's logo. Placed in elegant boxes, they look precious and beautiful, reminding of the number and the quality of the actors' and dancers' feet that had touched them, of all the hard work, sweat, tears, some accidents and bad falls. Ewa handed a floor tile to the students during her lecture. They passed it on to each other, touching it lightly and respectfully, sometimes caressing it with a sensitive finger.

3.6 Questions to reflect on

1. Stay at your workplace or university after most people have gone home. Take a walk along the corridors, take in the doors, visible workspaces, objects and think who was using them and what for, try to imagine what that person is like. How would you address this person? Can you think of ways of talking to her or him that would be likely to forge a bind between you?

2. Try to remember the dreams you had during one week. Write down as much as possible just after waking up. Recall not just what happened and what the setting was like, but how you felt, the mood, the aura of the dream.

3. Do you ever dream of flying? Try to recall several dreams of that kind. What was happening? How did you take off? Why? How did the others in the dream react? What does it feel like – to fly?

4. Think of the first day at your current work or university. Try to recall as much as possible from that day. What did you see? Whom did you meet? What were the colours, the lighting, was it cold or warm? Looking back now, which, if any, of your impressions from that day seem strikingly accurate when you come to think of them today?

Notes

1 1724–1804, Prussia.
2 1859–1941, France.
3 1904–1987, USA.
4 1875–1961, Switzerland.
5 The description is based on an interview with Ewa, my field notes, and Ewa's lecture at the University of Warsaw.

PART II
Organizing

Introducing the 3 S's: structure, space and synchronicity

Organizing is function concerned with the shaping of the idea or endeavour: *how* will it be done? In non-mainstream settings it does not have to be the most effective nor the most efficient constellation, but one that ensures smooth yet engaging ways of working together. Three key faculties are necessary to accomplish this aim: structure, space and synchronicity.

- *Structure* offers tools for ordering and arranging cooperation.
- *Space* is the frame and the primary resource for the realization of the idea or project.
- *Synchronicity* gives the project a consistent and right temporal dimension; things need to happen at the right moment.

4

STRUCTURE

At the end of the labyrinth
there is an empty space
where you and your shadow
become one

Structure is about the ordering of things and processes. Some objects, like crystals, have an inherent structure. Others, like social phenomena, need to be organized in order to get one. The ideas concerning the role of structure versus agency in social organizing differ a great deal. Some thinkers believe that structure precedes intentional attempts at organizing and that, in social life, as in nature, there exist underlying structures implying how things should be done and how power should be distributed. Some consider structures to be more of guiding lines than absolute rules determining how people interact. A number of people believe that structures are just social products, nothing more, and that we can influence them the way we want, even if we usually do not recognize it. Finally, there also are those who, like me, think of social structures in terms of human creations, that nonetheless serve as guiding lines for people.

Structure as a quality of social phenomena can be conceived of either as something permanent, a form that frames the organization or social group, something like the structure of crystals, or, possibly, as a way of doing things, a pattern of interaction, an order of flows, like the structure of performing live music. Structure as form can take different shapes, from hierarchy to network, and structure as pattern can also run along differing arrangements.

Structure influences important qualities. In the case of crystals, it determines such key properties as transparency and cleavage. In social settings it has an impact on important features of the lives of individuals, such as power, wealth, access to education and in many societies it defines, more or less permanently, the standing and life prospects of a person. Even if social structure is a human construct, it still affects the way chances and wealth are distributed: a woman still earns less than a man in most countries, even if her work is just as valuable, an immigrant with a foreign looking name will not have equal chances to be called to employment interview in many societies, etc. A rigid structure turns these limitations into absolute rules. The kind of structure most famous for being rigid is hierarchy, where every person responds to one above him or her in the hierarchy and power is distributed on a strict top down basis. It does have its merits in some circumstances, for example, there are thinkers who praise its effectiveness in organizations such as the army, but very often it prolongs decision making processes, puts the organization out of touch with its environment and oppresses the employees. However, a too loose structure can also have its drawbacks. When nobody is sure whom to interact with and which rules to follow, it not only makes cooperation difficult, even unlikely, but it sets people apart from each other. Faced with too much uncertainty in the collective sphere, people see themselves more in terms of individuals, having to fend for themselves alone best they can. Bonding is replaced by impression management and social ties dissolve.

Structure defines the way the whole is made up of its parts, the inner mechanisms or rhythms of the working on the whole system. In social settings it is much more than just an arrangement of elements, as it implies patterns of communication between people. Do they communicate with each other? Who with whom? In what manner? For what purpose? Cooperation needs both stability and freedom, because, together, they create a context where trust can develop and flourish. Without trust there is no community. Swift communication is also important for the sheer effectiveness of the system, if it is able to pass on information and make vital decisions, if it encourages responsibility. Structure may also influence the intensity and quality of the exchange with the environment: rigid structures are known to obstruct good exchange, as do dissipative, fragmentized structures.

4.1 A short history of structure

The Chinese philosopher K'ung-fu-tzu, better known in the West as Confucius,[1] believed in an ideal, harmonious social structure where every part contributes to the good of the whole, based on the principle of compassion. It should, according to the sage, be based on merit rather than traditional (feudal) distinctions. Education would enable social mobility and even a person of low origin could become a government officer of high status. At the centre of this structure is the charismatic king, its calm core, around which everything revolves (Xinzhong, 2000).

The Christian philosopher Pseudo-Dionysius the Areopagite[2] had a vision of a harmonious hierarchy, where all the celestial spirits were arranged in three spheres, each containing three kinds of beings. The structure is based on their proximity to God. The social structure of the Church should be made as a likeness to this celestial order to ensure participation in the holiness and beauty (Dionysius the Areopagite, 1899).

> Hierarchy is, in my judgment, a sacred order and science and operation, assimilated, as far as attainable, to the likeness of God, and conducted to the illuminations granted to it from God, according to capacity, with a view to the Divine imitation.
>
> *(Ibid.)*

The aim of the hierarchy is union with God.

The English philosopher Thomas Hobbes[3] conceived of social structure as a means of achieving greater good for a society:

> The finall Cause, End, or Designe of men, (who naturally love Liberty, and Dominion over others,) in the introduction of that restraint upon themselves, (in which wee see them live in Common-wealths,) is the foresight of their own preservation, and of a more contented life thereby.
>
> *(Hobbes, 1651)*

In order to achieve that aim, people consent to 'to conferre all their power and strength upon one Man, or upon one Assembly of men, that may reduce all their Wills, by plurality of voices, unto one Will' (ibid.), or they agree to submit to the authority of the ruler in exchange for the protection of their rights and needs.

The German sociologist and thinker Max Weber[4] believed that the most rational type of authority, power based on the rule of law, was best realized through the bureaucratic structure, which is also effective and the most technically superior, even if not always good from the point of view of individual freedoms. Bureaucracy is based on several principles, among them foremost: strict hierarchy based on the rules and regulations, defined lines of authority, formalization, that is, written rules concerning all of the organization's activities, and professionalization based on merit and expert knowledge (Weber, 1992).

4.2 Reflection 1

Only some 40 years ago structure was a very popular topic of study and while many theorists and practitioners looked for an optimal structure, some, as notably as Henry Mintzberg (1983) did, showed the variety of different structural configurations available to organizations and suitable (or not) for different purposes. Structure was often considered central to organizations and many considered it something of a cure for all ills of organizations. Perhaps it was so because it was fashionable, or many people trusted solutions that had a systemic air. Consultants often had toolkits of suitable structures and when they were given a specific problem to solve, they fitted it with a structure. Krzysztof Obłój (1986) shows how this style of thinking was attracted to certain 'general' solutions which, however, rarely lived up to real systemic challenges. Restructuration, yes, but only so that the system may continue to perpetuate itself. Nowadays management theorists rarely speak of systemic change and structure seems to be decidedly passé, judging by the amount of more recent publications, but there is yet some faith in its effectiveness. Organizational structure has been tested and proven to have an effect on the number of initiatives pursued by organizations and whether they were able to avoid decision making errors – in general, a structural decentralization was more beneficial for mutual funds management in several important respects (Csaszar, 2012). Organizational structure is shown to be positively related to knowledge management – the less centralized, less formalized, more complicated and more integrated, the more the levels of knowledge management were demonstrated to be enhanced (Mahmoudsalehi *et al.*, 2012). These more traditional perspectives on structure are, however, much less prevalent today than they were a few decades ago. Yet, there is a lively research activity focused on alternative structural ideas and different perspectives, not aimed at establishing a link between structure and effectiveness but rather using it as a means of organizing collective action. From this perspective, structure is seen as the ordering basis for collective effort. According to Karl Weick (2001) organizational structures that work particularly well in changing contexts are based on loose coupling. Each interaction needs a definition of the conditions and there are few assumptions as to its results.

> Loose coupling suggests that any location in an organization (top, middle, or bottom) contains interdependent elements that vary in the number and strength of their interdependencies. The fact that these elements are linked and preserve some degree of determinacy is captured by the word *coupled* in the phrase *loosely coupled*. The fact that these elements are also subject to spontaneous changes and preserve some degree of independence and indeterminacy is captured by the modifying word *loosely*.
>
> *(Orton and Weick, 1990, p. 204)*

Such a structure enables ordering while at the same time does not limit autonomy which makes it particularly suitable for self-management. It also has a beneficial effect on decision making, as it allows more freedom to point out errors and problems, and some discretion to act from different standpoints. Thus some decisions with catastrophic effects may be avoided. It has positive effects on job satisfaction because people have more agency in such organizations. It is also advantageous for adaptability, as the organization has a greater potential to respond to different signals from the environment if it is not determined and bound by a tight structure. Loose structure prevents spread of problems and enables buffering. It allows both the rational and non-rational processes that work together in organizations to be shown. Loosely coupled organizational systems tend to thrive in environments that are complex, indeterminate and fragmented (Orton and Weick, 1990). This seems to describe quite well the typical current organizational context, and so it is perhaps not surprising that this type of structure is currently quite often the topic of interest of researchers of a variety of organizational areas, from customer relations (Danneels, 2003) to asset management (Marriott *et al.*, 2011).

Another popular alternative structural idea is the heterarchy, a form based on decentralization and diversity, where power is dispersed and every actor's uniqueness is recognized (Hedlund, 1994; Grabher, 2002). Heterarchy is 'an ideal type in opposition to hierarchy' (Hedlund, 1994, p. 87), where 'several strategic apexes emerge, that these shift over time, and that there are several ordering principles at work' (ibid., p. 87, emphasis removed).

In firms that are constructed around projects the traditional stability is undercut but not necessarily substituted by the dynamics of the project. Personal ties and geographical contexts make such project oriented organizations multilayered structurally. Gernot Grabher (2002) proposes to regard them as project ecologies, meaning spaces of collaborative practices, containing some temporal and some stable features. Their basic structure is heterarchic – the diversity of the participating actors is one of the fundamental characteristics of such project teams. Collaborative relations develop over time and become stable relations. Different kinds of loyalties develop, from personal to industry-based. The projects are also embedded in much wider, global corporate communication networks. Another feature of project heterarchies is the rivalry which drives potential reconfigurations. It is the core of the structure and all the social actors

> [orbit] around and in the contested terrain of boundaries between professions, project teams, organizations and, in fact, in the understanding of the sub-sectors of the trade.
>
> *(Ibid., p. 255)*

It ascertains that the diversity is not limited in time, even though there exist strong ties of loyalty between the participants. Stability is derived from this supportive social network rather than from rules, regulations or a tendency to imitation and convergence. Organizations that are concerned about their creativity prefer heterarchies rather than other structural types because they provide an institutional support for diversity (Spelthann and Haunschild, 2011). Heterarchy consists of forms that are multilayered and overlapping and may be incongruent and dynamic, where the diversity is guarded by the coexistence of different organizing principles. This ensures that no hegemonic tendencies or routines survive on a more permanent basis. Inconsistency, slack and redundancy are constitutive characteristics of organizational creativity, and heterarchy is best suited to safeguard their existence in the longer term. Managing creativity is a latent activity and should not take on more active, controlling roles. Its role is to bring in creative people into the organization and to ensure the diversity that is necessary for them to be able to practice their creativity. Heterarchy turns out to be a good structure for such leadership, as it prevents more intrusive management practices through its inherent power instability. In sum

> the diversity of organizational forms and practices constitutes a potential for organizational creativity that gets activated through a particular organization of diversity, which is characterized by multilayeredness, duplication, overlap, incongruence, redundancy, organizational slack, rivalry and latency.
>
> *(Ibid., p. 106)*

Another example of organization, where heterarchy is seen as particularly desired is the entrepreneurial firm, or event as Bengt Johannisson (2005) calls it. It is based on action and reflection, all individuals are treated as unique, and even though they enact the event together and cooperate, they need a dynamic of rivalry in order to prevent clustering of power which has the tendency to block entrepreneurship. Heterarchy ensures that all are considered different yet equal. Entrepreneurship is a dynamic collection of contradictions which cannot and should not be harmonized or stabilized: anarchy and ordering, individuality and collectivity, work and play, organizing and affirming uncertainty. It is both reflection and action at the same time, a kind of creative process where the organization is the medium. Heterarchy also provides a structural context that does not prevent entrepreneurial learning, a process which demands much experimentation and experiencing, and abhors tight rules and regulation, as well as formal authority, which often blocks individual courage and passion to explore and question certainties (ibid., 2005). Finally, heterarchy has a potential for self-organizing, which gives the entrepreneurial firm a potential for a long term survival, despite all the inherent contradictions, and a development of an identity as well as a capability for endurable sense-making (Johannisson, 2008).

4.3 Sounds, images, dreams

Franz Kafka's novel *The Castle* (2012), first published 1920 in Munich, tells the story of the encounter of a man and a powerful yet inscrutable organization. The protagonist, K., tries to get access to the Castle governing over a village where he is working as a land surveyor – and ultimately, to be accepted as an inhabitant and employee. He is sent from one official to another, but no one seems to be willing to speak to him, claiming that there is another clerk more suitable for making such a contact. When he succeeds in talking to some of them, they remain for the most part completely unhelpful, or else obliging in a bizarre kind of way, giving advice that is absurd and confusing. K., regardless of the unwillingness of everyone he encounters to pursue the matter, insists on trying to get in contact with a character whose name he has heard in the village and who, he presumes, must be the one knowing what is going on – a man called Klamm. The villagers themselves never explain the nature of their relationship with the Castle, nor the rules embedded in it; they are more than willing to talk about the officials, but only to make excuses for their, at times, strange and disquieting behaviour, or to engage in lengthy and obscure storytelling about the culture of the Castle, of which they seem to be in awe. However, K. can clearly see that there is an underlying order of everything that happens here, a structure so potent that it is a taboo, while at the same time determining everything, providing the firmest foundation for all that the people do. He has an overpowering need to find out what it is, and, at the same time, the Castle is demanding that he justify his presence in the village. He feels that he cannot work without establishing some kind of meaningful link to what he sees as the ultimate source of the ruling order. Waiting, he listens to the villagers' stories, which are contradictory, obscure, more confusing than helpful. K. tries to keep his mind as clear as possible, he takes it all in but does not adopt the unstated rules as his own. He realizes that nothing is as voluntary or mutually agreed as the villagers claim; he comprehends that the Castle controls the village completely and unidirectionally, even though he seems to be the only one seeing this. He is increasingly lonely and isolated; the reality he perceives is different from anyone else's, and with the Castle's enduring elusiveness and thus refusal to justify his being there, he becomes more and more something of a vague presence himself, maybe wicked, possibly foolish, probably paranoid. If it is at all recognized by the reality based on the structure of the Castle, then he is, at best, its chief visible error: he has, after all, been called upon to come to the village and once there, there does not seem to be a place for him in the system. But even worse from its point of view, perhaps, he is wide awake within a reality whose main organizing principle seems to be oblivion.

I read *The Castle* for the first time when I was a pupil in secondary school in southern Sweden. From the first pages I felt a strange connection: it was as if Kafka had written this book especially for me. My school was just like the Castle, resting on an invisible but all powerful structure, unknowable but imperative, closely knit together by the understanding of all the teachers, administrators, school nurses, pupils, even librarians. I was the only alien element, unfit even to be given a place as an outsider. It was like an immense ship drifting on an ocean by a perfectly renewable force, in an unchanging landscape of perpetual grey dusk. In this school I kept silent for two years, only K., and later a Polish teacher, coming to my rescue.

An equally powerful but much more dynamic and constructive sense of structure can be found in the paintings of Pablo Picasso, the Spanish twentieth century painter, sculptor and peace activist, known foremost as the precursor of cubism. Picasso and Braque pondered how objects and people were visually set together as shapes, imaginatively took them apart and then painted the different structural principles they found. Instead of adopting the principles of perspective, canonic, since the Renaissance, the cubist painting presents several planes, revealing the structure in the process of seeing itself. That way, the work of art actively co-created reality, together with the viewer, instead of re-creating it, for the viewer to more or less passively absorb. Picasso sought out the basic geometric shapes and framed them the elements present in his artwork. In his oil painting *Three Musicians*, from 1921 (MoMa, 2013), this is very visible both in the silhouettes of the three men, their musical instruments and the furniture, but also the colours, with dominating brown tones and inky blues, emphasizing the structure rather than, as in many other directions in art, serving to convey the experience of either outer, natural, or inner, spiritual light. The *Musicians* speak much more to my senses of touch and hearing than most other paintings, and the impression they make on my sense of vision is very dynamic; looking at the picture feels like seeing a short trailer of a musical video, perhaps uploaded to YouTube. I clearly see the noise they are making, and the fun they are having by playing together. I gather they might not be very talented musicians but certainly good friends, their faces vibrant with joy and they feet impatient to stomp the rhythm. Are they, however, able to hold a common rhythm? Of that I am not entirely sure; they seem too eager and too exuberant to be capable of producing an orderly structure. But I feel invited to share their joy as a viewer, stomp my own rhythm if I like, as long as I do not impose it on the musicians in the painting. It is said that the *Three Musicians* are an homage to a bygone bohemian era in Picasso's life, it is indeed himself, portrayed in a harlequin costume, and his two artist friends who are represented in the picture. One of them had recently died when Picasso made the painting. The harlequin costume was used by Picasso in his earlier pictures as a statement of his identity as an outsider, not quite fitting in the bohemian ideal. Being able to catch something of the dynamic structure of the memory, Picasso has avoided sentimentality and idealization of the past, while strongly playing upon the tones of nostalgia, a longing for a younger, more boisterous world.

4.4 Reflection 2

It is not only heterarchy that supports the construction of organizational identity. All structures have this ability potentially and Anthony Giddens' (1979) structuration theory helps to describe the processes that underlie it. Giddens focuses on the pattern of ongoing interactive processes between structure and human actors. Structure at the same time enables human action and hinders it: it provides rules derived from past actions as to what actions to take in the future. When used anew, these rules are reinforced, or else they vanish if abandoned by new actors. The duality of structure refers to the essential recursiveness of social life, as constituted in social practices: structure is both medium and outcome of reproduction of practices. Structure enters simultaneously into the constitution of the agent and social practices, and 'exists' in the generating moments of this constitution.

(Ibid., p. 5)

Structure is thus both the process and the result. Not a solid or material fact, but rather the abstract feature of human action, structure is real because it appears as real to the human agents but it is not able to exist without them. There is both an aspect of agency and of determination in the process of structuration. Furthermore, agents are reflexive, that is, they actively observe and reflect upon what they are engaged in (ibid.). The recreation of organizations can be viewed in terms of 'interlocking modalities comprising interpretive schemes' (Wilmott, 1981, p. 472). A focus on schemes such as hierarchy makes it possible to see the underlying cultural meanings (ibid.). Yolanda Sarason (1995) proposes a model of organizational transformation based on Giddens' theory with reference to the role of identity and change. Structuration theory enables managers' action to be regarded as conscious work, undertaken in a concrete context. Seen that way, strategic change may be explored as a creative process. Not just the manager's vision, however, but also the organization's identity is an important component of this process. Organizational identity is the shared and endurable sense of what is central and important about the organization and, 'like personal self-identity, presumes reflexive awareness and focuses on the set of shared beliefs agents hold about their organization' (Sarason, 1995, p. 49). Identity influences strategic action, but the reverse is also true: strategic action has an effect on identity. The stabilizing factor in this ongoing process is held by structure which, itself, is also a process with a dual character.

The ability of agents to effect organizational action and structure is a function of the agreement on desired action as well as the power and influence of agents to change routines and resources. Change in strategy and structure would be a function of the degree of agreement on the direction of the change and the power to influence the rules and routines of the organization.

(Ibid., p. 50)

This implies that methods of communicating identity, embedded in the structure, are of utmost importance. The managers could use them to acquire valuable help and support from the participants.

Another valuable benefit that can be derived from structuration theory for the study of organizations is its ability to lead theorizing away from reductionism, determinism and functionalism when considering the role of structure (Fuchs, 2003). Structures can be seen as recreating and self-organizing dynamic social systems that are realized through the actions of the participants. Such systems generate information and so it is important to consider the role of an organization's history when considering the present and the future. This way of thinking also supports the significance of cultural identity. Self-organizing systems cannot be seen in terms of linear determination – similar causes may have different effects and cause and effect interplay and interact in creating sometimes unforeseen consequences. A centralized, rigid structure does not allow for sufficient flexibility and adaptability and may limit the organization's ability to respond to signals from the environment. The dual nature of structuration means that people reproduce the system but also make new rules as they go.

> [H]uman social activities are recursive because they are continually recreated by the actors whereby the latter express themselves as actors. In and through their activities agents reproduce the conditions that make these activities possible.
>
> *(Ibid., p. 140)*

A social system achieves continuity in time and space through the duality of structure. A sense of identity that springs from the consciousness of this continuity is central for human beings that need an ontological security in their life. However, social systems are parts of constantly changing environments. In order to survive, they need to be able to adapt. Structure seen as a dual process makes it possible to both eat the cake and keep it: identity can be preserved in and communicated through the recurring rules, while creative action by the participants is allowed or even encouraged in reaction to important new occurrences and developments. Such self-organization is possible only through human actions and agency and it demands both consciousness and reflexivity. This puts communication in a quite central position in organizations:

> If one observes society or a social system, one will not find either communications or interacting individuals, but both at once. Separating communications and individuals into two separate domains results in a rather dualistic and nonconsistent conception.
>
> *(Ibid., p. 163)*

Communication and social interaction are, indeed, not separate but part of structure that unites and supports the processes of meaning making in organizations. Furthermore, recent work (Vogus and Sutcliffe, 2012) suggest that structures and routines embody organizational mindfulness, or cultures 'encouraging thinking and capacity for action' (ibid., p. 724). It is a culture that results from initiatives taken by the leaders, supporting the participants' freedom to think. It is important because it may prevent dangerous surprises in the environment from destroying the organization and may produce strategic and operational reliability. In order to do so, it needs to be spread over the entire organization. Routines communicate expectations and therefore it is so important for organizations to make use of structures to spread these throughout the system.

Structure and ordering can be very useful, if not regarded dogmatically, but, rather, as a kind of practical ordering (Law, 1994). According to John Law organizing is about ordering, more or less obsessive, more or less precise. It concerns people and things. The entire is a strategy, not necessarily conscious, called the mode of ordering; the way of forming the process of organizing by concrete actors. The specific mode is regular and repetitive, providing a stabilizing framework that the actors can use as a safeguard, making it possible to engage in other, more adventurous plots, such as acting as a competitive enterprise on the market and acting as a network of colleagues, friends and enemies. An obsessive ordering, supporting hierarchical rigid structures is said to be one of the greatest obstacles to creativity, change and entrepreneurship (Johannisson, 2005). Hierarchies have a tendency to be used as a tool of oppression to undermine creativity and limit the quality of the interactions and involvement of employees. This creates a loss of energy, a loss of trust and impairs the organization's ability to read and interpret signals coming both from the inside and from the environment. Rigid structures were shown as the source of dysfunctional behaviours of companies, reinforcing solutions that caused the problems in the first place (Obłój, 1986). However, the opposite tendency, towards 'flexibility' understood as shapelessness, living in a constant present without even considering the past, so common in today's organization, is just as destructive. Richard Sennett (1998) describes the new flexibility as a kind of contemporary corporate dogma. It does not mean, as the original word, an ability to regain the original shape but, rather, a readiness to abandon all form, a kind of shapeshifting strategy, based on identitylessness. Identities, shapes and structures are forsaken, as is stability and organizations become domains of an ever changing present. Such organizations are not structureless, but their structures are less transparent and amorphous, responsibility is hidden or altogether gotten rid of (Sennett, 2006).

4.5 Stories from organizations

It was right after the fall of the Berlin Wall. I was a young assistant and PhD student, and as was the norm in the highly hierarchical academic world in my country then, I was the main tea making and cup cleaning force of my department. As an English speaker, I also got to accompany foreign visitors, one of whom was Alice, an American professor, then my current age, powerful and famous.[5] She wanted to visit some factories in the Łódź region and so we ended up in Gloriatex one gloriously sunny morning, together with a mustachioed driver who, on Alice's invitation, followed us inside. I was a kind of guide and hostess, as well as a translator, as most people in Poland did not speak English then, and even though I was never any good at simultaneous translation, I tried to do my best. We were led into a vast room, with a large antique table taking most of the space and heavy chairs of dark wood around it. Not a fan of antiques and palaces, I was feeling intimidated and dwarfed, but I was also, in spite of myself, in awe of the splendor of the decor. This was not a typical office of the time, in fact, I had never seen anything like it in a Polish workplace before: they usually had a rather drab or cheaply modernist outlook, with lots of concrete, wooden panelling and perhaps some folk art. This was different, it literally screamed opulence. After some 10, maybe 15 minutes, the door opened, the director entered and proceeded to shake hands, first with the driver, then with Alice, last, me. Alice gave me a tired and ironic look: myself, I was not surprised but, yes, ashamed and guilty. This was the spontaneous manifestation of social structure: it was obvious for the director that the man must be the most important guest. I felt this was partly my fault. I realized that I was staring up at the stucco ceiling instead of doing my job. I hurried to make the presentations and if the director regretted his mistake he made no big show of it. He bade us welcome and sat down at the head of the table, a large, confident figure in a sombre suit. A secretary came in with tea (I felt smug, at least I did not have to do it this time) and after some small talk: did we know that the portrait of a girl in the lobby was the original owner's daughter? She died in Auschwitz, together with the entire family, except the owner himself, he was shot in the massacre of Polish officers in Katyń;[6] the office space looks much as it did before the war, etc., Alice started grilling our hosts with questions about the company's strategy and financial standing. He answered smoothly and shot many English phrases into the conversation, relying on me when he was explaining issues related to the management of the company, but otherwise quite fluent himself. He was going to turn the company into a subcontractor for Western firms. Yes, he was sure that this was the best way to proceed. Well, yes, the company did have a brand, but it was Polish, was it not? He did not explain that but I knew: Polish brands were considered unattractive back then, only because they were Polish and not Western. Some new entrepreneurs who were starting their ventures made sure to name their companies in English, sometimes coming up with unintendedly funny 'Pinglish' labels. I made a mental note to explain that to Alice later. The director made it clear that he was committed to the cutting of costs. Now, at last, it was possible to do so. He was not bound by over-protective labour laws any longer, he could fire and hire people as he deemed sensible. He lifted the receiver of the greenish plastic phone, such a discordant element in this magnificent room. Soon a young man in a dark suit entered and after having greeted the director, turned to us. Eager not to repeat my mistake, I urgently made the presentations and he bowed to plant a profusely salivating kiss on Alice's hand first, and then, mine. She looked up at me with a puzzled look on her face. I rolled my eyes discreetly and nodded. He was to be our guide on a tour of the factory, on which Alice has been insisting, much to the director's surprise ('But why do you want to see the factory? It's old, nothing of interest there at all'). The director shook our hands, now in the 'right' order: Alice's, mine; the driver was greeted only by a nod this time. Good naturedly, he mumbled something, nodded his head and asked whether he could wait for us in the staff cafeteria, which was, of course, not a problem. We were led through the marble corridors, beside the painting (I almost stumbled when I looked into the girl's serious black eyes), then, an unkempt yard and into another building. I could see at once that this one has not been renovated since the Nazis grabbed it from its owners. Grey on the outside, it looked even more dilapidated on the inside. The young man escorted us into a huge hall, where rows and rows of looms were operated by women, clad in cheap colourful smocks, swiftly moving their hands and fingers to the rhythm of the machine. The noise was alarming, the pace very fast. The women did not have the time to look up, all they could spare were quick glances, expressionless, mute, as we passed by. There were no conversations or songs, the machinery did not make room for any of that, being too fast and too loud, overpowering. It was with relief that I left the room, even though the corridor was dark and noisy as well. We climbed the stairs to the first floor and entered another hall, furnished with another set of machines. I had no idea what they were doing, perhaps some kind of treatment of the yarn. The noise was less oppressive here, the women acknowledged our presence, nodded to the young man, some smiled at us. I smiled back, noting how efficient the workers were, how their fingers moved even without them looking at what they were doing, like a professional typist, as familiar with the keyboard as with her own hands. We entered the corridor again and were about to descend the stairs when Alice shook her head and emphatically pointed upwards, to the stairwell above. The young man said something, which I did not hear in the noise, Alice insisted; he excused himself and asked us to go ahead without him. We did. The last floor greeted us with an almost overwhelming rhythmic blare and something like a haze of tiny snowflakes whirling around in the air. In the large room the haze turned into a thick white soup of cotton wool, almost suffocating and blinding us upon entering. When my eyes, ears and the rest of my body recovered from the shock, I saw a room full of huge greenish machines, again, an all-female workforce, women in white covered smocks, in headscarves, with a harried look on their faces. They looked up at us but did not smile, their faces remaining as opaque as the air around us.

We went to the bathroom on the second floor ('look, both male and female bathrooms, what the hell for?', Alice pointed out to me; I had a urge to go in there and see if it is used at all, which I resisted), a grey faced woman was standing alone by the window there and longingly smoking a cigarette. When she saw us, she extinguished the cigarette and hurriedly left; I thought of running after her but refrained, thinking how that might have unnerved her. So we stood there in silence, Alice and I, brushing the white dust off our clothes. Days afterwards I found tiny balls of white fluff in my bra, in my shoes; I had the big room before my eyes with the constantly falling dust, as if inside a snow globe.

Since, Gloriatex has been privatized, then sold off to a Western investor, restructured and liquidated, all of the employees laid off.

4.6 Questions to reflect on

1. Discover the structure of your shopping. Next time you go to buy groceries in a larger store, take your notebook with you. Did you make a shopping list? Where did you put it? Which path through the shop do you take? Do you take a trolley? Where do you focus your attention? Do you follow your shopping list? What do you do once you have put all the items from your list in the trolley or basket? How do you pay? Make a note of all your movements

through the store. Once at home, review the notes. Are they typical for how you usually go about your shopping? Would you say you are an effective shopper? Which aspects of the process are the most/the least pleasurable? Why?

2. Write a haiku poem about shopping; make sure it follows the traditional structure: 5–7–5 syllables in every verse.

3. Sketch a communication model for your typical day at work/university. Whom do you usually talk to for more than 15 minutes every day? Mark the most intensive exchanges. What did their contents concern?

4. Make a schedule of a typical weekday and a holiday. When do you get up, eat breakfast, go out? Do you have the radio on? Do you watch TV? Make sure to include all your main activities. Now compare the two. Do they differ? In what way? Why?

Notes

1 551–479 BC, Ancient China.
2 Fifth to sixth century.
3 1588–1679, England.
4 1864–1920, Bavaria (Germany).
5 Story based on factual material.
6 A massacre on Stalin's orders – the director did not need to say it was the Russians who did this; we knew.

5

SPACE

Stars and eyes
against a cosmic blackness
Jacob, my brother,
I think I'm drowning

Space is what surrounds us, the medium in which we move physically, intellectually and in other ways. There are two main kinds of space: intersubjective, that which is shared with others, and internal, the space we have access to through inwards journeys. Intersubjective spaces make bodily movement possible, and can be physical, biological or social. Physical space was, since the Renaissance, believed to be absolute, that is, independent of other aspects of reality and objectively existing outside of the human psyche. Nowadays, after Einstein, space is usually conceived of as relative, or an extent in which objects have a relative position and movement. It consists of matter and energy. Space has three dimensions, or four, if we think in terms of spacetime, and is considered boundless, extending far beyond the reach of human access or perception. The space past our planet, Cosmos, is known only to a certain degree, surrounded by a deep space of unimaginable immensity and age.

Biological space is limited to Earth's ecosystem and is an environment supporting life. It is made up of the living organisms and other elements, such as soil, climate, etc., as well as the relationships between them. Biological space, like physical space, and all other kinds of space, contains energy, such as nutrition, which makes it possible to sustain life.

Social space consists of physical elements, like distance and material objects, but it also includes certain objects and phenomena which are abstract or immaterial such as culture, social structure – which some people regard as existing objectively, and others believe to be socially constructed – or virtual space, an abstract space made possible to access and share due to technology. Whatever their origin, they appear real to many human beings, as well as external to their selves and not easily changeable. These spaces are intersubjective because people are able to agree on their characteristics and able to share many of their experiences and perceptions which take place in them.

Internal spaces, which can be accessed by focusing of consciousness to the psyche within, is not as easily shared with others as the intersubjective spaces. They are, however, experienced as real spaces by the people who regularly get into them, by creative activity or meditation. There is an imaginative space, or the one used for creative activity; a spiritual space, where it is possible to gain spiritual insight and perhaps meet with spiritual beings; intellectual space, which is abstract and can be used by the mind to perform reasoning; and others. Different types of energy exist in these spaces and are available to the subject moving around in them, for example, imaginative space is rich in creative energy, which can be received in the form of inspiration (see Chapter 2).

It is often observed that even intersubjective space can be differently experienced by people inhabiting it, depending on its role in their lives. It can be regarded as completely external, not linked with some important events taking place from the point of view of the person. Or, it can be concrete, the setting of a certain life story, a meaningful place. There are also spaces in between, ambiguous, not definable as one or the other kind, perhaps even blurring categories, existing on the boundaries between known and unknown, physical and social, even external and internal. An example of such liminal space is an old haunted churchyard after dark, a place where some people claim to see and hear things out of this world: do they actually see them with their physical eyes? Or are they figments of their imagination? Or, perhaps, objects intuited by faculties other than the ordinary senses, originating beyond the earthly realm?

5.1 A short history of space

Aristotle[1] was one of the first thinkers to conceive of a definite space, having dimensions and extent, which he called place, *topos* (Mendell, 1987). Prime matter includes everything. Space is, therefore, a kind of an extension of matter and void does not exist. Topos is 'the inner limit of a containing body' (ibid., p. 206), dependent on the body. Movement takes place within it, or, rather, 'place as matter is not separable from the moving substance' (ibid., p. 225).

Marcus Vitruvius Pollo, better known as simply Vitruvius,[2] was a Roman engineer who considered space as a medium for urban architecture. He was one of the first to reflect on the utility and organization of space, and he was also interested in its beauty, which he mainly found in harmony and symmetry (Vitruvius, 2009).

> Beauty will be achieved when the appearance of a building is pleasing and elegant and the commensurability of its components is correctly related to the system of modules.
>
> *(Ibid., p. 19)*

The modules are measures adopted in architecture and Vitruvius describes carefully how different architectural elements relate to each other using this system.

The German mathematician and philosopher Gottfried Willhelm von Leibniz[3] sees space as a collection of places (occupied by objects) and the relations between them. It is an abstraction deriving from the sum of the concrete. He does not believe in an absolute space, but one originating from relationships (Northrop, 1946).

The Chinese geographer Yi-Fu Tuan[4] regards place and space as fundamental elements of reality as perceived through the lens of human experience. Concrete place and abstract space are connected to each other: space requires movement from one place to another, whereas place needs space in order for the subject to be in a concrete place. Place stands for security and space – for freedom (Tuan, 1977).

In a similar train of thought, the French philosophers Gilles Deleuze and Félix Guattari (1996) consider territorialization as the result of interaction processes between physical and/or psychosocial forces. The ascribing of meaning is a reterritorialization process, consisting of material and a phenomenological aspect, as it settles the event in a spatially concrete frame. Territories and territorializations are not only physical but also psychological and spiritual.

The French sociologist Henri Lefebvre[5] looks upon every human experience as spatially constructed around three aspects of space: imagined, perceived and experienced space (Lefebvre, 1991). As his theories are extensively used in theorizing about organizational spaces, more about them will be said in the section Reflection 1. Similarly, I will return to the work of the polymath scholar Michel de Certeau[6] (1984), who considered the relationship between the story and spatial action. Space is to him a practiced place. Stories turn places into space.

5.2 Reflection 1

According to Henri Lefebvre (1991) all human experiences are spatially constructed. He identifies three interrelated aspects of space: spatial practices, or space perceived in the commonsensical way; representations of space, or space conceived of, our knowledge and ideas about space via sets of symbols; and spaces of representation, lived or experienced space. Lefebvre also discerns three kinds of space, from raw space, or the space of nature, through mental space, containing abstract and formal symbols, to socially constructed space. Social spaces are objects of contest between different cultural representations and meanings; all social relations derive their meaning through space. Societies construct their own spaces in a way characteristic for their culture and social structure; it is the basis for their self-reproduction.

Ceri Watkins (2005) argues that Lefebvre's spatial triad enables a nuanced and integrated approach to organizational analysis, taking into consideration social, physical and mental aspects of organizational space. Traditionally theorizing of space has been dominated by a Cathresian imagery of an abstract space. However, bringing in the additional aspects into the picture, allow to move beyond the customary analyses of parameters and classifications of mental spaces. It is important, because

> [a]n abyss has opened up between the theories of space and the empirical world of actions, interactions and understandings, leaving our lived experiences estranged from the conceptions that purport to represent them.
>
> *(Ibid., p. 210)*

Everyday life and practices have been almost completely omitted from those theories and in order to re-engage with that dimension of organizational reality, the researcher needs to take into consideration other aspects of space. Lefebvre's triad is embodied and experienced within culture and human life, it needs to be used in a context of real incidents and relationships.

Timon Beyes and Chris Steyaert (2012) propose a concept of spacing, based on Lefebvre's work on space, which directs attention to the embodied and experiential aspects of performing of everyday organizational space. Inspired by the visual artist's Bill Viola's video *The Raft*, showing, in slow, motion, a group of people surprised by a deluge while they are waiting on a bus stop, Beyes and Steyaert show how space becomes spacing, 'cracking open usual horizons of space and time into a chronicle of passion and pain, a story of bodies and faces, water and sounds' (ibid., pp. 46–47). This shift of focus entails a rethinking of space as processual and performative, open-ended and multiple, practiced and of the everyday. Such a reframing of space as spacing implies exchanging a vocabulary of stasis, representation, reification and closure with one of intensities, capacities and forces; rhythms, cycles, encounters, events, movements and flows; instincts, affects, atmospheres and auras; relations, knots and assemblages (Foucault, 2007).

(Beyes and Steyaert, 2012, p. 47)

The concept of spacing is performative: it helps to bring attention to the embodiment and everyday creativity and the potential of transformative construction. Organizational space is 'performed through the simultaneous and excessive coming-together of multiple trajectories along (and exceeding) the full range of the senses' (ibid., p. 53). A performative organizational geography should encompass various sides of organizational experiences, including material and emotional, as well as drawing attention to the aesthetics of the research process itself. Writing about organizational space is, too, an act of spacing the organization and equally, as in experienced organizational space, has an aesthetic dimension. Its role is not just to analyze and evaluate but to invoke rhythms, invoke images and insights.

Michel de Certeau (1984) presents the links between spatial practice and spatial narratives. He conceives of space as practiced place. A place is concrete but also limited.

At the outset, I shall make a distinction between space (*espace*) and place (*lieu*) that delimits a field. A place (*lieu*) is the order (of whatever kind) in accord with which elements are distributed in relationships of coexistence.... The law of the 'proper' rules in the place: the elements taken into consideration are *beside* one another, each situated in its own 'proper' and distinct location, a location it defines. A place is thus an instantaneous configuration of positions. It implies an indication of stability.

(Ibid., p. 117)

A space has none of this stability of 'propriety', it can bring freedom, and is transformed and brought into becoming by practice.

A space exists when one takes into consideration vectors of direction, velocities, and time variables. Thus space is composed of intersections of mobile elements.... Space occurs as the effect produced by the operations that orient it, situate it, temporalize it, and make it function in a polyvalent unity of conflictual programs or contractual proximities.

(Ibid., p. 117)

Places turn into spaces with the deployment of narratives: everyday stories are guides of spatial practices. Key practices operating in space are strategies and tactics. Strategy shapes its autonomous space, imposes rules on it and orders it;

whereas tactics make use of cracks to make opportunities for uncontrolled movement or subversion. The latter is 'calculated action determined by the absence of a proper locus' (ibid., p. 37). It is operating on others' territory and does not have the options of planning, but works step by step, tentatively and taking advantage of opportunities. Strategies are utilized by institutions of power, whereas tactics are adopted by individuals acting in environments defined by strategies.

Hervé Corvellec (2009) adopts de Certeau's notion of spatial tactics to risk management, which he believes should be reconsidered in terms of its boundaries and nature. Risk management is embedded into the tactics of managerial practice in organizations where it is not the main area of activity, such as the public transport company the author has studied: 'organisations are populated with street-level risk managers' (ibid., p. 287). Managers deal with risk in the spaces they create by adopting tactics of everyday management. This may take significant amounts of time and presumes trickery and craftiness. They involve surprises.

> Risk management tactics evolve incrementally, for example, from interactions with heterogeneous and circumstantial elements such as a breakthrough in regional infrastructure planning, political whims, engine technology innovation or an increased awareness of climate change.
>
> *(Ibid., p. 299)*

Even more outside of the most trodden paths are heterotopias, or, according to Michel Foucault (1984), other spaces, beyond hegemonic institutions but at the same time connected with them, existing between meanings, moments in time and geographic areas. Heterotopias are intended for certain actions of special significance, such as rites of passage, certain social actors, such as the mentally ill, from outside of the main stream of culture. They function as liminal places, indeterminate and undefined, such as museums, containing several temporal moments or exotic gardens where plants from different climatic spheres coexist.

Daniel Hjorth (2005) shows how entrepreneurship is let in and allowed to develop in some organizations. Through the use of art, not necessarily high art but preferably street art, created by the workers, there emerge areas where normal rules do not apply. Places of work, as defined by strategies, are thus transformed by the materialization of spaces for play. These are not part of the dominant place but rather designed as visibly separate, different – as heterotopias. Tactics enable the workers to find cracks in the system and come up with their own ideas, some of which are pure play and some supportive of entrepreneurial activities. This unwritten, non-managerial and perhaps even counter-managerial side of entrepreneurship needs to be recognized and understood, Daniel Hjorth argues, and this can be made possible by the use of de Certeau's ideas of spatial tactics. As with Hervé Corvellec's street risk managers, so with Daniel Hjoth's worker entrepreneurs: silence does not mean that they do not exist.

Increasingly throughout the 1990s and onward, managements seek to secure a creative organization. As a result, entrepreneurship has become an interesting solution to this problem. However, the history of management thinking and practice reproduces a managerial form of entrepreneurship. In the wake of the present hype for entrepreneurship, we have to distinguish between this official-strategic (management literature) version and local-tactical events of entrepreneurship.... Simplifying the matter, we might say that the tension between the tactical art of making spaces for play and invention in work and the strategic, managerial appropriation of specific places for work is thus in focus.

(Hjorth, 2005, p. 388)

George Cairns, Peter McInnes and Phil Roberts (2003) believe that heterotopias are appropriate for all kinds of organizing processes and that they should be seen as a realistic and desirable alternative to traditional means of control. They are suffused of knowledge and power, both through their physical characteristics and the meanings ascribed to them. Their rich symbolism is a treasure trove for leadership, although not of the hegemonic, traditional kind but particularly well suited for self-management and self-organization.

5.3 Sounds, images, dreams

I was fortunate to get a private tour of the 1998 James Turrell exhibition in Warsaw by the curator, Milada Ślizińska (CSW, 1998). The two presented works, *Wedgeworks* and *Aperture*, were both installations of light and space, embedded in the architecture of the Ujazdów Castle hosting Warsaw's Centre for Contemporary Art. I learned that the installations were typical of Turrell but more intimate than in many galleries of the West, due to the character of the castle. After having passed through a completely dark corridor, we entered a room where one wall was a shining blue film, through which a further shining blue room was visible. The whole area then began to feel as if it was enclosed within a wider space, the room itself made up of planes of light, turning the material walls translucent or, maybe, enabling to see beyond them, making visible a perspective that felt, at the same time, both transcendent and more real than materiality. One of the installations moved me particularly strongly; it was made up of very dim light, on the border of visibility; I would have problems in deciding what its colour was, the only thing I can say about it is that it felt ancient, old as the Pyramids, older than any traces of human civilization. It was an experience of a self-reflection so powerful that it short-circuited the ego; a meditative moment of awareness of being embodied within a vast and immeasurable space and time, experienced by something beyond the sense of self. It is not an exaggeration to say that this was, for me, a life-changing experience, like being on the verge to perceiving reality unmediated by the human senses, while, at the same time, seeing something that so obviously has always been there, only the experience of it gets lost in the grey noise of everyday perception.

James Turrell was born in the USA and had his first exhibition in the 1960s. He is an artist using light and space as his direct media, perhaps best known for his work in progress, *Roden Crater* in the Arizona desert, an extinct volcanic crater with a network of corridors, that he is turning into an observatory of different fragments of the skies; as well as several *Skyspaces*, enclosed spaces with an opening towards the sky. His art is about seeing itself, the awareness of being present in space, and is to be experienced on the boundary between 'within' and 'without'. It is, in a way, an outer and inner journey at the same time.

> 'I want to create an atmosphere that can be consciously plumbed with seeing', says the artist, 'like the wordless thought that comes from looking in a fire.' Informed by his studies in perceptual psychology and optical illusions, Turrell's work allows us to see ourselves 'seeing'.
>
> *(Skystone Foundation, 2010)*

It is difficult, if not impossible to describe Turrell's work using language, which so obviously is not part of it. Milada Ślizińska described it to me as relying on spatial thinking, a fundamental aspect of visual arts and human experience.

Thomas Tranströmer, the Nobel laureate in literature of 2011, is a Swedish poet and translator, as well as a talented pianist, and has been much praised for his ability to express musical experience in words. The Swedish Royal Academy of Music has awarded him an honorary membership for his role in the creating of links between music and poetry. But his work has also another distinctive ability, which has struck me particularly strongly while reading his haikus: they evoke an experience of space and spatiality, touching, by the medium of words, several senses simultaneously and almost transporting the reader into different spatial settings. The following three lines, which are one of my favourite poems in the Swedish language, recreate an aura of the far North and an intense and acute sensation of presence in the reader.

> The high-tension lines
> taut in cold's brittle kingdom
> north of all music.
> *(Tranströmer, 2011)*

It is the coming together of several distinctly Northern impulses through sounds, images and senses not comprised by the traditional Aristotelian five: the sense of temperature, and orientation. The inner migratory bird directs itself toward the magnetic north invoked by the poem, it is almost a physical attraction.

Tranströmer's spatiality is not static, he tells about movement: both of the experiencing subject and of the space.

> The sun lies low now.
> Our shadows are goliaths.
> Soon shadow is all.
>> *(Tranströmer, 2011)*

Dusk is very physically falling, as we move along a darkening path. The suggested outcome of the journey is truly enlightening, albeit it does not involve light but quite the opposite: darkness is the space of union between the outer and the inner spaces. There is a suggestion of emptiness but it feels warm and liberating, as in the Buddhist phrase: emptiness is form and form is emptiness. A different sensation of emptiness emerges from the next haiku.

> Medieval fortress,
> a foreign city, cold sphinx,
> empty arenas.
>> *(Tranströmer, 2011)*

This is a lonely emptiness, a lack of presence, marked by a sense of time passed, moving away from the centre of life and towards its opposite. The reader becomes aware of two different spaces: one bustling with human life with a clear direction and intent to please, to draw attention, to make an impression; and another, lonely and forlorn. Momentarily, they overlap.

Another of Traströmer's poems transfers several coexisting spaces at once; they have no other link between them than the author, and the reader.

> Oak trees and the moon.
> Light and mute constellations.
> And the frigid sea.
>> *(Tranströmer, 2011)*

Parallel spaces of nature, cosmos and humans exist and intersect, one using the other as a background or frame. The biological space of the oak trees is held together by the rhythms and flows, with the moon serving as a fulcrum for the changing of tides and seasons. The constellations belong to a context of stars and infinite distances, they circle and move away from each other in their own unfathomable rhythms. The sea is an ecosystemic space with a different quality of light, gravity and cycles but its coldness suggests the presence of a human subject, unable to return to the underwater gardens of Eden from the beginnings of life's story on Earth, and neither belonging in the other two spaces. Between the two symbolic sides of the poetic space suddenly a bond is forged: the author and the reader, freezing together.

In his poem *Outpost*, Tranströmer explains perhaps most succinctly his relationship to all these spaces:

I am the place
where creation is working itself out.
(Tranströmer, 2006, p. 116)

5.4 Reflection 2

Space has a symbolic and ordering role (Yanow, 1995). Buildings can be read as narratives and communicate important aspects of culture between social actors. These readings depend on the observer and do not have to follow the intention of the city planner or architect. The researcher may try to understand what the buildings say, taking in the symbols encoded into them and around them, and in particular: the material used to their construction, the typical path of different social actors within them, design and decor. They will reveal the designer's intention, for example, an impressive form and expensive design tell the story of vying for attention and respect, seeking to impress. On the other hand, the client of a public office located in such a building may feel the institution is inaccessible, unmoved by the problems of the people who approach it. Space can inspire or even invoke an urge to act or to remain passive, it may encourage or discourage reflection. Paying attention to spatial contrasts can also help to understand the working policy of the organization in its cultural context. They are best visible when the observer takes into consideration the relationships between the elements of space. Dvora Yanow (2005) suggests that the researcher can use his or her sense of embodiment in space to enter such relationships and help to interpret them. The language of design can also help, such as the height of the building, where the management is situated, how people read the messages of the design, what it does to the perception of different social actors' status, how it influences the mood, whether it creates a sense of distance and closeness, etc. Such languages are embedded in the cultural context and should be analysed while taking it into account.

Karl Weick (2003) carries this argument a bit further, arguing that architecture and design can indeed actively co-create the cultural context. The experience of physical space in organizations may help to develop diversity. Using the example of Frank Gehry, who often invokes awe by the apparent chaos of his architectural projects, Weick shows how space opens the mind. Gehry's architecture is about balancing on the border of what is possible to express and what defies all attempts at definition. This tension creates a very dynamic space which teaches how to manage paradoxes, how to live with irreconcilable differences and both respect them and not become overwhelmed by them: 'that's precisely what it means to coordinate variability, complexity, and effectiveness' (ibid., p. 96).

Jerzy Kociatkiewicz (2004) also considers the symbolic dimension of space and brings attention to spaces absent from the dominant discourse within organization theory. He shows the significance of different spaces for human actors interacting with IT in their everyday work. The traditional Cartesian division into body, existing in a physical space, and soul, functioning in virtual space, does not describe satisfactorily the way in which people and computers interact. To this traditional division the author adds technical space, the domain of the mind; personal space, where experience takes place; and abstract space, which is the domain of logic. All these kinds of space overlap in a particularly powerful and multidimensional space where transformation can become real, the space of the alchemical marriage. Here incongruous energies meet and dynamically complement one another. This is where all aspects: body, soul, mind, logic and experience interact synergetically and their communication produces new qualities and potentialities. Moreover, this space makes it possible for human actors to meet and communicate intensely, for example, to be creative together. The division of attention into rational and emotional spaces does not diminish people's concentration in this space, on the contrary, they become the more energized the more they engage in both. This synergetic effect shows that such spaces are not contradictive or mutually exclusive but can work very well together, if a right frame of mind is adopted.

The empty space as another powerful kind of space is located outside of the dominant intersubjective ones. According to Peter Brook (1995), the empty space is the minimal theatre, where the performance becomes possible. There also exist such organizational spaces, which emerge as potentialities, *becomings*, open to different enactments and meanings. Together with a co-author (Kociatkiewicz and Kostera, 1999), I have explored through non-participant observation, spaces existing at the margins of organizations such as fire escape stairs, cellars or unused storage spaces. They remain outside of rules and cultural meanings as defined in these organizations. They are indefinite and invisible to most participants, even though they may be an integral part of the organization's space, not even necessarily cut off by fences or barriers, because of their uselessness, in an epistemological sense, from the point of view of the dominant culture. They offer a meditative freedom to the observer who claims them.

> Emptiness does not exist. It is an anti-frame of reference, becoming pertinent only in some scientific theories, such as the theory of black holes, or in some legends, such as the story about the Bermuda Triangle.... Emptiness is generally associated with death or non-existence. Thus it serves the role of the other side, the contradiction of life, or its only meaningful form – social life. Emptiness as such does not exist, it can only be defined negatively, as the opposition to what it is not. Through its indefiniteness and undescribability it gains supernatural aspects, becomes like God, who, according to some, can be described through the use of words like: void, loneliness, silence, absence (Eco 1986/1987), expressions which refer to emptiness in the first place. Emptiness is infinite, as a form of time and as a form of space. It is not defined by any target points, any cognitive structures, habits, expectations. It is everywhere and nowhere.
>
> *(Ibid., p. 49)*

Bengt Gustavsson (2001) reminds us that emptiness can be negative or positive. Negative emptiness is characteristic of the traditional knowledge and ideas of organizations – it brings no more inspiration, it closes the mind, as Socrates used to reveal in the case of knowledge of his contemporaries. Positive emptiness is different, it is a starting point for new thinking. Such a transcendent epistemology of organizations is based on the transcendental experience of emptiness and is a dynamic knowledge, closely connected to transformational change itself.

It can also bring phenomena into being. Tor Hernes (2004) claims that the notion of space can in some instances replace the notion of organization. Space epistemologically represents a set of various ideas such as culture, structure and many others – it is a generic construct for organizations that is the underpinning of them all. It is a useful analytic tool because it can simultaneously show how actions influence contexts and vice versa. A key idea is that of boundaries, as space can only be meaningfully considered when they are present. Hernes proposes a typology of boundaries for organizational analysis: boundaries as ordering, or tolerance limits, boundaries as distinction, or markers of identity, and boundaries as thresholds to the import and export of resources. They are used in a variety of configurations in the three different fields of spaces: physical space, where organization is achieved by regulation; mental space, where organization by thought takes place; and social space, the domain of organization by bonding.

Space may also contain, oppress and disenfranchise, by trapping the body and the spirit in prison like structures. Spaces can be claustrophobic and confining, haunted by ghosts of unacknowledged pasts, resembling the Panopticon (Foucault, 1991) and enabling constant surveillance over social actors. Ann Minton (2009) presents public spaces in many modern British (and, indeed, existing all over the world) cities organized to be 'clean and safe', which are subjected to constant control, where people are discouraged from personalized use of the space and some social actors are prohibited from using them altogether. These ends are achieved by means of spatial tools and techniques such as 'slippery spaces', or spaces that cannot be reached, 'prickly space', or space that cannot be comfortably occupied, 'jittery space', or space constantly controlled by surveillance and monitoring, etc. (Flusty, 2004). In the world of organizations one of such popular uses is the so called open plan office. Mats Edenius and Ali Yakhlef (2007) describe this seemingly 'open' spatial idea as in fact enclosing and inhibiting – for the participants, and enabling of extended control for management. They also support extraverted communication, small talk and rapid exchange of interactions, but limit or prohibit altogether deeper kinds of communication and sharing. Also, they make concentration virtually impossible. Open space offices are particularly devastating when one considers deeper learning processes, as they rely on concentration, understanding and sharing, beyond the superficial level.

5.5 Stories from organizations

Many years ago, my co-author and I did field observations of the space of various public buildings, where we discovered empty spaces, the godhead of the margins of becoming and perception (Kociatkiewicz and Kostera, 1999). Among other places, we explored universities. It was the days before the current omnipresence of security measures: no magnetic swipe cards, no gates, only perhaps an elderly guard watching the faces of people coming and going. Yet these were also the days when the numbers of students and possible visitors were more limited and one tended to recognize many of them or, at least, a gut feeling could actually be depended on to work, of who does and who does not belong. Strangers who were visibly out of place were often stopped and asked their business. We never were; as professional strangers (Agar, 1996), with no socially recognizable purpose, no active intentions and no agenda, we remained almost completely invisible during all of our explorations.

The old building of the Warsaw School of Economics dates from the 1950s and is a striking architectonic landmark, rather straightforwardly majestic from the outside but intricate and complex on the inside. It is perhaps most known for its vast hall in the middle, called the parachute hall, because of the glass dome covering it, resembling an opened parachute. The light coming in through the glass tiles spreads softly over the central open plane, where groups of people stand and chat. We are surprised[7] how many they are, it is not like those central ceremonial spaces in public buildings which remain reverently unoccupied and it is only on formal occasions such as openings and press conferences that they become populated by officially dressed men and women. Here the space reminds us more of a market place, an impression reinforced by tiny stands advertising books and tables with information about some students' events. We enter the old cafeteria, looking much like it must have done in the late 1950s, filled with gentle light filtering in through the chiffon curtains, with a prominent glass-enclosed counter of a an ovoid shape and several square tables covered with white cloth; even then a relic from a past none of us remembers, nobody sane has been using white cloth in student cantinas for decades. But the students here seem peaceful enough, conversing demurely over cups of tea. We decide to move into the shadows. The corridors and staircases around the central area lead us to small enclosed spaces, populated with students sitting on benches and floors, holding on to books, talking more loudly than in the cafeteria and behaving much more spontaneously: some flirt, some talk exams; the furniture looks old and used but not in the majestic, historic way it did in the spaces below. We have a look into classrooms: all with a central blackboard, light wooden floors, rows of tables and chairs that are not quite orderly. It is a time between classes so most of the rooms are empty except for some students chatting in the corner or a solitary figure, looking as if she is preparing her presentation. Or maybe just writing. We move further, into the most shadowy corners of the building, the hidden stairwell, where we encounter a lonely smoker. He is not embarrassed by our presence, in fact, he makes no pretence of seeing us. Before leaving the building we have a look into the main lecture hall, grand, amphitheatrically descending towards a huge sliding blackboard. There is one thing many of the spaces of the School have in common: clocks. They seem to be omnipresent.

By contrast, there is not a single clock in sight in the building of the Polish Academy of Sciences. Who would have thought, judging from the compact bulk of the building, as seen from the outside, that it contains such a labyrinthine interior. We almost imme-diately get lost and we abandon ourselves to the feeling, letting the winding corridors take us wherever they please. Some are solid, the floor covered in thick, velvety carpets, dominated by solemn greens, earnest burgundy reds. The doors are made of dark wood and bear plates explaining that the room belongs to professor so-and-so or such-and-such department. We go astray in the meandering grey passageways, with a heavy smell of dust and laminated floors, with a hint of soap. The silence of the space is not unfriendly, it is somehow enclosing, motherly, even though it compels us to be as quiet as possible. There are few people around, most of them solitary, walking rather slowly and determinedly, not looking up. Only the entrance hall had hosted voices and echoes, conversations of which it was impossible to discern a single word, as if they were conducted in a foreign language. We go down different flights of stairs which range from the red carpeted ceremonial steps at the end of the marbled entrance hall to a dusty stairwell which looks as if it is never used and where we are, indeed, all alone. Nonetheless, this hidden place has windows, covered with a filter of fine dust, through which an almost otherworldly light spills in, descending softly on the stone steps, as if in the shape of plumes. We sit in silence for some time before we move on, descending into the underground world of almost black passages, smelling faintly of chapel and coal cellars. We pass by a dark room, lit up by a vague spotlight. A dark face of a man looks up at us, and for the first and only time we are asked what we are looking for. We say we are ethnographers and, amazingly enough, this is accepted without any further probing. But then, again, this building is full of fuzzy scientists of all possible denominations. A long time passes before we find ourselves in a place we recognize. Time to leave.

The neoclassical buildings of the Academy of Fine Arts hold a completely differ-ent mood. We are struck by the complexity but also the vivacity of the building: smells of paint and turpentine, a faintly rushing sound accompanying the buzz of voices and an indefinite suggestion of music somewhere in the distance. The hall is dominated by a huge sculpture in the shadow of which there stands a small cabin for the guard. He nods to everyone, including us. We change buildings and dive into narrow passages, filled with stuff: empty frames, paintings facing the walls (we take a look at some of them, most of them are gaudy, sketchy, hesitant, but we also emit the occasional 'mmm'), plaster sculptures in pieces or more or less desolate wholes, rags, planks, objects the purpose of which we cannot identify. The walls covered with peeling oil-paint are marked with the sporadic splash of colour or the name of one of the students or perhaps his or her beloved one. We stumble upon things we did not expect in such a space at all, such as a wash basin, neatly folded clothes lying on the floor, looking surprisingly new and clean in this otherwise chaotic milieu. We also pass by people, clad in stained gowns, perhaps students, in pairs or small groups, who take no notice of us at all. They carry or touch the things which inhabit this space, they stand around, sit or walk quite slowly. Then, sud-denly, we stumble into a largish room, reminding me of the loft of my childhood, full of dust-covered furniture, shapeless cloth, where the tiny windows are almost completely shrouded by rags and obscured by huge pieces of cardboard and wood.

It is almost dark here, a dusty, powdery smell, and much more silent than anywhere else in the Academy's buildings we visited. For some unexplained reason I am seized by a compulsion to sneeze, which is entirely psychical, not embodied; it is strange but not entirely unpleasant.

How simple, compared with that, is the School of Agriculture, dominated by straight, greyish corridors, punctuated by the occasional potted plant, exuding the familiar smell of floor polish and lit up by modest but cheerful light coming in from the large square windows with traditional wooden white-painted frames. The windowsills provide ample place for students, sitting in large numbers with or without books. On both sides of the main corridor there are glass cases with topical books, presumably authored by members of faculty. The doors are all tidily equipped with placards spelling out the names of the occupants or types of classroom. In a certain distance of the Dean's office the floor is covered by a carpet and nearby there stands a potted palm. This is the current standard; this is how we have learned to recognize the part of the building where a Dean's office is located. The Dean-less floors are usually devoid of large plants, as they are here, and the floorboards are made of oblong wooden tiles. Students laugh, talk and move uninhibitedly, and it is quite easy to spot the teachers, who walk with a more purposeful stride, usually solitary. Classes begin and we are left alone. Surrounded by a more focused, distant murmur, we leave the building. I think of school and, for some reason, of sparrows.

5.6 Questions to reflect on

1. If you live in an apartment block with several floors, take the elevator to a floor where you or anyone you know does not live, for example, the upmost floor if you live on the fifth, and take in the space: in what way is it different from your floor? Be attentive to details such as shades of light, colors, sounds, smells. Now go slowly down the stairs, and pause by each window (if there are any). Compare with the view from your window.

2. Explore the underground at your university/workplace. Try to look inside the rooms: what do they contain? Take time to observe details. For what purposes is the basement used? What kind of things are stored here? What are the smells like? What shade is the light? Is it quiet or do you hear any sounds? What does it feel like to be here?

3. Use the next free day to visit the three topmost tourist attractions of the city or town where you live. Imagine you are a tourist on holidays; take a camera and a guide with you. Read the guide, take pictures, buy souvenirs. When you return home, try to make comparisons with your everyday experiences of the city. Have you seen and learned anything new? What did the city feel like, seen from this perspective?

4. Visit a public administration building in your city. Concentrate on the space: what does it try to say? Is it friendly, intimidating, anonymous? Does it encourage you to sit down, walk about? Do you feel like a welcomed visitor or a trespasser? Is the space beautiful or ugly?

Notes

1 384 BC–322 BC, Ancient Greece.
2 *c.*80–70 BC–*c.*15 BC, Ancient Rome.
3 1646–1716, Saxony (Holy Roman Empire).
4 1930–China.
5 1901–1991, France.
6 1925–1986, France.
7 Based on field material from 1998.

6
SYNCHRONICITY

Stars swirling
in the cosmic wind
carry stowaway worlds

Synchronicity is a temporal concept encompassing a non-linear organization of
time. It is a meaningful, but not causally connected, relation between events in

external and internal spaces. Events and things happening are ordered by an under-lying pattern of meaningful coincidence and timing is one of the vehicles linking them together. It can be narrated and envisaged but neither measured nor managed. However, it can be intuited (see Chapter 3) and, when taken into consideration in the realizing of any vision, be it artistic, scientific or organizational, its help is invaluable, as it helps to avoid some of the uncertainty associated with such an endeavour. Visionary plans are suffused with uncertainty and while some people advise going against the stream and forcing the vision into becoming – much of the current mainstream popular leadership and entrepreneurship publications advocate such a view – a harmonious and sustainable way to go about it involves sensitivity and cooperation with the environment rather than force, manipulation or incon-siderate persistence. With respect for synchronicity seemingly impossible projects may take root. It is vital not just to 'find time' but to find the *right* time. Therefore it is necessary to understand what time is about.

In post-Renaissance thought time was conceived of as linear, ordering of events from past through present to future, and absolute, independent of the perspective of the observer. Time was seen as that which is measured by the clock. Currently, after Einstein, many people see it rather as relative, depending of other elements such as the frame of the observer, in reference to the speed, and forming a larger entity together with space. Clocks are stationary and fail to accurately measure time when dynamic conditions are fundamentally altered, that is, when the object is travelling with a speed faster than light. According to some views, rooted in antique philosophy, there is more than one kind of time. The measurable time, imposing order on events and things, is one; and the meaningful, connected to things that make sense to a person, is another. In the second understanding, time is not a phys-ical characteristic or dimension, but an inherent part of human experience. It may take different forms in the different spaces (see Chapter 5); for example, time is usually experienced as flowing at a much slower pace in the imaginative space than it does in the social space, people 'forget time' when they are engaged in artistic activity and they 'lose sense of time', but artists and writers usually also report another, powerful sense of timing present in the space where creative work takes place. Time is not a necessary and inevitable aspect of experience: some mystics describe a state of timelessness in the spiritual domain. However, it seems to be indispensable in all the external, intersubjective spaces, where human everyday life takes place.

Time connects inner states of mind, feelings, thoughts and visions with each other and with events happening to us, in the external world. This serves as a common narrative device, enabling stories to be told of what happened. The most popular is the simple chronological order: first this happened, then this. But there also exist sophisticated temporal narrative orders, based on experienced time, for example, going back in time, or narrating memories, or juxtaposing different tem-poral instances, by narrating the train of experience leading to realization, insight.

Modernity has turned time into a management tool, quite effective, because it is so fundamentally linked to human experience and to ideas of measurement. In particular, speed is associated with modern mainstream management: the imperative to produce as much as possible in as short a period of time as possible. The acceleration seems to be unbridled and incessant; with the use of more and more advanced technology the management process is constantly breaking its own record. This attitude to time has, from the beginning, been at odds with any notions of meaningful, experienced time, and by now mainstream management has, perhaps, reached a point of no return, a kind of organizational events horizon, where return to sounder practices is possible.

6.1 A short history of time and synchronicity

For Artistotle,[1] there were two different ideas of time: *chronos*, the time that can be measured in motions 'before' and 'after', which he presents in *Physics* (Roark, 2011), and *kairos*, the opportunity that is right for the achievement of success in rhetorics (Coelho, 2013). It consists not just of temporal of units but of opportunities, space and other conditions, meeting in a way that is just right.

Lucius Annaeus Seneca[2] sees time as linked with the human subject and concentric, not linear.

> Our span of life is divided into parts; it consists of large circles enclosing smaller. One circle embraces and bounds the rest; it reaches from birth to the last day of existence. The next circle limits the period of our young manhood. The third confines all of childhood in its circumference.... The month is bounded by a narrower ring. The smallest circle of all is the day; but even a day has its beginning and its ending, its sunrise and its sunset.
>
> *(Seneca, 1917–1925)*

One should treat time carefully, not waste it and concentrate on today, as this makes one less dependent on tomorrow.

> Nothing, Lucilius, is ours, except time.
>
> *(Ibid.)*

The naturalist and philosopher Abu Ali Husayn ibn Abdullah ibn Sina, better known as Avicenna,[3] does not regard time as absolute. For him, there are events and beings that exist beyond time, notably God and the act of creation. Time itself is a creation – the first creation. Nature is limited by time-space in its process of self-movement since the timeless act (Afnan, 1958).

St Augustine of Hippo[4] famously reflected on the passage of time and the fleeting realities of the mind in his *Confessions*:

> What, then, is time? If no one asks me, I know what it is. If I wish to explain it to him who asks me, I do not know.... But, then, how is it that there are the two times, past and future, when even the past is now no longer and the

future is now not yet? But if the present were always present, and did not pass into past time, it obviously would not be time but eternity.

(Augustine, 1940)

According to Henry Bergson[5] time is neither objective and homogenous nor an attribute of the mind but is characterized by duration, a creative and experiential quality. No two moments are the same and duration must be understood in terms of qualitative multiplicity, which is heterogenous, yet transition is continuous (Bergson, 2002).

Uniting both external and internal notions of time, synchronicity refers to a meaningful but acausal relation between external and internal events (Jung, 1993).[6] It is located in time, but it cannot be measured or controlled. It can be approached not by means of rational planning but rather through aesthetics.

6.2 Reflection 1

Time has always been one of the central issues in management theorizing, at least since the era of Frederick Taylor and his famous *Principles of Scientific Management* (1911) where he presents time as a valuable resource that should be measured and controlled. Such an approach would fabulously increase effectiveness, as it reduces waste and at the same time it can be used as an incentive to the workers – fast work according to the rules would be rewarded with better pay.

> [M]anagement, on the contrary, has for its very foundation the firm conviction that the true interests of the two are one and the same; that prosperity for the employer cannot exist through a long term of years unless it is accompanied by prosperity for the employee, and vice versa; and that it is possible to give the workman what he most wants – high wages – and the employer what he wants – a low labor cost – for his manufactures.
>
> *(Taylor, 1911)*

These two aims meet thanks to systematic measurement and management of time, seen as an abstract, fully controllable entity. However, this classical managerial notion of time is challenged by views stressing the experiential and contextual aspects of time. Hans Rämö (1999) utilizes the two notions of time: *chronos* and *kairos*, and the two notions of space: *chora* and *topos*, to develop ideas of time-space for contemporary organizational settings and managerial ideas. *Chronos* stands for measurable time, while *kairos* denotes the right moment.

> The words 'due measure', 'proportion' and, above all, 'the right moment' are some of the English translations of kairos that carry ideas of wisdom and judgment in timely situations. In addition to administrating according to the clock of what already exists and is already known, all managers of organizations (and humans in general) also have to seize new opportunities, in 'windows of opportunities',

opportunities that exist for a finite period of time. Furthermore, all managers face timely situations characterized as 'moments of truth', which might imply judicious actions beyond the mechanically learned and beyond timetables.

(Rämö, 2004, p. 853)

Chora is abstract space, while *topos* stands for concrete place. The abstract *chronos* and *chora* are related to theoretical knowledge, whereas concrete *kairos* and *topos* characterize practical wisdom and judgement (Aristotelian *phronesis*). Rämö distinguishes also two other, mixed spatio-temporal configurations, which are particularly relevant with regard to managerial ideas. The first, *chronotopos*, is localized in concrete place but in abstract time and is characteristic of time management, Just-in-Time and lean production.

[I]n management, time has become a tool for organizational study, but also a means, a commodity, to gain competitive advantage in the marketplace. Thus, in management, time is frequently equated with speed and is regarded as an important yardstick against how we measure the value of our activities.

(Rämö, 1999, pp. 318–319)

We will return to this later in this chapter. Now let's consider that the second form, *kairochora*, takes place in meaningful time but in localized abstract space and is relevant for so called virtual organizations. Such structures are supposed to work independently of time and space to produce concrete effects. Information and communication technology keeps them organized instead of spatial foundations. Coordination is temporal: they have to perform in meaningful moments of time such as completion of projects or contact with client. Their work is usually not measured in chronological time, which means that the employees do not have to keep a defined schedule, show up 'on time' and are not paid by the hour. In the case of such organizations, it is important to remember that trust no longer derives from rules and regulations and thus control, as in standard organizations, but, rather, it springs from the kind of wisdom and judgement that the organization is able to exercise, that is, trust arises from action in concrete situations.

One example of organizations, where kairic time is particularly important, is projects. Hans Rämö (2002) shows how strongly project management depends on timely moments. Project organizations typically involve individual projects that are limited in space and time, relying on a prompt management of extemporaneous situations and unexpected incidents. In such organizations '[a]ction and communication based on right moments to act intelligently in a unique situation are ... encouraged virtues' (ibid., p. 571). Project organizations must follow a different logic of management, where not only the sense of time and timing but also the key principles of ordering and control are adopted to their specificity.

A 'kairic' feeling is accentuated by the importance in project organisations to do the right things at the right moment. Project organisations have to

> rely to a great extent on the ability to handle unexpected incidents in an impromptu manner, whereas more permanent organisations frequently have more institutionalised job descriptions and rules.
>
> *(Ibid., p. 573)*

Such managerial wisdom cannot be derived from textbooks and must be strongly linked with professional judgement and ethos.

Geoff Jones, Christine McLean and Paolo Quattrone (2004) propose to relate spacing and timing to fundamental issues connected to processes of organizing:

> Spacing and Timing are, in a second instance, an issue of mediation, negotiation, and opening and closings, for attempts to achieve order and organizings (in a sense of a centred, singular and coordinated form) require a great deal of work. This emphasis on negotiation and mediation introduces a third and final set of issues: the notions of alterity, absence/presence and engagement.
>
> *(Ibid., p. 724)*

The absence or presence of the Other is always about encounters in concrete space and time and, in organizations, it has vital consequences for ordering. Negotiations and mediations, involving an active cooperation of various social actors, are of key importance for this process. All these actors need to be aligned, as well as the intermediaries and it should also be kept in mind that such alignments may lead to unexpected and unintended transformations elsewhere (ibid.).

Richard Whipp, Barbara Adam and Ida Sabelis (2002) have edited a book on the role of time in organizations. In an introductory chapter (Adam *et al.*, 2002), the authors explain that, although often being taken for granted and not problematized, time is a principal organizing tool. The aim of the book is

> to describe and explain this temporal complexity as it occurs in management by working with a variety of specialist perspectives, such as strategic management, organizational theory, decision making, industrial relations, and marketing.
>
> *(Ibid., p. 1)*

Time is conceived of not as a linear (chronological) abstract but including broader and more paradoxical features, more directly connected to concrete practices and contexts. Some of the issues have been long recognized as having a temporal aspect, such as the case with strategy, change and planning. Some are being identified and reconsidered more recently, such as technology, relations with the environment and the processual nature of organizations themselves. Management is one of the cultural ways of overcoming transience. As a foundation for modern management, time has been commodified – 'time is money', and quantified. Such time became an abstract exchange value and separated from context. Traditional management is usually concerned about control of time. However, in everyday management practice, time is experienced and lived in many different ways, contextualized and made meaningful in interactions by social actors. Contexualized time is much more difficult to control, and, especially as the awareness of different worlds turning in their own way grows, a sense of loss of control is quite often present in contemporary management. Therefore the authors advocate for a time-sensitive approach to management, making it possible to avoid pitfalls created by the unproblematic forcing of concrete organizations into moulds created by the embracing of assumptions about time as an abstract, controllable resource.

Another important consequence of thinking in terms of the embeddedness of processes of organizing in (the right) time, is reconceptualization of organizational change in terms of becoming. Haridimos Tsoukas and Robert Chia (2002) show how such a view is more in tune with what change, and indeed organizations, indeed are, if considered from a point of view of process. Living organizations are about process and change. If devoid of these features they die or turn into abstract entities which are quite unhelpful as objects of study if we are to understand how they operate and develop. If the temporal dimension is made conscious then change has to be seen as an intrinsic part of organization.

> Change is ontologically prior to organization – it is the condition of possibility for organization.... Organization is an attempt to order the intrinsic flux of human action, to channel it towards certain ends, to give it a particular shape, through generalizing and institutionalizing particular meanings and rules. At the same time, organization is a pattern that is constituted, shaped, *emerging* from change.
>
> (Ibid., p. 570)

Finally, this leads us to an important insight about organizing itself, which is about timing and time. It presumes communication and action, interwoven naturally within the broader context: right things, right people, coming together at the right time, which, in fact, is the very point of organizing (Czarniawska, 2000).

6.3 Sounds, images, dreams

Hermann Hesse's novel *Siddhartha* (2008), first published in 1922, is a story of a quest for the meaning of time. Here, however, it is a process rather than a thing and it certainly is not monolithic, not even unique. The protagonist, a young man who accidentally but significantly happens to be called Siddhartha, realizes one day that he wants to leave behind everything he has: a loving family, a good home, a dedicated fiancée, and set out on a journey to seek wisdom, which he believes can be found through a life among religious ascetics. His friend Govinda goes with him, mainly out of loyalty but also, to some degree, driven by a similar urge to find meaning. Grateful to the ascetics for what he has experienced during his time with them, but now convinced that the truth he is seeking is elsewhere, Siddhartha, and Govinda with him, leave their company to pursue their journey. They encounter the disciples of Buddha Gautama and they get to speak with the master himself. Govinda is thrilled, he decides to stay. Not so Siddhartha: the Buddha strikes him as a truly enlightened sage, someone who has found the way, but it is *his* way, and not Siddhartha's; he feels compelled to go on in his quest. Even if the end result is true, it is not right to reach it by a short cut, even if it is cut out by an enlightened master. The path to wisdom is making one's own choices, including the wrong ones. Siddhartha does that; he gets entangled in life, learns to see it from the non-seekers' perspective, he falls in love, works for a local businessman, gains wealth and loses it by his own decision to, once again, walk away from everything he had built up. On his way to the land where he had settled down he had crossed a river with a remarkable ferryman; he now returns the same way and he understands that only the river is able to teach him what he needs to learn, and he stays with the ferryman and works with him until, now alone and a ferryman himself, he becomes enlightened. He has now realized that time does not exist and that

> the river is in all places at once, at its source and where it flows into the sea, at the waterfall, at the ferry, at the rapids, in the ocean, in the mountains, everywhere at once, so for the river there is only the present moment and not the shadow of a future.
>
> *(Ibid., p. 90)*

What separates us from what we had been, from the moments of our lives, are just shadows, not reality, 'nothing was, nothing will be; everything is, everything has being and presence' (ibid., p. 90). Siddhartha finally is happy. This realization had to be experienced, not verbally expressed or communicated.

I knew I wanted to be happy and know the meaning of time, I longed for it, when I read the book for the first time, at 17. But words cannot transmit happiness, they are just a signpost, showing that you are on your way somewhere, and there is a river to cross. You return, reread the book, your face now 'more and more like that of the ferryman, almost as beaming, almost as suffused with happiness, almost as shining from a thousand wrinkles, as childish, as aged' (ibid., p. 91).

People camping in the gallery, sitting and lying in the middle of the floor. I had not yet seen anything like it, so I first stood there, feeling out of place, awkward in a place where I did not know how to behave, before myself taking a look at the films projected on the walls. Soon I, too, found myself sitting on the floor. This was 2002, Bill Viola's installation *Going Forth by Day* in Guggenheim Berlin, an experience of a magnitude one associates rather with spiritual epiphany than with visual art. Although, perhaps, it was both.

Bill Viola is a contemporary artist whose primary medium of work is light. *Going Forth by Day* has light also as its topic. It was inspired by Giotto's fresco cycle in Scrovegni Chapel in Padua, but goes beyond the static aesthetics of the motionless image, as well as beyond the medium of video installation (Heyd and Heyd, 2003). The artwork consists of a five part projection of 35 minute long videos – panels showing the cycle of nature and human life, using imagery and sound. The first one, entitled 'Fire Birth', is located at the entrance; the viewer enters the gallery through it. It shows embryonic figures appearing in a fiery substance. The second, 'The Path' presents an endless procession of different people, walking through a forest from the left to the right. The third panel is called 'The Deluge' and shows a facade of an old neoclassicist building, which people enter and leave, and in front of which they incessantly pass, carrying a variety of everyday objects. Suddenly, water starts bursting forward from between the stones of the building's wall and a deluge roars through it, washing out people, bodies and things. The water recedes, showing the facade intact, and people gradually return to their activity. 'The Voyage', the panel situated next, shows an older man dying in a house by a lake, a young man and a woman sitting by his bed. At a certain moment they leave, and the old man dies alone. He then rises and walks out, toward the lake, where an older woman is waiting for him in a boat. Together, they sail away. The fifth panel, 'First Light', shows emergency rescuers trying to find a person missing in a flood, busying themselves with equipment, accompanied by a relative of the missing man, probably his mother. It grows dark and people on the shore fall asleep. Then a light figure of a man suddenly appears, coming out of the water and ascending towards the sky with the sun rising behind him.

The suite is rooted in Viola's profound understanding of several spiritual traditions and while the title itself is taken from the Egyptian *Book of the Dead*, the theme is not limited to its imagery. It is a reflection on the flow of the journey of the human soul and it tells the story of experience beyond earthly time. Time is only a medium but not the plot, nor the organizing principle, or, indeed, the objective form of life. In Viola's artwork, time is shown as an attribute of the narrative written in light, surpassing any other form of expression, by making possible an immersion in experience. The storyline is not linear, its pulse is based on the circle, and it is possible to view the separate projections one at a time, or in any sequence the viewer prefers, or, indeed, to try to take them in simultaneously, which is not possible: due to their visual and aural character the viewer can focus only on one panel at the time. However, sitting in the middle of the floor, one gradually grows an awareness of them all, and becomes able to concentrate on it, instead of any of the individual panels. Such a mode of viewing is literally transformative; it fills the mind with images and sounds that seem to connect with feelings and ideas of the entire lifetime and, like in the panel entitled 'The Deluge', wash through them all, and bring forward a profound sense of being present throughout.

We live in stories, stories written in light. Time is important, it is their poetic rhythm, nothing more and nothing less.

6.4 Reflection 2

Rita Durant (2002) uses the Jungian idea of synchronicity, or meaningful but acausal link between an event taking place in external and internal times: a kind of non-random coincidence, to propose a framework for understanding organizational creativity. The author conceives of synchronicity as a paradoxical narrative, supporting creative relations between the human being and the world.

> With synchronicity, meaning is more than cognition; it is a physical and emotional charge resulting from an experience of the force uniting inner and outer reality. Beyond understanding in causal terms, synchronicity is an archetypal experience of meaning, and meaningfulness, from the 'inside out'.
>
> *(Ibid., p. 491)*

It contributes to the feeling of being 'in the right time and place'; offers hope and a sense of unity with a larger whole. It lies at the heart of the issue of uncertainty which is a very timely topic indeed for today's organizations. Chance and contingency occur daily and despite modern technology not more, as was hoped in the last century, but perhaps less than before, can be predicted. Synchronicity offers a way of encountering these occurrences as meaningful and as parts of a relationship between the organization and its environments, not as estranging chance incidents. Synchronicity has two dimensions: the external, manifesting itself as serendipity, or fortunate discoveries or turns of events; and the internal, a sense of insight and things falling into place.

> Synchronicity is an effect without a cause. It is located in time, but it is discontinuous. Being alert to synchronicity means being open to paradox.
>
> *(Ibid., p. 493)*

Paradox is inevitable and part of the world of research and managerial practice, and learning how to deal with it is not only beneficial but a necessity. Synchronicity offers a sense of unity between the organization and the environment, helping to regard paradox as a meaningful link between them. Creativity, like synchronicity, has an inner and outer dimension, and, like synchronicity, is surprising and unanticipated. Both require humility, a sense that one is part of something bigger and not always in control. They are based on a kind of surrender, acknowledgement of wider contexts, courage to explore what is beyond the meaningful domain of culture.

> Both synchronicity and creativity indicate a union of the timeless with the empirical stuff of life; both hint at the presence of eternity in a single moment.
>
> *(Ibid., p. 496)*

The author believes that organizations can benefit from an openness to synchronicity and creativity not just because they support innovation, present a good and timely response to current challenges of the environment such as increasing uncertainty and they support such solutions as self-managed teams as they do not presuppose control. Furthermore, their connection to narrativity makes them innovative management tools to establish connections with imaginative energies of people. Synchronicity can be endorsed by work environments where sufficient freedom is offered to people to encourage them to experiment and use their imagination and creativity. People need to feel safe, allowed to play and interact. However, the author also warns against a misuse of synchronicity: overreliance on chance breeds fatalism and may encourage hubris in managers who claim a special link to fate.

Foo Check-Teck (2011) presents the benefits of synchronicity for managerial decision making. Explaining synchronicity from within a Buddhist context, the author points to existing Chinese techniques for using synchronicity to make better, timely decisions. These involve the achievement of an appropriate state of mind through meditation and the use of a symbolic language of oracles and ancient Chinese divination tools such as Kuan Yin Qian. While it is advisable to use rational decision making techniques as an answer to problems that are certain and logically determinable, there is a group of problems and situations where such an approach is not only futile but also counter-productive. Such is the case of many contemporary issues, due to the increased uncertainty and changeability of the environment.

The external dimension of synchronicity, serendipity is valued especially by entrepreneurs and researchers involved in studying entrepreneurship. Nicholas Dew (2009) believes that the ability to use serendipity is one of the most important abilities of the entrepreneur. An entrepreneur reminds us to a certain degree of an artist or a discoverer. Both artists and discoverers often come up with ideas by inspired chance and not necessarily by rational search. They may set out for one destination or artistic goal, but end up with an altogether different one which turns out to be their great discovery – Columbus and Picasso being cases in point. Scientists, too, sometimes make great discoveries by what looks like pure chance, such as was the case with Fleming's discovery of penicillin. Similarly, a great number of entrepreneurial tales contain such elements of lucky break, fortunate accident, albeit not in the shape of pure and random events but rather a sort of 'answer to the entrepreneur's dreams'. The success of many entrepreneurs is a result of serendipity and the ability to use it. Dew believes that for an entrepreneur it is essential that three domains overlap: domain of prior knowledge, domain of search and domain of contingency. Prior knowledge does not have to rely on education; in particular formal schooling does not ensure it in a way most productive for the entrepreneur. It is earned through idiosyncratic life experience and is quite individual. Contingencies are events that do not have to happen, they are not logically necessary. They have to be seen and grasped by the entrepreneur, not by means of rational scanning or formulation of a good business plan. Search is the third element and encompasses an intensive engagement with the environment to find information that the entrepreneur can use. Some people seem to be more able seekers than others; this quality may be what distinguishes a good entrepreneur from a mediocre one. The three domains overlap creating spaces in which lucky chances may materialize. At the intersection of search and knowledge lies systematic exploration, or discoveries based on undertaken search. The domain of search and domain of contingency overall in an area of pre-discoveries, that may lead to later discoveries, can occur. Pre-discoveries are hunches that there may be something to a certain idea but without pre-existing knowledge it is impossible to judge the truthfulness of such an intuition. In the space where contingency intersects with knowledge there take place moments of spontaneous recognition, useful entrepreneurial opportunities that take place without search: the lucky breaks and sheer surprises. The area where all the three domains come together is the space of serendipitous discovery. Entrepreneurs are active in all of the three areas and once in a while the domains coincide in such a way as to produce a serendipitous discovery. However, the bulk of entrepreneurs' creative work consists in provoking situations where several, at least two of the model's elements, overlap, typically: knowledge and search, as the third one is uncontrollable. The ability to recognize this and be open to such factors beyond one's control may prove to be the greatest of the temporal challenges and, simultaneously, talents connected with sensitivity to internal and external aspects of time, present in the work of an entrepreneur.

> Enduring entrepreneurial firms are often products of contingencies. Their structure, culture, core competence and endurance are all residuals of particular human beings striving to forge and fulfill particular aspirations through interactions with the space, time and technologies they live in.
>
> *(Sarasvathy, 2008, p. 90)*

A talented entrepreneur does not treat time as a linear factor to control, instead, he or she needs to understand that there are different times and that the balance between them is of key importance: what many of the authors cited in Reflection 1 in this chapter have referred to as kairic time.

However, most of the mainstream management literature, whenever it speaks of time, is in fact interested in speed, even if such approaches as 'just in time' managements are in fact concerned about methods for speeding up operations, ideally to the level of *instantaneity*, via perfect coordination (e.g. Zimmer, 2002). According to Andrzej K. Koźmiński (2005) high-speed management, together with flexibility, is suitable for systemic transformation of the European economy. In fact, speed should be maximized as only the top performers can win the competition game in the changing world. This development necessitates a management education programme that would enable the formation of niche finders, people able to identify and exploit niches in the market. Management education should promote speed and flexibility through the ability to adapt instantaneously and cope with radical change. John Jones (1993) also advocates high speed management as a response to the ever changing environment. Time based management strategies are aimed at working faster than the competition, knowing that time is money and using time as a most valuable resource. All processes, including culture management, should be sped up to market and instant adaptation processes. Similarly, Pierre Mourier (2001) calls for a new velocity management, based on 'decision making at lightning speed' (p. 24). Velocity management enables management to develop an instinct for immediate reactions to errors and disturbances. Thus improvement can take place in 'off-schedule conditions' (p. 27).

6.5 Stories from organizations

Yga is a living legend of the Polish LGBT movement. She is a management graduate, working in marketing, interested in a variety of things such as cooking, arts, music (she used to play drums in a rock band when she was in school), poetry (she had the most poetic coming out I heard of, distributing her poems to friends and fellow students at the University). I asked her for the milestones of the Polish LBGT movement, as seen from her place in the world. She told a story of the struggle of getting time on her side. There were moments when things would flow smoothly, and there were moments when the organizers were fighting against a powerful current. There is still no possibility to marry a same sex partner in Poland, there is even no civil partnerships legislation. Yga[7] is living with her partner of 18 years, neither of them giving up hope to be able to get married one day. Hope is a way of propelling one's own time towards the main stream of others, and attracting their larger stream to approach one's own; where everything falls into place. To be able to once say: it is so obvious that these things happened, they were waiting to happen. As Vaclav Havel said, hope is the certainty that something makes sense and the ability to work for it.

The journey began well. In 1932 the Polish government decided not to consider homosexuality an offence. Several well known Polish writers and artists of that time lived a more or less openly homosexual life, even if the general public did not mainly consist of paragons of acceptance. Then the war came and many gay persons were murdered, sent to concentration camps and brutally persecuted. The centrally planned system introduced after the war did not plan for the eventuality of someone being gay; the early years especially, still under Stalin, were dominated by an aversion to sexuality and to anything that had to do with close human bonds, as is typical for totalitarian systems. In later decades sexual orientation never came up as a valid subject for social debate, even if gay people have been pretty much left alone, until the 1980s dominated by martial law and the dictatorship of General Jaruzelski. It was during this decade that the secret police persecuted homo- and bisexual people and as many as 11,000 persons were registered in the infamous 'pink files' for further use, mostly in blackmail. After the fall of the Wall, in 1990, Lambda was registered as the first Polish LGBT organization and began its work with much energy and enthusiasm. The early activists were not very good at the formal side of organizing but, in the words of one of the pioneers, Kando,[8] they were rather good with the social and idealistic side. They managed to obtain a room in a very good location – at the central University campus, and they organized a number of meetings, seminars, discos and social events.

These meetings were not, as today, 20 people [in all], but for example, a huge classroom, 100 people came, for example, it would take place at on campus.... We invited guests, really famous people, such as well known film directors, ..., politicians. Lots of things happened.

(Kando)

But, as I said, the organization did not display a talent for dealing with procedures and formalities. Petty matters, such as the inability to call a meeting, to prolong the tenancy of the offices or the failure to register its assets, which later became symbolically known as the 'battle for the kettle', derailed the first Lambda in 1997. A new Lambda was born one year later, this time with two visionaries and co-creators at its helm: Michał and Yga.[9] They were both well liked persons and talented organizers, and no form, procedure or aspect of social entrepreneurship was abhorrent to them. They also worked very well together and, for many years, the tandem led the movement through a number of activities which became well known throughout the country, such as demonstrations, protests, social marketing campaigns, reports on discrimination, information campaigns before local elections, and many others. Yga is quite an icon in Poland; she is often interviewed by journalists and media campaigns frequently feature her smiling face. Unlike so many celebrities and politicians, she smiles with her whole face, her eyes express hope; as for Havel, hope is for her what makes her not just follow, but try to shape the stream of time. Michał and Yga would heartily tap into the streams of time that worked for them, in the EU and the Polish economy which, until recently, was doing quite well: they successfully applied for grants, looked for sponsors, placed their organization on the national and international map, cooperated with other organizations, helped authors to publish books and albums related to the history and culture of the Polish LGBT movement. They are, however, both refreshingly modest people. According to Michał, the role of the leaders consists, more than anything else, in allowing people to be active and that is also their most important success.

We [the leaders] delegate to people in the organization, for example, someone wants to do something and we formalize it when he or she presents arguments why this is important, makes sense, how they want to do it, and we grant them a free hand, so that they can do it their way, [...], and we do not get in the way.

(Michał)[10]

Indeed, the organization is mainly based on volunteer work and the enthusiasm of many people: old and young, male and female, gay and straight. Teresa, a straight psychologist, attending Lambda's helpline, explained:

[We dedicate] our private time, our private energy and health and everything that is our private thing to various problems, to others. [...] I believe [that we are doing this] because one has a deficit, a deficit, wait, how should I put it ... I think it is a certain possibility of the human being, a potential possibility

[...] to do good. All of us have, perhaps, such a margin in our personality, to do good. And if one grabs such an opportunity, if one has the chance to do it, one will use it, I think[...]. You give your time, not taking anything back, and at the same time you have an enormous satisfaction because you feel you have, as if, subtracted some iniquity from the world.

(Teresa)[11]

Lambda's journey was, and still is, a collective one, built on sharing, common responsibility and a feeling of community, stretched in a time that, for the larger Polish society, was mainly about other things: surviving in a transition economy, not losing one's cultural identity, history. It brought hope to many people, both inside and outside of the organization. A hope which Yga has in abundance and which she often and generously shares with others. But the journey was also rocky at times. In 2005 the right wing authorities prohibited the demonstration for LGBT rights in Warsaw. However, instead, an illegal demonstration marched through the city, and many people, not just gay, joined, condemning discrimination, invoking human solidarity and reminding of the dark times, such as the Nazi rise to power in Germany, when a contempt for minorities led to a global tragedy of human civilization. Repeated attempts at getting a legal standing for same sex couples: 2003, 2011, 2013 on Yga's list of milestones, failed. However, as she promptly points out, the attitude of the public has changed enormously during this period of time. In 2003 a significant majority was opposed to civil partnerships of same sex couples, today 33 per cent of the population is for[12] and the figure has been constantly, even if slowly, growing with time.[13] At the same time, a majority admits that homosexual people are being discriminated against in Poland.[14] She recalls a question from a journalist in the 1990s about who, in her partnership, played the role of 'man' and who of a 'woman'. Today, journalists ask instead: 'which are the most important issues that a civil partnership law should regulate?'. Yes, things have changed, and Lambda has helped these changes to happen. She points out that politicians are quite another matter; it is much more difficult to change them than the mood of the general public. However, they can be changed too: either their programmes or they themselves can be exchanged for others. It will take work and time but it needs to be done.

We have to be aware, disappointed and angry [with the last vote over civil partnerships], yes, but most of all, aware.

(Yga)[15]

Yga's list of milestones contains not just disappointments but several dates marking celebration and success: 1992, the year of the first public coming out of a well known actor; 2001, the first Pride in Warsaw, which, in Poland, is taking the shape of a human rights demonstration; 2003, the law prohibiting workplace discrimination of LGBT persons is passed by the Polish parliament; 2010, the first openly gay person, Krystian Legierski, elected to the local government in Warsaw; 2011, two LBGT persons: Robert Biedroń and Anna Grodzka, elected to the Parliament.

Did you have any use of your management studies?, I ask Yga, as I write this story. Sure, she says, organizational psychology and sociology proved very useful for her sociological imagination, such things as group dynamics, communication, how people work together. But also about organizing, how to organize oneself and events, how to manage projects, actually, all the basics were seeds that grew with time, with the help of practice and imagination.

6.6 Questions to reflect on

1. Is it a period of time, such as a certain decade (the 1920s, the 1960s, the 1980s, etc.) that you identify yourself with particularly? Is it a period from within your lifetime? Why is it important to you? In what ways are you linked with that period of time?
2. Make a list of 12 temporal milestones of your life up till now. Why were they so important? Whom did you meet? What happened? Did you feel aligned with the times (zeitgeist) or not? Did you feel you were going with or against the tide?
3. Are you always too early or always almost too late? Are you usually way ahead of time for planes and trains? Or do you arrive at the last minute? Think of a friend who is your opposite in this respect. Invite him or her to 'swap times' with you for one to two weeks. Be very disciplined and always do what your friend would have done at that occasion. Write everything down in a note-book. Then meet again and 'swap back': tell each other stories of how life in that other person's shoes were like, what happened, how you felt about it.
4. Draw a representation of what time is like, for you. Is it a line? A circle? Something entirely different?

Notes

1 384 BC–322 BC, Ancient Greece.
2 4 BC–AD 65, Ancient Rome.
3 980–1037, Iran.
4 354–430, Numidia.
5 1859–1941, France.
6 Carl Gustav Jung, 1875–1961, Switzerland.
7 Material obtained from Yga, 2013; interviews conducted 1999–2000.
8 Interview from 2000.
9 There was also a third founding member, Krzysztof, who, however, preferred to work only with the helpline.
10 Interview from 1999.
11 Interview from 2000.
12 CBOS, 2013.
13 25 per cent in 2009 (GfK, 2009).
14 60 per cent according to PBS (2008).
15 Yga, private communication April 2013 (after the voting of Parliament on the proposition of the Law of Civil Partnership).

PART III

Motivating

Introducing the 3 L's: leadership, learning and love

The function of motivation stands for encouraging, causing the people in the organization to make the effort. In non-mainstream management it does not refer to persuasion, manipulation or exerting of power, but rather to finding a reason for doing something, one that matters: *why* should this be done? The idea or project has to move the inventor and the result should make a difference. The main fundamental reasons of this magnitude are: leadership, learning and love.

- *Leadership* is about being a visionary or putting trust in one; it is important to be able to tell whether the leadership is constructive and helpful for the organization.
- *Learning* makes the development of new projects meaningful; it can be an aim in itself or an important side product.
- *Love* makes effort worthwhile.

7
LEADERSHIP

Darkening
of the light
Closer
and closer
changing sides
Now I am it and it is me; it is
Not

Leadership is often regarded as a special quality of an individual, the talent or destiny to lead other people. The leader is thought to have an innate propensity, perhaps of a hereditary nature, to gain followership and be revered, admired and deferred to. In other words, many people conceive of innate leadership, a quality that a person has got, be it as a gift of nature or from the gods. Myths recount the supernatural origins and childhood exploits of great leaders, such as Alexander the Great, pointing to the more than human character of such individuals. Analogous modern stories emphasize the inborn skills of successful business leaders, perhaps due to them being alpha males or females, awakening loyalty in others by sheer genetic makeup. Another well founded tradition of understanding leadership is the epic origins. A person embarks on a heroic adventure, which teaches him (or more rarely, her) how to be a leader. In the beginning, he is more or less ordinary, but by a successful completion of a quest, becomes recognized by others as the true king, the rightful chief, the good boss. Instead of a mythical quest, the person may undertake a learning project, a version much more common today, for example, by completing a challenging MBA programme at a prestigious institution or by facing a difficult managerial turnaround endeavour. Such an approach rests on the assumption that it is possible to become a leader through education, practice, or both.

There is, however, another way of perceiving leadership – as a role within a community or organization, rather than a characteristic of a person. One *is* not, then, a leader; rather, one *stands in the place* of the leader. Like most roles, the leadership role can be seen as based on a contract, offering benefits to both sides, an occupation, or a vocation. Some people are more willing to assume such roles than others; some are also more gifted, they may possess a special quality, charisma, which makes it more likely for others to notice and follow that person.

Leadership encompasses the power to organize others to reach a common goal. It may also be regarded as a symbolic representation of the group, of its cohesion and legitimacy. Leaders offer a sense of shared meaning, a trust in a common future.

There are two main ways of fulfilling the role of a leader: through vision or representation. A visionary takes responsibility for an idea about the shared goals of a group, and of the ways that they can be reached. Such a person is associated with the idea by others; if it succeeds, he or she is hailed as the author of the success, but if it fails, then the leader is blamed and many of the followers may be exonerated. This is an intense shared learning situation, but there is no guarantee, of course, that the goal is successful or just. History knows as many examples of brave and enlightened visionaries, such as Buddha Gautama or Martin Luther King, as it knows leaders proclaiming a corrupt, murderous vision, such as Josef Stalin or Adolf Hitler.

A leader who represents a group tries to be as sensitive as possible to its aims and desires, often by empowering the goals of the majority, but some leaders take it upon themselves to also satisfy some of the needs of minorities. Part of the responsibility is reflected back to the group and the power may be more dispersed, but the situation of such groups is often experienced as static, even stagnating, and there is less hope for change.

Leaders are important for communities and organizations, because they offer a sense of direction and unity. However, there is also a distinctly dark side of leadership: people in this position often come to believe that they are better than others, even more than human. This makes them reckless and narcissistic, they abuse their power and act in harmful ways, focusing on their ego, instead of the needs of the group.

7.1 A short history of leadership

Ancient and classical philosophers considered leadership through the lens of the archetype of the King (Kostera, 2012). Plato[1] (2007) reflected on the ideal leader in the *Republic*, where he stated that, just as boats need a steersman, societies require leaders. He depicted the ideal as the philosopher king, someone with a passion for truth and wisdom. Not prone to illusions like ordinary people, he is able to see the truth itself, usually hidden from view from the eyes of mere mortals. The world is like a cave where people, chained to face the wall, can only watch a theatre of shadows passing in front of their eyes. Most of them do not realize that behind their backs there is a vibrant world, full of light, which falls into the cave and animates the shadows on the walls. The philosopher king is different. He knows the real nature of the world. He is able to experience the real pleasures that only beauty and truth can give. His, or indeed her[2] role is to guide his people towards them and to share the wisdom that he or she is able to gain from them.

The ancient Far East philosopher Sun Tzu[3] (2008) was also convinced of the necessity of moral superiority of the leader as compared with ordinary people, the subjects. The leader is someone who is able to affect fate and, if used from a morally higher position, can bring all kinds of success to the people. He is obliged to guide and to share, which means that a communicative talent is required, especially as the leader's intellectual capacity and thinking style surpasses the abilities of others. The leader should be modest, not attracted by fame or wealth, only driven by the ideals of common good. Just like Plato's philosopher king, Sun Tzu's leader is an enlightened Taoist master and a sage.

Thomas Aquinas[4] (1949) shared some of the central convictions of both Plato and Sun Tzu (although he was probably unaware of the latter's existence). In *De Regno* he depicts the king as someone endowed with powers given him from a higher source, from God. He uses them to impel towards a common good. Aquinas discerns between different types of rulers, from the unjust tyrant, to the ruling group and just king, seeking common good. According to Aquinas, however, it is 'best for a human multitude to be ruled by one person' (ibid.).

Max Weber[5] (1992) did not subscribe to the view of the superiority of such leadership. Instead, he proposed that there are different types of power: traditional, based on what is customary; charismatic, or resulting from a unique bond between the leader and the followers; and legal, based on the rule of law. It was the latter that Weber considered superior to the others: more effective and modern.

7.2 Reflection 1

Much of the mainstream management literature dedicated to leadership focused on the special innate traits of the leader, a kind of talent that needs to be identified and perhaps developed (Stogdill, 1974). Among these traits Ralph Stogdill counted assertiveness, cooperativeness, adaptability, decisiveness, dependability and tolerance to stress. There were also leadership skills, to be enhanced, such as intelligence, creativity, fluency in speaking and persuasiveness. Other authors, such as Kurt Lewin, Ron Lippitt and Robert White (1939) believed that there were different styles of leadership the effectiveness of which depended on the situation and the characteristics of the group. There are three main leadership styles: autocratic, democratic and laissez-faire. Autocratic leaders formulate tasks and expect subordinates to conform. In an organization managed by an autocrat there is a clear hierarchy and usually a centralized responsibility and authority. Autocrats do not consult their decisions with others; they make them on their own. This style is the most effective in unmotivated and rather immature groups, when the task is simple and the outcomes easily measured. In the researcher's experiment, this style causes the most discontent. Democratic leadership is oriented towards achieving a consensus. Decisions are made collectively, and different perspectives and opinions are sought and used as valuable input. This style was found to cause the most satisfaction among people, and proves to be effective when the group is fairly motivated, the communication between people is working well and the task is not easy to measure or structurize. Laissez-faire is a style of minimal involvement; people are left to their own devices as much as possible. The leader only sets the goals and perhaps also shares the most important values with the people. It works well when the group is highly skilled and motivated and where no external control is necessary. More contemporary work on leadership styles (e.g. Hersey *et al.*, 2007) emphasize the necessity of matching individual leadership styles to the characteristics of the context, such as the group, the environment, the type of tasks, etc. Skills can be learned and need to be adapted to the situation.

Another approach regards leadership as an archetype, or a pattern hidden deep within the collective unconscious or within human culture (Kostera, 2012). Czarniawska and Wolff (1991) present the three interconnected roles: manager, leader and entrepreneur. They argue that these are all archetypical because they have a relevance unrestrained by the passage of time. The manager is concentrated on more mundane things, such as the everyday workings of an organization, the entrepreneur creates and brings new organizations and ideas into existence, and the leader takes centre stage by giving the possibility to control fate.

> Leaders serve as symbols representing the personal causation of social events.
>
> *(Ibid., p. 535, emphasis removed)*

They do so by bringing together elements and resources and providing them with agency in such a way that they get to symbolize the whole organization. Manfred Kets de Vries (2003a) depicts an exemplary leader, Alexander the Great, king of Macedonia, as an archetypical leadership character. He was undoubtedly one of the greatest leaders in known history, not just from a military point of view – he created one of the most powerful empires of the ancient world – but also as a philosophic and scientific guide, one who successfully gathered new knowledge and encouraged others to do the same. He was also a great propagator of Greek culture and the Hellenization of many of the contemporary cultures was due to his advocacy. He was magnanimous, courageous and open minded, he knew how to communicate with others and was fiercely loyal. But he also had a dark side that got enhanced with time. He increasingly saw himself as someone more than human, a god, and this caused him to be suspicious, even paranoid, self-obsessed, and in the end, unfeeling and cruel. Kets de Vries holds that this historical figure has an archetypical relevance for today's bosses, as a story resonating with some of the central issues that business leaders have to deal with. Leadership is critical as a way of life, in the sense that leaders bear a responsibility for more than just themselves, more than the family or closest surroundings. They do not make innocent mistakes, as their blunders almost always have consequences for others as well. All this uncommon aspects present a temptation to regard oneself as more-than-human, which brings forward dark tendencies which only can be transcended through awareness. More about the dark side of leadership will be said in the Reflection 2 section.

Now let us return to some more ideas about leadership archetypes. Together with a co-author (Kociatkiewicz and Kostera, 2012b) I explore the potential for what we call morally sustainable leadership, that is, leadership with an awareness of both its light and dark sides. We look at the symbolism contained in the archetype of the king and its consequences for the management of organizations. We carried out a study in the domain of imagination with the help of the narrative collage method (Kostera, 2006). Respondents were asked to write a fictive story, belonging to a chosen genre and, with plots and characters of their choice, on a given subject or beginning with a phrase verbalized by the researcher. In this case, we used the following phrase: 'Upon a certain Anniversary Day the good manager had come from London, and had held a very magnificent reception at the HQ as was fitting on such a day.' It is a paraphrase from Chrétien de Troyes' (1988) introductory sentence of his tale of King Arthur. The respondents – management theorists and practitioners from different countries – wrote 23 stories which we then interpreted in order to see how issues of leadership and goodness are related to each other and to other themes. The stories are archetypical tales, touching profound aspects of culture and the mind. Taken together, they tell yet another tale, the narrative collage, a tragic and ironic representation of a goodness that has absented itself from the world's organizations, but which is necessary, and very real indeed, even if hidden, waiting to be gained yet again.

Paul Moxnes (2013) looks for the implications for leaders in another classic archetype, the Hero. Traditional heroic narratives and organizational stories often share the motif of an individual overcoming a number of obstacles and, in the end, achieving success. This is certainly a transformation role, invoked especially during times of crisis or stagnation. Even though such characters have little or no effective impact on the organization's performance, the symbolic potential of a 'saviour' is significant. People want such stories not just because they give hope, but because of their considerable educational potential. Moxnes has found that heroic stories have a real and lasting effect on internalizing knowledge by students. Learning is not just a conscious process, but relies also on process outside of awareness. Archetypical narratives have, therefore, a great learning potential. Finally, leadership itself has an irrational side, and archetypical stories can guide leaders through this domain far better than many other, more rationalistic knowledge.

A related quest has been undertaken through the use of fully realistic stories, as presented by famous CEOs in interviews published in the *Harvard Business Review* (Hatch *et al.*, 2005). The storytelling talent of these managers, together with a kind of aesthetic sensibility, if not always necessarily consciously sought for, result in a collection of compelling narratives, full of metaphors, dramatic effects, mythical and archetypical characters, which have the potential of expressing responsibility for organizational maturation and transmitting the experience of change to others. Leaders can derive from stories, and more generally, from aesthetics, a holistic understanding and practical human wisdom. Stories link everyday events and facts with universal human experience. The tools that aesthetics offer leaders, such as storytelling, dramatization and mythologization, may be used to develop practical wisdom. Leaders know how to recreate real life experiences and influence it by the telling of stories, and they change their stories as organizational life develops and transforms. Thus management can use aesthetic methods to actively co-create reality (see Chapter 2, Section 2).

7.3 Sounds, images, dreams

Little Matt in Janusz Korczak's unforgettable children's book (2011a) did not want to be king, but after his father's death he had no choice – he was made to accept the crown and the symbolic responsibility for the kingdom. It was thought to be just a symbol, nothing more; until he grew up the country would de facto be ruled by his advisors and secretaries. The neighbouring countries saw it as an opportunity to attack and conquer the land. However, they turned out to be wrong: little Matt's army won the war. The victory was but the beginning for the child king, who might have been small but had some big ideas. More than anything he wanted a childhood, he missed his parents very much, and wanted to play and to study like other kids. But during the war he had met other people, coming from very different backgrounds to his own, made friends with Felek, a boy from a poor family. All this had taught him to see the world differently, to understand problems no one at court seemed to be able to deal with or even face. He felt responsible; even though he was still too young to even read and write, he set out to change the world and started to introduce radical reforms. To the displeasure of advisors and secretaries of state, King Matt signed a peace treaty with an African ruler, traditionally regarded as an enemy. He refused to submit to the rituals of the court, he made friends with his subjects and finally decided to introduce constitutional monarchy, giving people citizenship rights and a say in the rule of the country. This included the children who got a parliament of their own. He also encouraged the children of the world to stand up for their rights. This made the neighbouring rulers very cross. Another war began and King Matt was treacherously captured and sent into exile to a desert island. This is how the first book ends but Korczak's young readers demanded a sequel and so he wrote the story of King Matt's exile and return (Korczak, 2011b), how he managed to escape and get back to his kingdom, where he established full democracy for all, of course, including the children.

The author, Janusz Korczak, was a Polish-Jewish pedagogue, famous for his activism for children's rights and his work on re-education of young delinquents (Olczak-Ronikier, 2011). Together with Stefania Wilczyńska, he directed a home for Jewish orphans before the Second World War, which was relocated by the Nazis to the Warsaw Ghetto in 1940. Despite the horrifying conditions in the ghetto, he and Wilczyńska succeeded in giving the children a relatively decent life, by virtue of their brilliant managerial skills, perseverance and sheer courage. The orphans were sheltered from the horrific brutality of the ghetto life and the pedagogues viewed it as imperative to give them, even if food was lacking, a sense of meaning and justice. Korczak was asked several times by his friends, living on the so called Arian side, to let them rescue him. They wanted to get him out of the ghetto and, realizing that he was a precursor of pedagogical ideas that lay much ahead of the times, tried to persuade him that his work was too important to be cut short by the war. He refused, and when the order came to liquidate the orphanage, he chose to follow his children to death in Treblinka, as did Stefania Wilczyńska. Witnesses recall that even on this last horrendous march to the Umschlagsplatz, from which people were packed into cattle trains carrying them to the death camps, the children walked orderly, neatly dressed and looking well cared for, holding on to flags with King Matt the First (Szpilman, 2000).

The main protagonist of Werner Herzog's (1972) film, Lope de Aguirre is a Spanish soldier who leads a group of people in search of El Dorado down the Amazon River in the mid sixteenth century. He is an enthused visionary, guided by the conviction that the journey through the most inaccessible parts of the Latin American continent will eventually lead them to the legendary city of gold. Although originally entrusted with the task of second in command of a rather straightforward reconnaissance party, he soon takes over the leadership by inciting a mutiny against the commander, who appears to lack faith and be too weak to succeed. Aguirre seems to know that El Dorado is within their reach, and that they are on the right track – if only they persevere, success is not only possible – it is certain. Apart from the fearful nature surrounding them, which they are neither used to nor equipped for, they are threatened by the natives who observe their progress from the banks of the river and shoot poisoned arrows at them. They suffer from the poison and diminishing supply of food, but perhaps most perilous of all is their own persistence, held up by Aguirre's incessant proclamations of his vision of imminent success. The only source of conviction and meaning, Aguirre remains unquestioned and unquestionable, maybe because no one has the courage to challenge him, or perhaps, because doing so would mean the necessity of giving up hope, something no human being is ready to do, if he or she has even the smallest will to live left. The journey goes on and all the men and women die, one by one, and at last Aguirre remains as the only survivor, but even then he does not lose his vision of success; neither does he give up his role as leader. Drifting around and surrounded by corpses, he continues to be in charge of the dead men, a group of monkeys that had boarded the raft, but most of all, the dreams of reaching the city of gold and becoming its magnificent ruler.

Aguirre keeps calling himself the Wrath of God, he believes he is on a mission to found a new dynasty and become the ruler of the continent. Obstacles do not deter him; impossibility looks to be just that only before the successful reaching of an end; afterwards it seems like necessity, like fate. Aguirre's vision enables him to reverse the sequence, fate goes before him. The filmmaker Werner Herzog is, not unlike his creation, known for trying to do the impossible, even if it means putting himself and the crew in danger (O'Mahony, 2002). In the words of Klaus Kinski who played the role of Lope de Aguirre,

> he creates the most senseless difficulties and dangers, risking other people's safety and even their lives – just so he can eventually say that he, Herzog, has beaten seemingly unbeatable odds.
>
> *(Ibid.)*

7.4 Reflection 2

Manfred Kets de Vries (1998) depicts two contemporary business leaders: Richard Branson and Percy Barnevik, who are famous for the ability to transform whole environments. They not only create and radically change their organizations, but influence institutions: set the standards for whole businesses and industries, generate visions that others try to live up to. They have charisma, a combination of dreams, visions and expectations that form a special bond between them and other people. This quality enables them to act as agents of change.

> In order to move the change process forward, such leaders know that every individual should be empowered to consider him- or herself as a crucial player. If employees are inspired, empowered, and free to act, they will stretch themselves to make exceptional efforts, demonstrate a high degree

of commitment, and be willing to take risks.... The blueprint for the change process is drawn from the leader's ideals and a shared vision. The bricks and mortar are communications, trust, and reward.

(Kets de Vries, 1998, p. 8)

The charismatic leader should be able to communicate his or her vision, engage others and make them able to feel proud of a common effort or the achievement of a shared goal. They are able to bring the best out of people, inspire them to want to develop and offer them the possibility to develop a basic sense of trust that makes individual and collective growth possible. Furthermore, they can utilize the normal, usually gigantic potential of energy present in most organizations, that may be aggressive or affectionate, and they channel this energy in one shared direction (ibid.).

Barbara Czarniawska-Joerges (1993) portrays visionary leadership as heeding of future rationality, acting as if the change has taken place already. Culture can be profoundly changed, but not by superficial manipulation or pronouncement of new mottos and slogans, but through symbolization and the giving of a convincing example: at the same time practical and spirited, such as by responsible and visionary leadership (Hatch, 1993). On the other hand, the allure of making noise around oneself, to pose as a management guru, is very attractive to some leaders, while the media and popular culture seem never to tire of such 'loud managers' (Mintzberg, 1999). Contemporary media are full of stars and celebrities of management, presenting themselves as brilliant strategists who singlehandedly succeeded in turning around a failing business and making it a goose that produces golden eggs. Yet so many of them are so busy with self-promotion that they lack time or heart for anything else. Their formidable changes prove to be superficial manipulations, often undertaken at great human and material cost, their grand successes turn out to be nothing but inflated egos and their allure is not due to charisma but a collective infatuation. The facade of greatness often turns out to cover a bland and shallow interior. They are visible and they are loud but if one listens carefully, one hears that what comes out of their mouths is just a cascade of fashionable slogans. In contrast, good management is silent, modest, perhaps even a little boring. Good managers are first and foremost responsible and they do what should be done in order to take care of their organizations. They act globally and they introduce changes but they do so with care and they do not make much noise about it.

Quiet management is about thoughtfulness rooted in experience. Words like wisdom, trust, dedication, and judgment apply. Leadership works because it is legitimate, meaning that it is an integral part of the organization and so has the respect of everyone there. Tomorrow is appreciated because yesterday is honored. That makes today a pleasure.

(Ibid., p. 30)

Noise interferes with thoughtful and considerate management, based on respect for people, the organization and for real time. Change takes time; fast 'solutions' more often kill than save.

> Might not the white knight of management be the black hole of organizations?
>
> *(Ibid., p. 27)*

Many workplace problems of our times are caused by organizational narcissists who seem to thrive in modern corporations (Kets de Vries, 2003b; Kostera, 2012), so much so, that recently there have been some attempts to declare it a non-problem (see, e.g. Pfeffer, 2013).

> People want to associate with winners: people who are going places and therefore can help them. Narcissists, who have higher levels of self-esteem, display more confidence and do more things that will cause them to stand out – such as being assertive – thereby attracting more people and greater talent to their team.
>
> *(Ibid.)*

Therefore there is no need to worry that business schools promote a pathology, according to the author.

> Maybe business schools are doing just what they should: selecting precisely the people who have the greatest chance of being individually successful and putting them in environments that reward self-promotion and competitive success.
>
> *(Ibid.)*

However, researchers of the phenomenon, such as Clive Boddy (2011) claim that there is compelling evidence that the harm, both in human and material terms, done by such and other pathological leaders, is enormous. They create workplaces where such phenomena as conflict, bullying, low levels of job satisfaction and overall human suffering are everyday, and they tend to be destructive from the point of view of their organization as a whole. They are attracted to managerial positions because of the high rewards connected with them, as well as the great risks that go with the job which they experience as thrills. They are seen as ideal for the job because they are excellent at selling themselves and many of their pathological traits, such as great resistance to stress or determination and assertiveness, are valued by corporations. Indeed they are positively value thriving, 'the higher up one goes in an organisation, the more likely one is to find Corporate Psychopaths' (ibid., p. 108). People with high levels of narcissism are arrogant, self-centred, maladaptive and exploitative and they make terrible leaders, interested only in their own aggrandizement, even if it is achieved at disproportionate cost or built upon a lie. Psychopathy, which Boddy primarily focuses on in his book, has many common characteristics with narcissistic personality disorder but there are some differences. Psychopaths lack a conscience altogether, while narcissists have feelings, albeit mostly directed towards their own behaviours. However, if needed they may be willing to change. Psychopaths do not care about such 'trivialities'. Yet indeed, both groups are focused on something other than the wellbeing of the organization and the employees. Organizational psychopaths may even get a thrill out of hurting others and there is nothing at all that can stop them in their drive towards domination and what they perceive as 'victory'. As with kingdoms, societies, so it is with organizations – much misery is caused by tyrants, great or small. A leader who compromises his or her humanity, perhaps believing that they are more than human, degenerates into a tyrant, devoid of conscience and empathy and therefore sliding into a less than human condition (Kostera, 2012). The tyrant becomes obsessed with his or her position and with the preservation of power, feeling entitled to all measures, including violence. This leads to a self-destructive price cycle that erodes the moral fabric of an organization or society (Kets de Vries, 2006). Opposition is seen as a dark force, and its proponents are proclaimed to be non-human, and to be annihilated and gotten rid of (Arendt, 1999). Tyranny

> alienates people from themselves and gives them over to others. Whatever victories may ensue must be pyrrhic. Whatever happiness is to be attained here is not the happiness of the individual. Indeed, it is no happiness at all. It is the drama of happiness attaching to a role that the person performs in a play that is written and directed by others.
>
> *(Schwartz, 1990, p. 16)*

Erich Fromm (1994) has famously considered the reasons why people let themselves be enslaved and has come up with a sobering answer: many people seek dependence because it frees them from responsibility, it helps them to escape from their identity and the dilemmas posed by conscience. Becoming part of a totalitarian society and succumbing to a tyrant's power, may free a person from the suffering and uncertainty caused by the seeking of one's place in society and the world. Both the leader and the led thus avoid moral or spiritual dilemmas, or existential questions, the choice is one and it is given: there is no alternative. But freedom is what makes us human, choices are what we live for. If we deprive ourselves of freedom we may avoid the pain of conscious living, the uncertainty of human fate, but it also robs us of our humanity.

7.5 Stories from organizations

Leadership is creation. Milena[6] is the founder and the leader of the team of teachers at the kindergarten Little Croc. Its aim is to inspire children to explore the world and to develop their imagination, to lead them into a world that they would want to embrace as their own. According to the mission statement:

> We want to create a place where the small and the big will feel secure. We want to create and learn together, explore new ways to knowledge.
>
> *(Eko Przedszkole Mały Krokodyl, 2013)*

Leadership is bringing together people and ideas. The young team love learning themselves and they think this is the natural way for everyone: learning is inherently human, it brings joy and fulfilment.

> Learning is a natural activity for the child. In our kindergarten learning is joy, and most of all, great fun.
>
> *(Ibid.)*

The children play together with the teachers. They are encouraged to solve problems, use their inventiveness and ask questions. Milena believes that the whole fun part about working with kids is that they are active and creative persons who have a need to express themselves, each in his or her individual way, and in a tempo that is best suited for them. There are children who are naturally 'fast', and some are 'slow', no mode is better or worse and each should be allowed to follow their own inner time.

> We believe that each child has a great potential which should be supported from his or her earliest years in a way that fits him or her best. Learning should be an awakening of the child's internal will, the freeing of its potential and intuition.
>
> *(Ibid.)*

Leadership is taking care of relationships. Milena has selected a team of people who love what they are doing. She sets an example, she is always first to test ideas, she lives as she teaches. Teachers are there to have fun together with the kids and to support them. It is a mutual relationship. They are interested in the children's development, but also their own. The staff of the Little Croc are all young passionate people with higher education in everything from pedagogy, through management to classical music. They all say that they love what they do and that working with children brings them authentic joy.

Leadership is teaching and learning. Many of the methods used in the kindergarten are based on Maria Montessori's ideas, but new elements, derived from the programme of the Polish Ministry of Education, and an ecological groundwork, are also included in the curriculum. Much of the time is dedicated to various creative games and play, but there are also possibilities to attend special classes for young children. The children can learn English, music, ceramics, cooking, ecology and other subjects. It is up to the parents and the children, to decide whether and which of them to include in a child's individual programme.

Milena holds two university diplomas: in pedagogy and in management, and the kindergarten is for her a much beloved brainchild. For her master's thesis she did an ethnographic study of an organization, the aim of which was to support and propagate culture. However, the director and most of the staff were rather uninterested in any active pursuit of this goal and acted in an uninspiring and dispiriting way. Milena got the impression that the organization was an empty shell, only nominally fulfilling its aim. If anything, it seemed to have a reverse influence to the one intended on the people who came in contact with it: art seemed to them to be something distant, not meant for them to engage in, and indeed, not really interesting. She decided to take a different path when she graduated and the Little Croc was from the beginning meant to be such an antidote to the tedious reality of much of contemporary organizational life.

> When I come to think of it, I become more and more convinced that the basis for the whole idea of my kindergarten was provided by my own childhood experiences and, possibly, also the all good educational experiences I have had. I was raised to believe that the child is a value all by itself. I had a lovely childhood, full of fun and people who loved me. That's why I chose to base my kindergarten on a mood like that: uninhibited play, mutual trust and a feeling of profound security. I wanted to create a place where the children, their parents, the teachers and me too, would all come with pleasure. An own kindergarten gives the possibility to realize one's vision of elementary education, a remarkable opportunity for self-actualization. Just to be able to be together with the kids is enormous fun. I can't think of many other examples of a job where you can play every day, paint, make origami with the children and observe how they develop.
>
> *(Milena)*

Leadership is sharing. For Milena it is very much about supporting and taking an active part in the team's activities and in the development of the children's creativity. Apart from her own experiences and her profound inner sense of joy, Milena also draws on the knowledge she had acquired, mainly during her pedagogic studies.

> My personal view on education is close to John Dewey's pragmatic philosophy. Freedom is the most important thing, we learn through experience and action. Every child has different needs because it is different from everyone else. In my everyday work I use so called alternative pedagogy a lot, that is, mainly the educational ideas of Maria Montessori and of Rudolf Steiner. We also use the method of educational projects. We try to select topics that would be of interest to our children. We make our teaching aids ourselves, as well as many of the toys. The kids often help.
>
> *(Milena)*

These toys are often indeed quite inventive and always very colourful. For example, it is a Polish custom to send winter, personified as the Marzanna, to sail down the river and away to the sea on the spring equinox. The children prepared their own Marzanna dolls for that event, beautifully dressed in vivid outfits, quite often bright green – perhaps the common choice of this colour was due to the unusually long winter of the year 2012 and our common longing for more green around us? In

December they made trolls dressed in cosy felt coats and fantastically vibrant fish, also made of felt. Of course, they prepared their own Christmas tree decorations. During the carnival the children dressed as fairy tale figures, using multicoloured fantastic costumes, original and not aiming to imitate the readymade templates for imagination as provided by the big corporations of mass culture. The more colour the better, or so it seems from the photos of a carnivalesque kindergarten, where the kids' ideas are not criticized or inhibited and where it is perfectly okay for a little girl to dress as a funny and also slightly scary clown with a bright red wig full of curly hair. Also the teachers can be seen wearing handmade headwear such as crowns. The kids sometimes make quite mundane things such as a gutter pipe of a recycled inner tube of kitchen paper, which one of them has described as 'beautiful'.

Leadership is vision, and the responsibility for it. Milena decided that her kindergarten would be ecological, because the human being is a very complex creature: 'body, mind, soul, and perhaps something more'. Ecology has been an inspiration to her in developing an idea of an organization that would acknowledge this complexity, and also the interconnectedness of everything and everyone as a planetary living system. It does not necessarily mean that everything is to be recycled in the kindergarten or that only organic substances are used for all of its activities. Yes, they try to be as friendly towards the environment as possible and they aim at teaching such an approach to the children. All meals are ecological, organic and prepared on the spot. No soft drinks, fast food or ready meals are used. A dietician is employed by the kindergarten to develop an attractive and balanced diet. But the main idea of ecology has been, for Milena, the sense of belonging to a wider context, the belief in a harmonious, symbiotic relationship between humans and the natural environment. It is good for us to conceive of ourselves that way, good not only for our bodies but also for our souls.

7.6 Questions to reflect on

1. Recall a situation when you were in a leadership position. Make a list of seven things you enjoyed the most and of seven you disliked the most. Now compare the two lists – what do they say about you as a leader? Is there any particular kind of group you think you would be best suited to lead? Are there any groups or organizations that you know you should avoid?
2. Think about King Arthur today, born around the same year that was also your year of birth, as a leader of a contemporary organization. What kind of organization would that be? Imagine him sitting around a round table with his 12 key co-workers. What are they discussing? Write a short story.
3. Think of the best boss or teacher that you ever had. Why was he or she so good? Try to list the most important qualities that made him or her such a good boss or teacher. Would you want to be like him or her? What can you do to follow the example? Make a to-do list. Now think of your *least* favourite boss or teacher. Why was he or she so bad? What can you do to avoid becoming like that?

4. Tell the story of a fictional leader who has impressed you, in a positive, negative or ambiguous way. It may be a character from a novel, film, a mythical hero or heroine, or from a folktale, legend, old or new. Why is the character so interesting to you?

Notes

1 424/423 BC–348/347 BC, Athens, Ancient Greece.
2 That Plato does not speak of women leaders does indeed not mean that the archetype he described excluded women. The King is both male and female (see Kociatkiewicz and Kostera, 2012b).
3 544 BC–496 BC, Ancient China.
4 1225–1274, Italy.
5 1864–1920, Prussia.
6 Based on field material collected 2012–2013.

8
LEARNING

This is the centre of the Earth
here all roads come to an end
Time to begin anew

Learning is an activity inherent to the human kind. Ecosystems and all living organisms learn, but it is humanity that has made a special virtue out of it. It is considered by many to be one of the most important activities of individuals and societies alike, and some regard it as a calling and a meaning of life. It is about gaining insights into how and why things work and being able to deal better with oneself and one's surroundings. There are several ways of doing that, from simple adaptation, to posing big questions. First of all, one can learn how to do things, and how to do them better – techniques and methods. By grasping and perfecting them, the learner gains a skill, such as how to bake bread, or becomes a more well-behaved, civilized person, by, for example, having the right table manners. People acquire skills and behaviours all the time, most intensively in childhood. Much of basic and elementary education is aimed at the developing of competences considered crucial by a society, such as how to read and write, how to brush one's teeth, how to address teachers and parents. Second, learning can bring knowledge about oneself and the world, for example, the awareness that there exist different cultures with different customs and languages, or that the burning of certain substances produces energy. This is also an important part of the contents of education, not just on the elementary level, but on all stages. Then there is a kind of learning that develops independent thinking, the ability to solve problems, usually regarded as a more advanced capability. The student holds a certain body of knowledge and has mastered the methods and techniques how to do things; now he or she is trained to use all that when facing a problem in a novel and creative way. For example, a person has been taught Swedish grammar and words and is, on this level, encouraged to make conversation, to use the language for expressing thoughts and feelings. Or, an apprentice has grasped all the cooking methods and the knowledge about different foods and tastes and is now ready to become a master chef, able to create new, original recipes and prepare a delicious dish out of more or less random ingredients. Often problem solving is taught together with skills and knowledge, because it engages the mind and makes the learning process more meaningful, probably also more effective. For example, foreign languages are nowadays often taught simultaneously on all these levels, students are encouraged to create sentences almost from the very beginning of their studies. Finally, learning can mean seeing things in a broad context, questioning the rules and the given order of things, inquiring into the reasons and meaning of things. This is possible by radical criticism: the questioning and problematization of what appears to be most obvious; and radical creation: invention for which there is no demand, but whose aim is to test the boundaries of the real and the possible. The latter often takes the shape of highly unique art or groundbreaking theories and is not immediately recognized or appreciated by the public. Nor, by the way, is radical criticism: it provokes and irritates, infuriates even, because it questions the fundamental social institutions. By practicing the last level of learning not only the individual learns, but so does society as a whole; it acquires the ability of creative *autopoiesis*, to renew itself, to constantly be able to solve the problems it produces and invent new ways of dealing with threats and taking advantage of opportunities. This level has to be taken care of and made secure by special institutions of society, because no 'free market forces' or individual interests are likely to support it, and without it society becomes sterile, loses its ability to survive in a longer term. It is the unique role of decentralized, widely spread and self-managed public universities, granting academic freedom to learners operating on this level; a role which cannot be replaced by other institutions such as corporations' R&D departments, research institutes funded by private means or government agencies.[1]

8.1 A short history of learning

In *Apology*, Plato[2] (1999) presented Socrates,[3] one of the greatest philosophers of antiquity, who believed that wisdom is a quality of the gods, whereas human wisdom is the knowledge of the limits of one's ignorance. He provoked people to question widely held truths and search for true knowledge, by asking questions that made them think. Inspired by Socrates, Plato founded the Academy in Athens in the sixth century BC, the first institution of learning in Europe.

The Roman philosopher and statesman Marcus Tullius Cicero[4] believed in learning and education, as a good in itself but also as a bringer of happiness.

> There is supreme satisfaction to be derived from old age which has knowledge and learning to feed upon.
>
> *(Cicero, 2004, p. 232)*

However, he did not support traditional forms of schooling based on a total subordination of the pupil and insisted that the authority of the teacher may be an obstacle to true learning rather than support it.

Education, traditional or more liberated, has been discussed throughout human history and in all parts of the world, by philosophers, politicians and the interested themselves. But it was perhaps the Enlightenment that brought a real explosion of interest to the topic. Thinkers from all countries where it reached expressed their views on learning, often very positive. In Poland the philosopher Hugo Kołłątaj[5] was a spirited advocate of popular emancipation through education. He believed that being able to acquire learning, the people would take co-responsibility for the state and the culture. He was a proponent of equality, including the bourgeoisie and the peasants. He not only authored philosophical treatises and letters addressed to the broader public, but also actively took part in the political processes leading to reforms of education (Buczek, 2007).

The anthropologist and social scientist Gregory Bateson[6] considered the levels of learning (1972). First level learning means the gaining of skills; the learner learns *something*, such as how to use a tool. One can proceed from this to the second level, deuterolearning or learning *about* something, through reflection, problem-oriented learning and the development of intelligence. Now the problems are given a frame of reference and situations are more easily understood. The learner puts together the rules that enable to learn – he or she learns how to learn. The third, highest level of learning, trito-learning, is a spiritual and existential level. On this level the learner questions his or her role in the world, considers the meaning of experience and acquires a chance to change his or her identity and fate. This is the level of acquiring wisdom.

8.2 Reflection 1

Learning is one of the most important activities for many humans and non-humans alike, perhaps one of the greatest joys in life, as Cicero (2004) pointed out. It is, in Batesonian terms, a path toward the ecology of mind (1972). Chris Argyris and Donald Schön (1978) applied Bateson's ideas to organizations. They believe that organizations cannot be reduced to sets of individuals.

> An organization is like an organism each of whose cells contains a particular, partial. changing image of itself in relation to the whole. And like such an organism, the organization's practice stems from those very images. Organization is an artifact of individual ways of representing organization.
>
> *(Ibid., p. 16)*

The kind of learning that is relevant for organizations understood this way concerns active processes of organizing, which are, at their root, of a cognitive character. They present two levels of learning: single and double loop. The first is an adaptive kind of learning, aiming at achieving skills and adapting means to ends. People discover errors and their sources, and they invent strategies to adjust them in the future. The second level is reminding of deuterolearning: innovative, introducing a new quality and questioning the existing norms. For organizations this may mean strategic change or a cultural reorientation. This type of learning is of key importance for organizations and consists of

> those sorts of organizational inquiry which resolve incompatible organizational norms by setting new priorities and weightings of norms, or by restructuring the norms themselves together with associated strategies and assumptions.
>
> *(Ibid., p. 18)*

An organization can be seen as an expression of the shared knowledge of how the whole system operates in its environment. This knowledge is dynamically used in its daily problem solving and decision making. Learning organizations are not just collections of procedures and objectives but ways of doing things, dealing with situations that come up embedded in the knowledge of the organization as a whole. People should therefore be encouraged to get to know, and even question, their organization. If learning is to take place the 'learning agents' discoveries, inventions and evaluations must be embedded in organizational memory' (ibid., p. 19). Otherwise only individuals may learn and not the organization as a whole. Excluding certain issues from organizational communication and discussion, a wish to avoid conflict and keep hierarchies intact makes it impossible to develop second-level learning in organizations. Instead, a complex system of learning that actually prevents change emerges: people are unable to face the underlying problems, just deal with the most apparent and superficial issues. Furthermore, it is important to keep in mind that organizations are not only formal systems but they also comprise much informal activity. Both make up the actual learning system and so they should be both opened to communication and inquiry of the participants. The authors propose practical programmes for the development of such open ended learning systems in organizations, including mapping the processes of organizing, generating solutions and generalizing leading to further mapping. In any case, it is important to take under consideration what the authors call theories-in-use: a set of cultural assumptions about how things are supposed to work. These often block or hinder learning. Max Visser (2007) proposes to reformulate the concept of deuterolearning for contemporary organizational use, following Bateson, and Argyris and Schön, as 'behavioral adaptation to patterns of conditioning in relationships in organizational contexts' (Visser, 2007, p. 660). It is continuous, communicative through behaviour, rather than verbal means, and largely unconscious. It tends to evade attempts at direct control and, if efforts at verbal steering are made that seem to lead in a different direction to the non-verbal communication associated with deuterolearning, people feel caught in a situation of conflicting communications and may lose their trust in the communicator or even the whole organization. Deuterolearning in organizations does not always lead to improvement, learning resulting from simple adaptation may be much more functional from the point of view of the system. Paul Tosey, Max Visser and Mark Saunders (2011) critically consider the idea of organizational triple-loop learning that has been proposed in more recent literature. This idea is not derived from Argyris and Schön (1978) but rather loosely rooted in Bateson's (1972) writings. It is often presented as superior or equal to double-loop learning, as a kind of strategic choice. Instead, the authors propose to regard it as a possible mode of learning, aimed at transformative change, and a possibility of gaining wisdom. But it is neither necessarily superior to nor always desirable for organizations. It is also important to keep in mind that this is no mere tool, as

> higher levels of learning cannot be actively planned and may not necessarily have beneficial outcomes. It provides a clear warning against the one-sided preference for higher levels of learning that is sometimes discernible in parts of the organizational learning literature and in consultancy practice.
>
> (Tosey et al., 2011, p. 304)

Peter Senge (2006) is also considering learning on the organizational level, but not from the point of view of processes as such, but rather from the perspective of the entire system. Learning can become part and parcel of the organizing processes, an inbuilt systemic feature. Yet whereas people are naturally disposed to learn, organizations need to be taught how to. First, the organization should be designed in a way that it enables it to fulfil the assumed goals as effectively as possible. Second, there should be a mechanism present ensuring feedback whenever the organization's functioning diverges from the desired goals. Then steps should be taken to correct the incongruity. This creates the foundation for the development of a permanent learning culture in the organization. The quality that supports such a culture is system thinking. It helps to see the broader context for all the actions undertaken and decisions made: as part of the larger organizational whole which, in turn, is the part of an even broader environment. The system is seen as a whole made up of its parts and the complex relationships between them. Everything that happens is then an aspect of a much wider and dynamic net of elements and connections. It is never advisable to try to solve a problem without consideration for where it has occurred and what role it plays in the context of a larger whole. The same applies to learning: it should be built into a broader context of the system and thus give rise to learning organization, with an ability for autonomous self-creation:

> [it can] create the results [it] truly desire[s], where new and expansive patterns of thinking are nurtured, where collective aspiration is set free, and where people are continually learning how to learn together.
>
> *(Ibid., p. 8)*

A learning organization is more flexible in its responses to the environment and gives more freedom to its participants than in other organizations. Constant learning is characteristic of the whole culture – and connected with thinking, and with ideas and practices of the sharing of knowledge. People are not resources or elements but co-authors, co-creators of the system. This does not mean consensus or lack of tension: creative cooperation often produces conflicts and disorder, as it is driven by a diversity of ideas, attitudes and methods. People need to be able to make mistakes if they are to learn, and they have to be able to admit to not knowing something. This refers to ordinary participants, but also to managers. Managers' defensiveness is a gigantic barrier to learning. Leadership based on a fantasy of omniscience and infallibility easily degenerates into narcissism and tyranny (see Chapter 7, Section 4). To prevent this, diversity should be built into the structure of the organization, so that no simple hierarchy or attempt at ordering inhibits people from seeking creative solutions and new ideas (ibid.).

But good plans for the future are not all that needs to be prepared, in order to make sure that the organization will develop a learning culture. Karl Weick (2001) reminds us of the importance of continuity and identity for learning processes. Quick fixes, programmed changes and managed reorganizations, even if they invoke ideals of learning, do nothing to help lasting learning processes. Organizations need a sense of identity and memory of the past, not just good system or effective structures. An organization with a sound learning potential is rooted in a shared sense of stability and connection.

8.3 Sounds, images, dreams

The Spanish modernist architect Antoni Gaudí believed that architecture should be learning from nature. He is famous for the irregular, organic forms he used in his designs, curved shapes, asymmetrical and uneven edges, details that make his buildings seem to be alive and breathing. On the roof of Casa Batló there are elements that seem to be fantastic hybrids of a church tower and a mushroom, a mountainside and a lizard. The famous La Pedrera is equipped with chimneys looking vaguely humanoid, like bizarre heads; they appear to be manifestations of what our imagination may make of an old fashioned chimney, seen at dusk and from a distance. Gaudí's buildings look magical. When my husband and I arrived in Barcelona for the first time and were about to leave the Sants railway station by a long grey underground tunnel, I was having a travel-weary moment and was soliloquizing about the futility of voyage. Is it not so, that reality is always underwhelming? If you have seen a few places, you have, in fact, seen them all and nothing is likely to surprise you? At a certain point travelling becomes just a tiresome and disillusioning pastime, and it cannot reach the level of excitement that music or reading provides. We were ascending the stairs and I interrupted my monologue in mid-sentence, breathless, from the climb, which is something my body sincerely dislikes, but also because I caught sight of what was right in front of us, glowing softly in the warm night, a magical house that seemed to hum and shift, like a giant cat or, rather, sleeping dragon. That was my first encounter with Gaudí and even though the effect is less dramatic these days, his work never fails to move me. His designs are unlike any other, seemingly impossible to realize, but, on reflection, so obvious, even if based on calculations that evade linear geometric thinking. Indeed, nothing he authored has the aura of artificiality and hypocrisy that so much of modern architecture suffers from. Also, he never tried to shock or distinguish himself, make an impression just to have a say. He was a faithful and profound learner, using inspirations from oriental and gothic styles and designs, as well as shapes and engineering principles derived from nature. His successive buildings reflect a process of development of an own personal style which would gradually encompass all that he had learned and epitomize the path towards sublime originality. The ultimate step was to be embodied in the work of his life – La Sagrada Familia, a modernist cathedral, a design of outstanding wisdom and imagination (Zerbst, 2005). Since Gaudí became involved in its construction in 1883, it is still a work in progress, carried out according to his projects. It was declared a UNESCO World Heritage site in 2010 (UNESCO, 2013a) and is celebrated worldwide as an unsurpassed masterpiece of art, unique and standing out among all church buildings in the world (Zerbst, 2005). However, as the completion of the building is proceeding, many believe it is accruing not in accordance to what Gaudí himself taught by his designs; it is becoming too sane and too sanitized (Moore, 2011).

> [I]t is no longer a work of Gaudí. It cannot overcome the central paradox, which is that Gaudí's architecture was organic, living and responsive, whereas posthumous simulation of his ideas makes them fixed and lifeless.
>
> *(Ibid.)*

Perhaps Rowan Moore is right that only an arson attack would save the vision today, and 'erode that computerised precision, that deadliness, that lack of Gaudí's solubility, which is the worst feature of the new work' (ibid.).

The film *Himalaya* directed by Eric Valli (1999) tells the story of the last stand of an elderly chieftain of a village in Nepal's Dolpo, of the education of the village's new chief and future, and of an unusual learning experience of a Buddhist monk. The old leader, Tinle, has recently lost his son, for which he blames his son's friend, Karma. The latter was heading the expedition to bring salt from the mountains. Tinle's son was part of the journey and met his death in its course. Karma is now to become the new chieftain by public acclaim of the tribesmen, something to which the old chief is opposed. The salt is indispensable; the villagers exchange it for grain each year and the whole tribe depends on the perilous journeys to survive the winter. Karma is about to embark on such a trading expedition with a group of able men of the tribe. The old chief refuses him his blessing and sets out on a rival journey with a small company of completely unsuited people, including his other son Norbu the lama, who is living a peaceful life in a Buddhist monastery, and his young grandson, Pasang. The two caravans meet in an archetypical clash of power between the young and the old, the new and the traditional, but the meeting encompasses also other profoundly human feelings and attitudes, such as courage, tenacity and compassion.

The scenery of the film is truly grandiose and it is enhanced by the remarkable soundtrack by Bruno Coulais, based on Buddhist chants. The Himalayan landscape is indeed unforgiving, the Dolpo people living on heights 4,500 m above sea level are not spared any of life's difficulties. The surrounding mountains are perilous to move around in and the Dolpopas only have their yaks to depend on for transport. Every journey they undertake is essential for their survival, and each one is fraught with severe danger. As nothing much grows at this height, to get food they must acquire it in exchange for another necessity, such as salt, from villages living in lower areas. The air is thin and incessantly cold, and at times the weather becomes truly deadly, storms and avalanches turning the surroundings into an uninhabitable environment. The beauty of the mountains is as breathtaking as it is lethal, as far away from Demeter's lush fields as one can possibly imagine. It is a miracle that any creature is able to survive and even more miraculous that as sublime a culture as that of the Dolpopas has been able to develop under these circumstances. That in itself teaches respect for and awe of the human spirit. Norbu considers the experiences as lessons with his family as his teachers. He sets out to show glimpses of the journey upon return to his monastery. The film ends with a scene where Pasang is sitting up in a tree for the first time in his life, embracing its branch covered in green leaves: a lesson in happiness, one without which any childhood would be incomplete.

For the director, too, the making of the film was a learning experience. In his own words:

My work as director ... involved letting my characters express themselves in their own way. I had to be as transparent as possible; I had to make myself disappear before the power and wealth of their own lives. I was telling their stories; they were the teachers, I was their student.

(Valli, 2001, pp. 8–9)

8.4 Reflection 2

Learning, if it is to make a real difference, has to be a creative process. Daniel Hjorth and Bengt Johannisson (2009) present learning as an entrepreneurial process, showing the importance of considering knowledge as cutting: differentiating, setting up boundaries to help students make sense of the ambiguity that is associated with their entrepreneurial activity. Entrepreneurship is a creative process and in a way it is the opposite of management: it implies an active taking advantage of uncertainty, creation of opportunities, experimenting and questioning old institutions. Its genealogy can be traced 'along paths laid down by creation, desire, passion, play, spontaneity, immediacy and intensity' (ibid., p. 58). Learning, useful for the enhancement of this process, needs to mean an openness to the creative powers of life, approaching the world as becoming. It also is a process of self-creation and recreation, of moving beyond the proscribed identities, a road to self-actualization. It is 'about extending life beyond experiences' (ibid., p. 74), by introducing heterogenous, interdisciplinary programmes, with a large space for the students' initiatives and creative becomings. Entrepreneurial learning needs to actively promote continuous sense-making and reconstruction of self and the environment: the relations between self and others and between self and the world.

Humans can become more than they are in themselves by processes of becoming-hybrid with what is not itself. When education is also a creative process we become-hybrid by the help of co-learners as we desire images of the learned.

(Ibid., p. 63)

The necessity to consider meaning making as part of the learning process does not only apply to entrepreneurship, but to more conventionally managed organizations as well. Martha Feldman, Ruth Nicole Brown and Debra Horner (2003) consider organizational change as a result of learning processes. Planned change is often framed by management as successful when financial or other effectiveness related goals are reached. The authors, however, point to another dimension of planned change – that of the satisfaction of the involved social actors. Change as learning needs more than technical and quantifiable measures – a sense of meaning. Meaning is contextual and, in fact, different multiple meanings appear when organizations initiate change plans. These meanings concern the contents of the change plan as well as its implementation and may develop in time, depending on how the participants alter the plans and themselves change. The authors emphasize that no change programme can have lasting effects without the simultaneous change of rules and mindsets and this process is interdependent: learning needs to take place at the same time at the individual and organizational level if change is to be enacted and regarded as satisfactory by the people engaging in it.

James March (1991) takes up another important aspect of learning related to the link between the participants and the organization, and the organization and its context. He discusses exploitative versus explorative learning and shows how the former are more effective in short term processes, while the second is necessary for the long term development of organizations. Exploitative learning consists of making the most of old models, ideas and truths. Explorative learning involves a search of a quest and the new things that it has brought. A reliance on only one of the two is disadvantageous for the organization. Exploitative without explorative learning results in suboptimal equilibria, stable states that are sterile and unproductive in the longer run. The opposite situation: explorative without exploitative learning brings a chaos of new ideas without any benefits or stable competence. Both are then essential but as they compete for scarce resources, organizations tend to show a preference for one of them. This is due to them embedded in broader social contexts: the culture of the organization and the environmental context. Within the organization is

> mutual learning of an organization and the individuals in it. Organizations store knowledge in their procedures, norms, rules, and forms. They accumulate such knowledge over time, learning from their members. At the same time, individuals in an organization are socialized to organizational beliefs. Such mutual learning has implications for understanding and managing the trade-off between exploration and exploitation in organizations.
>
> *(Ibid., p. 73)*

Furthermore, organizations often compete with each other and consider knowledge an important resource for competitive advantage. These contextual frames influence the predilection an organization may show for the exploitative or explorative learning mode.

> The essence of exploitation is the refinement and extension of existing competences, technologies, and paradigms. Its returns are positive, proximate, and predictable. The essence of exploration is experimentation with new alternatives. Its returns are uncertain, distant, and often negative. Thus, the distance in time and space between the locus of learning and the locus for the realization of returns is generally greater in the case of exploration than in the case of exploitation, as is the uncertainty.
>
> *(Ibid., p. 85)*

It makes these two modes seem incompatible or impossible to combine. However, a preference for exploration is self-destructive in the longer term. It continuously degrades mutual learning between the organization and its participants as causes a divergence between people's beliefs and the organizational codes. The opposite imbalance also causes serious problems, as it may further knowledge but prevents discoveries. In other words, no matter how difficult it seems, the two modes of learning should be held in a balance.

Another popular skewed approach to learning is an excessive focus on the rational aspects or even isolating these aspects in managerial education. It is a source of numerous problems and does harm to the idea of good management that is based on the ideals of wisdom and maturity, unavailable to the purely rational mind.

> Although no one can isolate and deliver wisdom, inspiration or creativity as if they were technical skills or knowledge tools to be learned in an intellectual way, we feel that we share the obligation to train future leaders in ways that enliven their human potential.... In particular we would like to see leadership studies embrace the aesthetic approach to business leadership we promote throughout this book.
>
> *(Hatch et al., 2005, p. viii)*

Aesthetics brings back a holistic perspective, an equal focus on things rational and irrational in exploring and learning new things. Learning is not something one-sidedly positive or even morally neutral. Learning the wrong things can give birth to many demons of the mind, such as phobias and mental barriers limiting and perhaps even destroying enjoyment of life and human as well as organizational capabilities, shaping a psychic prison (Morgan, 2006). People and organizations sometimes learn to act as if they lacked freedom and train themselves into being limited by their own constructs such as oppressive management systems. Such systems are based on the modes of thinking, on the type of knowledge adopted as binding and on behaviour conventions. Some of these barriers are unconscious or subconscious, and they stem from learning processes. Often enough they are neither questioned nor made conscious. Sometimes organizational participants rely overly on procedures and conventions, even if they are oppressive and limiting, because it gives them a sense of security, makes them feel safe and does not put demands upon their judgement. Other barriers derive from the strategies of control introduced intentionally by managers aiming to extend their power and area of influence. The trust of employees is used to further leaders' own goals. An example of such leadership is described by Roy Lubit (2002). Destructively narcissistic management is common in contemporary organizations.[7] Their exclusive and unabashed concentration on their own image and success undercuts the employees' self-esteem and work satisfaction. The managers fail to learn from others' feedback and reactions, but other people may engage in a destructive learning process involving a spreading of narcissistic traits among other managers, focusing of energies on political strategies rather than work, concentrating on increasing power and prestige, instead on making experiences or developing oneself creatively. Learning itself can, alas, lead in destructive and toxic directions.

8.5 Stories from organizations

Schools are, in the minds of most people, organizations whose main purpose is to develop the intellect of the pupils and that includes their capacity to learn, think and be creative. And yet they all too often fail to fulfil that purpose and sometimes even work against it. I asked several friends and colleagues from three European countries: Poland, Sweden and the UK, if they knew of examples of such behaviour. The response[8] exceeded my expectations: almost all of the people I asked had stories to tell, often not one but several, and a few got back to me later and told even more stories. I will share some of these stories, the ones I consider the most typical or the most symptomatic of the phenomenon. Olivia speaks of elementary school, where the children are asked to write essays about 'what the poet had in mind' which then would be evaluated according to the textbook interpretation. Any flight of imagination on the side of the kids is punished or at best disregarded. So is their own interpretation of the poem. Exactly the same problem is mentioned by Martina, who adds that the teacher gave her a look like she was some strange and terrible creature, when she presented her own interpretation of a poem in class. She felt humiliated and quite silly. Maggie points out that kids are hardly likely to express their more imaginative thoughts: the teachers in her son's school always have the last word and they invoke regulations, norms and standards. The kids are allowed to voice their concerns and ask questions but, in the end, they will hear that this or that regulation says how the problem should be resolved and the discussion is over. Amazingly enough, this also happens during art classes. Her son once asked if he could use his smartphone to take pictures and was told that the rules oblige him to acquire a 'real' camera. When the music teacher asked the kids to perform their favourite song, he chose a metal tune and was rebuked for 'silly jokes'. Any irregular or unexpected ideas on the side of the children are either ignored or defined by the teachers as 'not fulfilling the norms'.

> As a consequence, my son dislikes his school, and when I ask him how school was, he says: boring.
>
> *(Maggie)*

He has already figured out that to do well, he has to mindlessly follow all the instructions and suppress his imagination. Robert gives examples of how kids only are expected to repeat something that has been said already and never to think for themselves. No wonder they then think plagiarism is something normal. Joasia recalls her elementary school where the children were divided in genders and made to learn either cooking and sewing (girls) or DIY (boys). She wanted to learn how to do bird feeders but was prevented from it, because she was not a boy. Instead, she was made to learn how to prepare sandwiches, a skill she does not care much for anyway. Marta expresses her exasperation with the omnipresent tests in her son's elementary school. The children are only taught to do well on tests, and not to write, interpret, question or indeed think on their own. Tests are applied in maths, geography, even literature.

The teachers do not even prepare these tests, they receive them from the publishers of textbooks. She has complained to the teachers, and one of them even agreed with her, and they had a long talk. However, such are the rules of the school, she was told, and even if some of the teachers have their reservations, they are powerless. Not only tests discourage pupils from learning how to think on their own. Olivia recalls how the literature teacher in her secondary school made them reply in class, using only specific formulations, which she had dictated from textbooks. Thomas, a high school teacher himself, tells how he was trying to 'fight the system' and introduced alterative history to the pupils (even though it was not part of the approved programme). The pupils loved it, even if they initially did not know how to deal with it, being completely unused to such forms of learning; the authorities did not, and, in the end, he was persuaded to stop such experiments before they even started to work. Formulaic writing seems to be a systemic standard, even if some teachers are more or less explicitly against it and even if many of the pupils sincerely dislike it. Natalia remembers her literature teacher in secondary school telling her how much she had liked her essay but how she was unable to mark it higher than 'satisfactory': it was written in 'her own words', and based on her own interpretations. The teacher explained that she was expected to prepare their pupils for their A level exams and thus any work that did not meet the formal standards could not be encouraged, according to the regulations that she had received from the authorities.

> I started to keep to those standards and now always received high grades for writing that was completely uninspired and devoid of imagination.
>
> (Natalia)

Gosia tells of her high school that had a mathematical profile, and while the maths classes were indeed very inspiring, the Polish classes, which seemed to have been organized to be as similar to them as possible, suffered from a dramatic lack of imagination. She happened to like Polish and be really good at writing. However, the teachers seemed not to know what to do with her and so simply ignored her. She was asked not to be 'too active' in class and the teachers did not talk to her about interests as they tended to do with more 'normal' pupils, i.e. those who did well in maths but not so well in Polish. Michał, who is an academic teacher, points out that the whole system of Polish A level exams (*matura*) strongly discourages the use of imagination and critical thinking, as it relies only on written tests. Pupils who learn the material by heart and are able to think analytically are those who do well on such exams. Having reservations or own ideas, especially if they are too original to fit into the preconceived standards, is not encouraged. What is more, the pupils do not learn any communicative skills. They only know how to do tests, and small wonder that they are unable to write any meaningful texts when they later go on to university studies.

> And what even worse, the new A level exam kills off any need the pupils may have to read books.
>
> (Michał)

Textbooks summarize all longer texts and books so neatly and helpfully, providing the pupils with ready answers for the exam. So why would they care?

University studies have problems of their own, one of them being the authoritarian academic culture. Michał points out that whereas there are no A level exams awaiting the students, the teachers expect them to repeat only what has been said in class, not to have any of their own opinions, especially not critical ones. Natalia has similar complaints, adding an illustrative story:

> Three students tried to argue for their own ideas and interpretations during the [oral] exam. They were thrown out from [the professor's room] even though they were very good students indeed.

Lena blames the university authorities for many of the problems: the programmes are developed at a level where presumably no one has any real contact with the students or the teachers and some abstract 'standards' of 'quality assurance' are invoked instead of the actual quality of the learning situation which is always unique and based on a relationship between the teacher and the student.

I also received some positive examples, of how schools at various levels encouraged my respondents or their children to learn to think and be more imaginative. Natalia recalls how her elementary school teachers supported the pupils' creativity and always asked them for their own interpretations during the classes in Polish literature. They celebrated the kids' attempts at originality and awarded the best marks to those who seemed to sincerely try to think outside of the box. Johanna praises her secondary school teachers in classical literature who encouraged the pupils to make their own connections between literature, art, geography and history – it was like discovering a whole world. They were to imagine walking along the busy streets of ancient Rome and narrate in class what they 'saw' and 'heard'. Julia also has some positive examples from her secondary school. Her music teacher asked the pupils to perform the songs they have been taught in class and then to tell, in their own words, how they interpreted them: their feelings, the images that came to their mind, the reflections that the song brought. He explicitly forbade mindless, repetitive answers. The pupils were compelled to use their imagination. Johanna tells of secondary school teachers who introduced alterative history to her, and other pupils', joy. They could invent own histories and also think critically, take a step back from the mainstream and engage in sociological imagination to their hearts' delight. Gosia praises her university teachers in German literature for being sincerely interested in communicating with the students. Students engaged in creative writing, after an inspiring contact with German poetry and prose, alone and together. The teacher would present them with an idea such as a colour, music, a quote, and ask them to creatively develop the theme. Olivia recalls a university teacher who always gave space for own interpretations of the students and actively supported their attempts at critical and creative thinking. She was, however, something of an exception rather than the rule:

I have the impression that creative knowledge among the students is not looked kindly upon by academic teachers, they fear it because it is not quantifiable and demands engagement on the part of the teacher, as well as the student. However, I think this is rather the case with many older teachers, the younger ones are much more open towards creative and imaginative learning and thinking.

(Olivia)

8.6 Questions to reflect on

1. What are the seven most important things about management and organization that you have learned? How did you learn them? How can you use them in your life?
2. Compared with the comments in the stories about schools that end this chapter, what were your experiences of primary and secondary school like? Which were your most inspiring moments in school? The most dispiriting ones?
3. In the film *Himalaya*, the monk Norbu was asked why he decided to go with his father on the dangerous journey which he was so ill equipped for. He answers: 'When two paths open up before you, choose the hardest one.' Discuss – what is your idea about such choices? Would you want to choose the hardest way? Provide examples from your life and from literature.

Notes

1 I would like to thank Michał Zawadzki and Carmelo Mazza for the talks that brought on these insights.
2 424/423 BC–348/347 BC, Ancient Greece.
3 *c.* 469 BC–399 BC, Ancient Greece.
4 106 BC–43 BC, Ancient Rome.
5 1750–1812, Poland.
6 1904–1980, UK.
7 Narcissistic leaders are characterized later in this chapter.
8 The section is based on quotations collected from my respondents via email and renditions of stories they told me in person; some of the names (where the respondents did not explicitly agree for me to use their real name) are changed.

9
LOVE

Drink wine to Omar Khayyam
Drink red to the shadows
Drink white to the light

Omnia vincit amor, love conquers all; it is what turns our minds and hearts towards the Other, brings us together and expands our worlds – even though we will never be able to see the world through another's eyes, never be anyone else than our-selves, love is what, albeit indefinitely and tentatively, shifts the punctual perspective we are constrained by to something embracing more dimensions that the unique one allotted to each of us. It can mean many different, if related, things. First of all, it can refer to embodied love, driven by biological impulses, such as physical attrac-tion, known as *éros* in Ancient Greece, and the affection between parents and chil-dren, which the Greeks called *storge*. Even though this type of love is underpinned by hormones and subconscious drives, it is not limited to the biological function of reproduction. Both comprise higher areas of the psyche and the soul. People attracted by the force of *éros* may get to love each other not just as sexual partners but for their beauty, elan, spirit. Parents may not only wish to protect their off-spring instinctively, but care for them because of their trust and vulnerability.

Both kinds of love can be the source for the development of something even more complex. Biologically defined love can pave the way for more profound bonds, acting on many levels, offering people the divine grace of sharing a whole world with the Other, a kind of love that the ancient Greeks called *agapé*. Whereas *éros* is powerful and compelling, with an ability to turn towards each other individuals who otherwise would have had nothing in common, *agapé* is mind-opening. It is truly able to break down barriers and make people receptive to things and ideas that had never mattered for them before. Lovers grow to care for each other as two parts of a greater whole, which makes life doubly worth living. Parents discover the uniqueness of their chil-dren in the difficult process of growing up, learn to see their individuality when they embark upon the arduous path of adolescence, and to respect it. Children understand and appreciate, when they grow up, that their parents are not just the gods of their childhood, but loveable human beings with their own stories, hopes and dreams. Yet such a journey is often bound to fail; people choose not to take upon themselves the arduous task of building a relationship, of staying constantly aware of and respectful to the Other's agency and individuality. Lovers part after the initial phase of fascination, or they marry but grow insensitive to each other, lie, ensnare, deceive each other; instead of opening up they close down and oppress the Other with their solipsist defi-nitions of reality. Parents do that quite often to their children: they refuse to see them as separate persons and try to prevent them from growing up and becoming them-selves, they regard them as things which they are responsible for to shape and mould; and they guard that form fiercely, at times without mercy.

Another kind of love is compassion, pure *agapé* without the drive of *éros*, encom-passing understanding, empathy and a deep sense of responsibility for the Other. It means caring regardless of the external conditions or the needs of the self in con-nection to the other person, going out of one's way to understand the Other and to act upon that understanding. It is a feeling of genuine connection with human-ity, a selflessness and generosity of spirit enabling to transcend the narrow motiva-tion of self-interest. Compassion is regarded a major virtue in most philosophical and religious traditions.

Finally, there is the bond between friends, members of family and community, which the Greek called *philia*, a social love: loyalty and trust binding together people who see each other as equals. *Philia* makes the world a safer place, less random and hostile. A friend can be trusted with secrets, may help out in difficult times, can be counted upon to take one's side and listen sympathetically to one's stories, sad and happy. Ultimately, friends and communities offer a frame of reference, they make real the values and aspirations we have and, if well chosen, help us grow as human beings.

9.1 A short history of love

In *Symposium* (2008) Plato,[1] through the character of Socrates,[2] describes love as a lack, an empty space, a longing for something or someone that is not. Any earthly fulfilment of this longing is not love, it is but a vulgar substitute of what is truly lacking: goodness and beauty. Love is, then, a reflection on the divine, the great indefinite. All sages are, indeed, looking for love. Love pushed us out into the unknown and guides us towards the unreachable, and thus is the drive behind all human quests and actions.

The poet and philosopher Lucretius[3] begins his *On the Nature of Things* with an invocation to Venus, the goddess of love. She is the inspiration for all living things to blossom and life to perpetuate itself. She is an elemental life force, the energy of Earthly life.

> Because you alone steer the nature of things upon its course,
> And nothing can arise without you on light's shining shores,
> And nothing glad or lovely can be fashioned ...
> *(Lucretius, 2007, p. 3)*

Lucretius' Venus is even more than a life force: she can be a bringer of peace, and it is to her the poet addresses a prayer to end wars, subjugate the fierce Mars to love.

The Sufi scholar and poet Jalal-ad-din Rumi[4] also conceived of love as the prime reason behind all being and becoming. It transcends all religions and merges humans with the divine, with wisdom and foolishness and moves us to seek God.

> Our desire for God is fanned by His love: it is His attraction that draws all wayfarers along the path. Does the dust rise up without a wind? Does a ship float without the sea?
> *(Rumi, 2000, p. 13)*

The Catholic mystic and theologian Saint Teresa of Avila[5] (2007) considered love to be the epitome of spirituality. Divine love makes the human soul alive, heals it

> and His love thaws
> the holy in
> us.
> *(Ibid., 2007, p. 63)*

She believed that love only can bring worth to us and our world. God is at the same time wisdom and love, combined and infinite.

> O love
> that loves me more
> than I can love myself
> or understand!
> *(Ibid., p. 70)*

The moral philosophy of compassion is perhaps a less commonly known side of Adam Smith[6] today, but to himself one of upmost significance. His *Theory of Moral Sentiments* (2010) is a treatise in support of altruism, which, Smith believed, was a natural and basic need of human beings. It is a need entirely upon the other's account, and so 'not … in the least selfish' (ibid., p. 329).

According to the philosopher Emmanuel Lévinas[7] (1999) when the Other reveals to us his or her face the epiphany of his or her Otherness, alterity, awakens us as ethical subjects and makes us infinitely responsible for the Other. It is a responsibility that precedes everything else and springs from our freedom, the core of our humanity. Our subjectivity is formed in this relationship: to encounter the Other means to gain an idea of infinity.

9.2 Reflection 1

Compassion 'is about love but not (or not intensely) directed toward oneself' (Frost, 2011, p. 396). It is more than empathy, 'it entails, even inspires, helpful and merciful actions' (ibid., p. 396). Love gives life meaning and direction. It is not true that its importance for humans ends when the working day begins. Also in organizations we have a responsibility for the Other, central to our being (Lévinas, 1999). Encountering the Other is a transcendent experience, revealing a reality beyond the limits of the self. The realization of alterity, that the Other is separate and different from oneself, makes one conscious of being oneself, it brings identity into being. The Other reveals a whole world beyond ourselves and the realization of this is an instance of infinity, thinking that recognizes the alterity of the Other. Oneself and the Other are linked but always separate, one can never experience what it is like to be the Other. But the openness to the Otherness creates an ethical relationship: in the Other one exists in another sense than for oneself. Organizations offer many such encounters, they are, in fact, journeys in alterity (Cunliffe, 2013). This brings us to the question of how alterity is treated and what roles love, empathy and compassion play in organizations. Let us begin the quest by considering individual empathy (Atkins and Parker, 2012). The authors observe that, even though a lack of compassion is usual in organizations, it is vital that organizations, which are human institutions, are based on sustainable human relations. Workplaces should be able to support compassionate behaviour and also enhance such behaviour in the employees. Paul Atkins and Sharon Parker propose methods that may prove helpful in this endeavour, such as noticing, appraising, feeling and acting. First of all, it is crucial to notice another's suffering. Second, a person who believes they have the essential skills to help is more likely to engage in compassionate behaviours, therefore appraisals may be a much more important element of the enhancement of compassion than hitherto thought. They may help to eradicate some negative but solidly rooted assumptions. It is often presumed that organizational goals demand human suffering, for example, in the name of greater effectiveness a reduction of employment is more than justified, and the feelings of the downsized people are not relevant. It is also assumed that managers, even more than others, should not empathize with the downsized people. So, even if a manager feels the pain of the employees he or she will not consciously consider his or her feelings of empathy and even less react, because of the lack of skill and resources to do so. Appraisal also includes values: the person must feel that the suffering person is deserving of help and that his or her feelings are relevant in the situation. It is therefore important to better understand the roles and identities of the participants in the organization, such as work related roles and skills, gender, etc. The appraisal of deservedness means that it is important to promote a taking of perspective and a discussion of values in organizations, through training and reconsidering of organizational practices. The authors also suggest that psychological flexibility, the combination of mindfulness and action directed by values, may be important in enhancing compassionate actions. Mindfulness should be encouraged, and not, as is usual in many contemporary workplaces, strongly suppressed by management values and procedures.

> [P]sychological flexibility provides a way of bridging the apparent tension between distancing and connection – distancing so that one does not become absorbed in another's suffering and one can place it in context, and connection so that one cares. In relational frame theory terms, psychological flexibility can be understood as the development of increasingly subtle and complex relations of distinction and similarity between aspects of self and emotional experience.
>
> *(Ibid., p. 539)*

Organizational compassion may involve collective appraisals and an inclusion of prosocial values into the everyday culture of the workplace. Individual empathy can be socially coordinated by compassion organizing, or

> collective response to a particular incident of human suffering that entails the coordination of individual compassion in a particular organizational context.... Compassion organizing creates a pattern of collective action that represents a distinct form of organizational capability that alleviates pain by extracting, generating, coordinating, and calibrating resources to direct toward those who are suffering.
>
> *(Dutton et al., 2006, p. 61)*

Ordinary work structures and procedures can be redesigned and redirected to fulfil compassionate purposes. The authors hold that individual agency and social architecture are forces that turn individual empathy into collective social reality. It is 'the amalgam of social networks, values, and routines that structure an organization and that constrain and enable individual action' (ibid., p. 74). Individuals are able to notice and respond to others' suffering through social architecture of the organization. One of the forces that activate compassionate behaviour are the values of humanity and holistic personhood. Organizational routines may enable or prohibit compassionate behaviour. If they are associated with service and notification of harm, they advance and enable compassionate responses of the participants. Another potentially helpful resource is social networks that the individual can mobilize when he or she encounters suffering in the workplace. Processes helpful in empathic responses include also the creation of unofficial roles enabling such a response, improvisation of routines that enable coordination of action and the existence of empathic leaders, with whom the participants may identify. The proliferation of compassionate stories in the organization's culture is another helpful factor. Thus, three main groups of factors: social architecture, individual activation and mobilization and structural and symbolic emergent features, may enable compassion organizing. Organizations need to pay attention to pain, enable the spread of emotions, rely on trust between the participants and on their knowledge necessary for the creation and improvisation of roles while responding to suffering. Finally, leaders create symbolic enrichment of compassionate behaviour and provide material for the creation of compassionate stories in the organization's culture.

Indeed, organizations as wholes can be compassionate and the need for this is increasingly being recognized, having such manifestations as the *Academy of Management Review*'s Special Topic Forum on Understanding and Creating Caring and Compassionate Organizations (Rynes *et al.*, 2012). Scholars contributed with texts refocusing theorizing around management and organization around care and compassion and aimed at exploring what happens to our understanding of how organizations work if we change perspective, and regard compassion as not an individual virtue or perhaps even less relevant private trait, as so often happened in the past of management theory and practice, but instead see it as an important organizational feature. The forum proposes that compassion should be taken to the forefront of the interest in organizations and management and become the responsibility of organizations.

> Rather than assuming that revenues, profits, and wages or salaries are the ultimate (and, often, sole) objectives of organizations and organizing, attention would be focused additionally or instead on the health, happiness, well-being, and sustainability of organizations, their members, and those they serve.
>
> *(Ibid., p. 518)*

Eastern as well as Western traditions can be helpful in the development of compassionate management (Opdebeeck and Habisch, 2011). Eastern wisdom carried in Taoism, Confucianism and Zen Buddhism upholds a compassionate way of life and the desire to help in all walks of life. That includes management and obliges them to create workplaces where they themselves and others can be happy. This involves mutually beneficial transactions, benevolent leadership and empathy with others. Many Eastern entrepreneurs aspire to holding these values as central in their work. Western traditions, such as Christianity and Islam, emphasize the necessity to treat the Other in the way one would like to be treated oneself. Many Western enterprising initiatives have, in fact, historically been as much economic as social initiatives and the attempts at reframing their history as purely effectiveness-oriented is a sad distortion of a potentially valuable lesson in managerial compassion. There also exist philosophical inspirations for compassionate management, present both in antiquity and in contemporary thinking. All these perspectives and traditions may help to develop management styles and cultures based on trust rather than fear. This is a key imperative for management education.

9.3 Sounds, images, dreams

Ko Ǔn's *Ten Thousand Lives* (2005) is a collection of poems written in a tradition reminiscent of Chinese calligraphy: each is a sketchy portrait of a person, albeit carried out with such mindfulness that it seems to reflect something essential about him or her. One of the translators to the English language, Brother Anthony of Taizé, explains that it is

> an immense mosaic narrative of Korean history. Instead of conceiving history as dominated and directed by a few powerful figures. Ko Ǔn insists that Korea's history is embodied and endured by its people as a whole, so that little children and poor old women are as significant as political leaders and famous public figures.
>
> *(Brother Anthony of Taizé, 2010, p. 44)*

Ko Ǔn's poetry carries so much compassion that it almost brings the characters alive, either known personally by the author or of whom he has just heard, they invoke experiences and feelings that had indeed been part of someone's life. In 'Beggars: Husband and wife' he tells the tale of the difficult life of two people during a spring famine.

> When they have no food left
> they go roaming around five villages ...
> 'If you've any food, please, could you give us a spoonful?'
> Their humility is so much humbler by far than
> even the wife from Sŏnun-ri in Jungttŭm could manage.
> The words 'please, could you give' are scarcely audible.
> During the bleakest days of harsh spring famine,

when they cannot see so much as the shadow
of a pot of cold left-over barley-rice, they say:
'Let's go drink some water instead.'
Off they go to the well at Soijŏngji
to draw up a bucketful. Then those two beggars,
husband and wife, lovingly share a drink, and go home again
In the twilight thick flocks of jackdaws settle,
daylight fades into twilight,
as husband and wife pass over the hill at Okjŏng-gol.
In the twilight, smoke from a fire cooking supper
rises from only very few houses.

(Ko Ŭn, 2005)

Times are hard for everyone in the villages, there is not enough food to feed the family, let alone share it with the two wandering people, who are, due to the famine, reduced to begging. Some of the villagers, while turning them down, might have felt genuine regret; doing so meant renouncing the last occasion for showing humanity. Yet they felt that they had to make such a choice or they themselves and their children would die of hunger. The husband and the wife go home hungry but not deprived of their dignity. Sharing a cup of water, they share, indeed, much more.

Some of the protagonists of the poems are Ko Ŭn's own relatives, such as in the case of 'Maternal Grandfather'.

Ch'oi Hong-kwan, our maternal grandfather,
was so tall his high hat would reach the eaves,
scraping the sparrows' nests under the roof.
He was always laughing.
If our grandmother offered a beggar a bite to eat,
he was always the first to be glad.
. . .
Once, when I was small, he told me:
'Look, if you sweep the yard well
the yard will laugh.
If the yard laughs,
the fence will laugh.
Even the morning-glories
blossoming on the fence will laugh.'

(Ko Ŭn, 2005)

The portrait is more than a beautiful tribute, it actually makes Ch'oi Hong-kwan's spirit speak to us directly, sharing his wisdom with us, bringing forward a smile and perhaps, if we let him, an enlightening moment, opening the mind to the infinite beauty of life. Ko Ŭn has been looking for enlightening wisdom himself: he used to be a Buddhist monk but abandoned the monastery to dedicate his life to poetry and activism for peace and democracy. A survivor of the Korean War, he saw many friends and relatives die. Much of his poetry is about giving those people – dead, forgotten, killed in wars – a voice, and letting them share their being with others, with us. Among them are sages, beggars, thieves, traitors, liars, lovers, abandoned spouses, dreamers...

Wim Wender's film *Himmer über Berlin*, known in the English speaking world as *Wings of Desire* (1987) is a story of falling, and of love. Angels exist, they are around us all the time, they listen to our thoughts and watch over our steps. They are there to 'assemble, testify, preserve', as one of them, Cassiel, affirms. The angels of Berlin had seen it all: from the beginnings of time, through the geological ages, then, human history, recently, the horror of the Nazi rule, despair, death, murder, a divided city.... But they only take in and do not give; they cannot become involved with what they see, and cannot be seen themselves. Whereas they are invisible to adults, children are able to see them. One of the angels watching over Berlin, Damiel, falls in love with a circus acrobat. When he sees her perform, he becomes moved, at the same time concerned and thrilled. She is a remarkable artist, flying over the arena like an angel, but being just human after all, she may fall to her death; she is risking her life for an uncertain art. She feels lonely, making Damiel realize his own heavenly loneliness. She cannot see him, and he is not able reach out to her or to comfort her. One day he decides to give up immortality and become human, to be able to tell her that he is there, maybe make her love him too, maybe be with her. He is risking his immortal life for an uncertain, but incomparably brief, future. It turns out he is not the only one who had made such a choice: he encounters Peter Falk, another of the angels who chose to fall to Earth. Immortality had become unbearable to him; he had only been able to watch, never to experience, become immersed in life. He fell and he does not regret his decision to face death, pain, uncertainty. Becoming human means becoming vulnerable: when Damiel takes the plunge, he discovers that his hand is bleeding; to him it means being able to feel pain, perceiving colours. At the same time, however, he has lost his ability to hear the people's thoughts. Nevertheless, meeting the Other is now possible, even if difficult – it requires a place, a right time, choices and serendipities. Love makes all of these conditions possible; a step taken in love opens the door to a path together, which is an entirely different world altogether. As Peter Falk so well realizes, echoing Emmanuel Lévinas (1999), the precondition for meeting the Other is seeing the Other's visage. When he is talking to an angel he cannot see but feels to be present, he repeatedly says: 'I wish I could see your face, just look into your eyes and tell you how good it is to be here.'

Wings of Desire was widely critically acclaimed and gained its director the main award at Cannes, as well as several other prizes. The screenplay was co-authored by the German film maker Wim Wenders and the writer Peter Handke, whose poem, 'Song of childhood', is recited at the beginning of the film.

> When the child was a child,
> it didn't know that it was a child,
> everything was soulful,
> and all souls were one.
>> *(Handke, as quoted in: Wenders,*
>> *1987)*

Growing up, we lose the sensitivity to one-ness, we begin seeing things separately, and we ourselves become separated from everything and everyone else. Loneliness is, however, a way of seeing, not the ultimate truth of our existence. We learn it as we grow up and thus fall from the grace of innocence, but it does not take inhuman effort to unlearn – all it takes is love.

9.4 Reflection 2

Peter Frost (2011) makes a strong case for compassion in organizations, based on a personal story. The author was recovering from cancer surgery in a ward together with a patient with a very serious health problem. The nurse offered him compassion, which made him feel more cheerful and perhaps even helped him to heal. Peter Frost believes that compassion makes a real difference in all kinds of organizations. Receiving and giving compassion creates a new quality, something important and enduring. But witnessing compassion is also an uplifting experience. It changes the meaning in organizations: people act with the intention to make the organization and others grow. As organizational practice, it is a kind of competence, which can be used but may also be misused or simply left unemployed. If not valued or celebrated, it may seem completely absent. When it is misused, for example by toxic leadership, it may lead to compassion burnout (we will return to this later in the section). Compassion may also help researchers to approach organizations and theory building with simultaneous love and detachment. This enables us to gain more insight and a fuller knowledge about the topic of our study. Practice and theory can finally meet on a solid ground.

> Compassion counts as connection to the human spirit and to the human condition. In organizations, there is suffering and pain, as there is joy and fulfilment. There is a need for dignity and self-respect in these settings, and to the extent that our theories, models and practices ignore these dimensions, so they distort our understanding of life in these enterprises. Looking at organizations through the compassion lens brings this 'disappeared' world into focus.
>> *(Ibid., p. 399)*

Ronald Paul Hill and Debra Lynn Stephens (2003) are also of the opinion that the time for compassionate organizations has come. The consumers are changing, becoming more diverse, more dependent on and proficient in technology. This is a challenge that contemporary organizations have to face. One of the important steps towards a shift in the necessary management perspective is a focus on compassion, beyond the traditional market-oriented approach. Organizations have to become better workplaces, recognizing

> their benefits and drawbacks for meeting the full range of needs of customers and employees, helping both to become and to remain productive and satisfied with their personal and professional lives.
>
> *(Ibid., p. 339)*

Enjoyment of work should be, once again, a legitimate idea to consider and focus upon. This means a radical change in management philosophy, but it does not imply a rupture with the past: organizations should acknowledge their history, but not become bound by it. People's needs and desires in their diversity should become part and parcel of the organization's strategy.

As I have already mentioned, such a radically new focus calls for a reorientation of management education programmes, which some of the authors reflecting on compassionate organizations recognize. Richard Kernochan, Donald McCormick and Judith White (2007) explain how compassion changes the teaching experience. Based on personal stories from their teaching practice, the authors propose that spiritual values including compassion be integrated into teaching, as this helps to deal with the emotional labour of teaching but also to transform the teaching experience into a calling, able to give something to the students beyond the technicalities of the subject taught. Teaching compassionately helps to spread and grow the compassion.

Compassion is also recognized as the missing link in economics and management. Debjani Kanjilal, Azam M. Bejou and David Bejou (2012) call for a shift in perspective, drawing the attention of companies and theorists to other factors than the now ever dominant focus on profit maximization. The current crisis calls for new solutions and radically new ideas about how and why to manage organizations. Some measures of quality of life are needed to be taken into consideration. Currently,

> one of the prime assumptions in economics is that economic agents behave rationally. However, this sometimes leads one to become selfish, thus engaging in opportunistic behavior with one another. What is perhaps more important is a sense of altruism and compassion as characteristics of rational behavior. Compassion is a missing link in mainstream economic theories.
>
> *(Ibid., p. 16)*

Compassion is missing from the economic and management models today, which encourage economic actors to behave in ways that are selfish, greedy, inconsiderate and call these vices 'rationality'. People, employees, consumers and communities of stakeholders, should be treated in a way that allows them to develop their integrity, to feel happy and productive, 'and the world will move toward attaining the economic efficiency, equity, justice, and quality of life that all people deserve regardless of their economic class' (ibid., p. 19). Compassion should, according to the authors, be the new philosophy of business.

Finally, love has been brought forward as a new managerial virtue (Harris, 2002). Based on the recognition of the centrality of the relationship between love and courage, Howard Harris brings forward a number of arguments from management literature, as well as from philosophy and ethics, in support of management being a managerial virtue. In fact, love can be said to be 'an organising principle for the virtues' (ibid., p. 180). It is regarded by managers as an important part of their role as leaders.

As valid and important as the argument for the inclusion of love into the practice and theory of management may be, there is also a dark side to be taken into consideration. Recent history shows how everything can be managed. Also the heart. Arlie Hochschild's (1983) well known book presents emotional work in such occupations as flight attendants, nurses and waiters. They are expected to play out feelings; sometimes their work embraces deep play and suppression of their real feelings. The actors develop numerous defence strategies to prevent burnout and the effect is often hypocrisy and cynicism. Sometimes people fail to defend themselves effectively and grow alienated from their own feelings. Heather Höpfl (1992) speaks of methods, reminiscent of those adopted by religious missionaries, used by business leaders towards their employees. They are aimed at eliciting dedication and identification with the organization, ideally a devotion so complete that it indeed brings to mind a religious conversion experience. However, it gives no profound sense of salvation of enlightenment in return. The person is not saved; he or she is not even recognized as an important spiritual being. Instead, he or she receives a mirage of meaning, so shallow it is unable to bring comfort to anyone but remains a broken promise, an organized deceit eating away on the social fabric of cultural confidence.

To those who are open to giving and receiving of feelings in organizations, contemporary workplaces regularly offer hate and contempt as a kind of dark replacement, perhaps derived from the organization's shadow, or collective unconscious of suppressed strong emotions, even positive ones such as passionate love, when these find no outlet and instead become managed and repressed (Kostera, 2012). Bullying is quite widespread in workplaces – a repeated attacking, harassing or humiliating of the same people, usually connected with power inequalities (Monks et al., 2009). As a result of the current proliferation of toxic leaders, bullying may become ingrained in the organization's culture and it erodes the basic principles of human relationships (Boddy, 2011). Not only do the people at whom the aggression is addressed become affected but also the witnesses and bystanders. Bullying demoralizes entire organizations and breaks down the fabric of confidence and trust that provides the basis for human interactions. Another common organizational product is humiliation (Czarniawska, 2008). Humiliation is the negative result of organizational authority, a common but not usually well documented phenomenon. Employees subjected to a ritual deprivation of participation rights become more easily controlled and passive; they also lose their agency and interest in the organization as a whole.

Both kinds of practices are frequently connected with power and then they erode love and compassion in the organization, as people, in fear of losing their jobs, train themselves not to react, and, even worse, learn to persuade themselves that this is a rational and therefore legitimate way to behave – the sign of being a socially competent adult.

9.5 Stories from organizations

This is a tale of two restaurants, where I worked as a student in Sweden over 30 years ago.[8] One had recently been opened, on the new wave of private business and entrepreneurship. Britta and Calle were harbingers of the dynamic era; upon their return from the States, where they had been working in restaurants, they decided to start an American-style chain of their own in their home country. They opened several outlets simultaneously, and one of them was Café Crystal where I started working as I finished secondary school. The first day I was mainly cleaning the floors and bringing things that the cooks needed from storerooms and the cooler. I also helped another student worker, who later became my friend, Anna-Karin, to take out the rubbish. We had lots of fun playing basket ball with the huge black bags, trying to send them with a perfect hurl into the bin. But most of all, we enjoyed throwing the big ketchup cans, they flew like rockets and landed with a clang, and the residual ketchup left a wonderful red splash on the wall. We wore the dark aprons of the low caste personnel and enjoyed the privileges: we were supposed to do the dirty work and we could be as dirty as we pleased. I do not remember having laughed as much for months as I did then, my stomach ached from it, even more than my muscles and back from all the carrying and scrubbing. The following weeks I spent doing similar work, on my own or with someone else, but increasingly often I was sent to the dishwasher by Ulla, the energetic personnel boss, who, I knew by now, would materialize suddenly and make sure we were working hard enough; shouting, reprimanding, redirecting us, sometimes sending some of the extra personnel, like myself, home. At last I became a dishwasher and acquired a blue T-shirt with the café's logo. The place got a restaurant extension and the kitchen employed Eva, a real chef with a diploma. There was, however, no table service and what in fact was offered was a kind of fast food, but the aura was that of a restaurant: earthenware plates and cups, cutlery, an interior that was at the same time luxurious and utterly fake. The customers had to queue up for their coffee and food, they also had to wait for it being served at the counter. It never took much time, all Eva did during rush hours was heating up food she had earlier prepared. For that purpose she used the microwave oven, an epitome of modernity. The personnel at the counter shouted in their orders through a hatch: 'one nettle soup, one!', 'one shrimp sandwich, one!'. Café Crystal was an extremely popular lunch place, maybe because it was, somehow, a combination of Burger King (the speed) and the nearby Mona Lisa restaurant (the decor), with reasonable prices and good deals for loyal lunchers. In the summer it was swarming with tourists and *flâneurs*, dropping in to buy an ice-cream or a soda. The all-knowing kitchen personnel told me conspiratorially that Britta and Calle were doing very well indeed and by Christmas they had extended the opening hours and huge crowds occupied the tables almost non-stop. We were told to 'effectivize' the customers, if they were sitting too long with a single coffee we should first give them a hint that they should move on, or, if they did not react, tell them explicitly that they should either order something or leave. However, Café Crystal seemed to employ fewer people. I was studying organization theory and reading Frederick Taylor's writings on 'scientific management' (1911),[9] and it made perfect sense: this was what Britta and Calle were trying to do, with the help of the omnipresent, eternally furious Ulla, they made us work harder and harder, for the same meagre pay, and with the help of 'organization' they were getting maximum profit from a constantly accelerating rhythm. When I began as dishwasher's help, we were always at least three, usually five during rush hours, operating the machine and cleaning the tables. By Christmas there were two of us, the anxious Madeleine, who was a permanent employee, and myself. A majority of the personnel at Café Crystal were extras, young students with a bitterly low pay. The pay in the restaurant branch was not much anyway, my friends in the kitchen told me, as the trade unions were weak and ineffective. Most of us were women; there was only one young man, Peter, who was studying medicine. All the kitchen personnel (they had the most fun, most of them were permanents, I loved the kitchen and was overjoyed each time Ulla directed me to help out there) flirted ferociously with the tall, blond young man, who was very shy and his face was always turning red behind the beard in reaction to their remarks ('you do have a great ass!') or furtive caresses and pats. I thought that was really funny at the time; I began to reconsider some years later when I became the youngest woman in an almost all-male team at work. We worked extremely hard but also had our deal of fun, usually at the expense of the bosses and customers. We loved stealing things from the cooler: stealthily drinking sherry, eating grapes, swallowing whole handfuls of shrimp. We enjoyed making fun of the customers: they were all ridiculous, and we pointed them out to each other from behind the round window in the kitchen door: 'look at that one! Silly cow...'. 'The customer is always right' we were taught, so we smiled at them and were offensively courteous to their faces, but among ourselves, what a ball we had laughing at them. We relished serving them something that had landed on the floor. We did not have much respect for the food we served; we were not supposed to touch it anyway, all the leftovers were to be thrown away. Ulla checked that very thoroughly; no food should be eaten by the personnel.

By Christmas Ulla called a meeting after work. We believed she was going to thank us for our hard work, but, instead, there was a short motivational speech by Britta and Calle, who left immediately afterwards, and then an impassioned lecture by Ulla about how we should and should not dress.

'Look at you', she said, pointing at me, 'the way you look in that T-shirt, so shabby [I did not protest that I was dead tired after nine hours of work and, furthermore, well hidden from view in the dishwasher all day], and you [a sharp finger went in the direction of Anna the cashier] – these shoes are atrocious. The customers deserve better.

You are all to be shining clean, with neat and fashionable hair styles, and you are to wear high heels from now on. Except cooks. That is all.'

Having said that, she left. We looked at each other. Anna shook her head. Madeleine suggested that we contact the unions.

'And what good will that do?' Eva wondered. But we did that anyway. As Eva foresaw, they were sympathetic but utterly unhelpful.

'Let's just boycott this. Let's wear our normal shoes tomorrow and the day after', Eva said. And we did. Ulla was furious and went to telephone her employers. She came out, smiling.

'You', she looked at us extras, hanging around in the passage, 'out. All extras, out.'

'Oh no' – Eva started cleaning her hands on the apron and then deliberately taking it off – 'you don't. If they quit, so do I. And nobody's gonna tell us to wear shoes like whores, this is not a brothel and we do not want to become handicapped at 50, we fucking *work* here.'

Ulla froze. We all did. For a deadly 10 minutes we watched her going into her office, and then, composed, coming out again. We could wear the shoes we liked but we had to look clean and decent at all times. Now get back to work! On that day I learned about the power of the chef – and of compassion.

I continued to work extra for one more year, wearing comfortable shoes. I was first allowed to work as cashier, then to help Eva in the kitchen with more serious cooking. When I finally quit, the café was as successful as ever, with crowds welling in at all hours, and just one dishwasher.

I then started to work as a waitress in a small restaurant many kilometres into the countryside, The Willow, founded by Olof, an older man, the ex-chef of the king, as the kitchen personnel immediately revealed to me. Olof was a kind person, with an open, round face, emphasized by the balding front. He loved cooking, he came in to the kitchen every day and in the evenings he cooked for us. Every day after work, we were served a most delicious meal, worthy of a king, for free. Olof loved us. He talked with us over dinner, asked about our families, problems. We also talked about the customers on these occasions. We liked the customers; we recognized most of them and called them by their names.

'Did you see? Malin brought her new baby today. What a cutie!'

'Does anyone know what's the matter with auntie Stina? Haven't seen her for awhile.'

After we finished eating, we could take home all the leftovers we wanted. It would be a pity to throw away food, prepared with so much love.

The tale has a postscript. When I visited Malmö a few years ago, it occurred to me to see what happened to the two places. I learned that the chain went bust in the late 1990s, and for awhile only two locations, including Café Crystal, still worked in a limited way, but then closed down, too. I also learned that The Willow was very much in operation. The old chef was dead, but his son had taken over, a good man, a good chef. I sat by a table in the corner. A tear rolled down my cheek, but if it was of sorrow, happiness or gratitude, I cannot say.

9.6 Questions to reflect on

1. Think of a very good friend (but not your partner), what he or she likes, how he or she talks, dresses, behaves. Close your eyes and concentrate on these thoughts. Now imagine you are the person. Open your eyes: what do you see? What do you feel? Think of what the world is like as seen through that person's eyes. Now call him or her and ask how they are. Listen.

2. Go to a café, sit down at a table with a coffee or tea and look, discretely, at the other people: sitting, queuing and working. Focus on where they are placed in the room, what they probably see from the perspective, what they do. Try to think well of each of them for a few minutes. Wish them good luck in your thoughts. Now shift attention to yourself. How do you feel?

3. Think warmly of someone you know. What would make that person happy? Is there something you could easily do to make him or her happy? Maybe pay a visit, invite her or him for coffee or to the theatre? Buy him or her a book of poetry? Do that. How did he or she react? How did that make you feel? Write a short poem about that person, paint or knit something that makes you think of him or her.

4. Cook something for someone you love. It may be simple or complicated, or perhaps just a coffee, but try to express your love through it. Ask that person afterwards how it tasted. Did you succeed in expressing your feelings? How did that make you feel?

Notes

1 384 BC–322 BC, Ancient Greece.
2 c.469 BC–399 BC, Ancient Greece.
3 c.99 BC–c.55 BC, Ancient Rome.
4 1207–1273, Afghanistan, Persia and Turkey.
5 1515–1582, Spain.
6 1723–1790, Scotland.
7 1906–1995, France.
8 Based on authentic material.
9 See Chapter 6, Section 1.

PART IV

Controlling

Introducing the 3 E's: ethos, ethics and ecology

The management function of control means in non-mainstream conditions, providing a fair and effective ground for common action: *how to make sure* that it will be done? It does not imply exerting power over others, making them follow rules, handed down to them, or checking on them to ensure that they act in these proscribed ways. Instead, non-mainstream control relies heavily on self-discipline, conviction and determination, provided in particular by the three key sources: ethos, ethics and ecology.

*   *Ethos* provides a higher bond with a group or a place, forging a sense of duty and an obligation to act in certain ways.
*   *Ethics* provide meaningful guidelines for how to act in order to increase the good and fair and avoid the wrong and unjust.
*   *Ecology* puts human life and activity in a global perspective.

10
ETHOS

Archangel Uriel, bring us water and wine
to pour out over the darkness
with which we collide

Ethos refers to moral character within the context of a group or a place. It can also be a rhetorical mode of persuasion, directed at a group of listeners, establishing legitimacy or trustworthiness of the speaker through the presentation of a moral competence that would appeal to the listeners, usually by creating moral links. In this sense, ethos is used as a bridge constructed between two areas of land: the speaker's and the listeners'. In the more general sense, ethos can be seen as the land itself and it is, indeed, often tightly connected with a physical place, such a village, region, landscape. Else, it is an attribute of a group of people sharing an identity, such as a group of professionals, for example, medical doctors, teachers, academics; or a movement, like the arts and crafts movement. Ethos invokes the values and norms constituent for the group, either because of the geographic and climatic peculiarities, or because of what it does and why. Only some places and some groups share an ethos; it is a (significant, yet singular) exception rather than a rule. Ethos can be derived from the special challenges posed by a place itself: for example, the Himalayas are an extreme environment for plants, animals and human beings, mere survival in such surroundings demands not only physical predispositions, but also a moral stance, based most of all on patience, endurance and courage. Many of the Himalayan tribes also have an ethos of cooperation, compassion and kindness, which is not a direct effect of the environment, but a moral identity making possible a life, even in such extremely difficult circumstances, which is worthwhile and happy. In places located in strategic spots of historical trade-routes, such as Sandomierz in southern Poland, there is an ethos of welcoming guests and of exchange, as much of goods and money, as of expressions of politeness and civility. Life has been, for hundreds of years, much easier for the inhabitants of Sandomierz than it has for the tribes of the Himalayas, for natural and climatic reasons. However, being regarded as an economically and politically attractive place also has its risks: the town has been invaded and robbed many times in its history. Its collective identity requires a moral unity and readiness to defend the group from aggressors, while at the same time not discouraging peaceful visitors, bringing trade and prosperity. The geographically determined sense of the sublime differs also: mountaineers have a daily contact with what most people readily see as awe-inspiring and even transcendent. The townsmen living among gentle green hills and lush meadows look for inspiration elsewhere: to the river which brings nourishment to the land but sometimes, during floods, rages and seizes the fields and houses of the villagers, or to the products of human thought and architecture. Ethos of occupational groups provides a sense of collective identity rooted in the ideals, goals and standards of a profession. For example, a nurse embracing the ethos of the medical profession believes that what he or she is doing makes a difference and deserves to be done carefully and well, with the patient's well-being in mind. Social movements provide a similar meaning by their ethos.

Unlike other constructs defining group identity, ethos does not attempt to classify the insiders versus the outsiders, it does not seek to invoke divisions or portray one group as inherently better than another. Even geographical ethos does not include xenophobia, nor is it particularly patriotic or makes a special virtue of belonging to this or that particular group. It is more about how to live in order to survive and be happy in a given environment. Professional ethos is exclusive, in that it regards unprofessional behaviour as a violation of the standards of the profession and maybe even a way of leaving the group. The ethos is, however, not an affiliation and it does not offer a sense of belonging, together with the other social mechanisms such as socialization and ostracism; rather, it is a higher ideal of the profession, something making it worth practising it and aspiring to fulfilling the standards. Ethos is not about checking on the inhabitants of Sandomierz to see whether they are welcoming, nor on nurses to see if they do their best to help the patient. Ethos is what makes them believe in what they are doing.

10.1 A short history of ethos

Ethos is a broad term in classic literature. For example, in Hesiod's[1] *Works and Days* (1914b) in its original Greek version, it signifies both human settlements and collective moral character, according to the classic scholar and translator Inga Grześczak (2012, personal email communication). Other meanings include: custom, behaviour, way of being, disposition, character in drama (ibid.). Aristotle (1991) describes ethos as one of the three modes of persuasion in rhetoric (the other two being *logos* and *pathos*) and involves a moral competence of the speaker and the audience. It refers to the general trustworthiness of the speaker, his or her likeability and authority. There are three types of ethos: *phronesis*, or practical wisdom; *arête*, or virtue; and *eunoia*, a positive predisposition towards the audience (Hyde, 2004).

Max Weber[2] (2012) understood ethos as a way of life, a collective moral and sociological predisposition, such as, for example, enacted by the creators of modern capitalism. Religion supports the development of such an ethos, some do it more and some less effectively. In particular, 'puritanism carried the ethos of the rational organization of capital and labour' (ibid., p. 103).

The sociologist Robert Merton[3] (1968) used ethos in the sense of attitudes and ideals attached to the engagement in science, or the academic profession:

> The ethos of the social institution of science is taken to include universalistic criteria of social validity and scientific worth, thus involving values easily integrated with the values of a free society in which it is men's capabilities and achievements which matter, not their ascribed status or origins
>
> *(Ibid., p. 588)*

The Polish sociologist Maria Ossowska[4] (2000) understood ethos in a similar way to Merton and used the term to describe the chivalric code of mores and its significance for the development of the modern society, especially social groups with a high sense of value and internal control.

The French philosopher and social theorist Michel Foucault[5] saw ethos as self-discipline, self-regulation, demanding self-reflexive practice and thought. It is

> the considered form that freedom takes when it is informed by reflection.
>
> *(Foucault, 1997, p. 284)*

The philosopher and sociologist Pierre Bourdieu[6] used the term *ethos* in the French original of *Questions de sociologie* (1980) in the sense of a set of moral predispositions.[7] In his understanding, the term *habitus* is broader than that of ethos and he preferred to utilize the former to refer to general dispositions resulting from socialization and accumulation of a history that each of us acquires. It includes formal and informal education and schooling, enculturation, upbringing, etc. It becomes part of the individual's responses and attitudes, often unknowingly, deriving from socialization. Through the habitus we reproduce social conditions but not in a mechanical way.

10.2 Reflection 1

Craig Kallendorf and Carol Kallendorf (1985) advocate for a conscious use of Aristotle's classic figures of speech, including ethos, which they see as intimately connected to public image. Businesspeople recognize the importance of image and they dedicate much effort to the development and maintenance of a positive image through dress, demeanour and adaptation to the style of their customers. However, too little effort is dedicated to the use of a cultivated, cultured rhetorical style or verbal ethos. This demands education and an appreciation of learning.

> Effective reasoning and a convincing *ethos* can only come from sound, broad knowledge.
>
> *(Ibid., p. 46)*

However, education may not only be connected to an ethos seen as trustworthy image, but a more profound value set. Ethos, understood as social and institutional context carrying certain dispositions, can be seen as a collective habitus, such as that of an organization, and in particular an educational organization, such as a school (Smith, 2003). People construct and reconstruct their habituses by their participation in the organization's culture. What emerges as a result is a collective organizational ethos, which may (or may not) be supported or undermined by an 'official' ethos, proposed by management. I would add to Edwin Smith's ideas of the links between learning and ethos that any organization, where learning is an important part of the everyday processes, can be said to hold an ethos, or at least a predisposition toward it. People learning together may create a cultural construct allowing for collective self-control, which is ethos.

Robin Snell (2000) calls for a greater interest in organizational moral ethos as a collective moral foundation.

> Moral ethos is a set of force-fields within organizations, comprising everyday norms, rules-in-use, social pressures, and quality of relationships, all of which impinge on members' understandings, judgements and decisions concerning good and bad, right and wrong (Jackall, 1984; Snell, 1993). As a 'hidden' curriculum (Jackson, 1990), of morality in the workplace, moral ethos is synonymous with moral or ethical climate …, culture … and mileu.
>
> *(Ibid., p. 267)*

The currently dominating liberal individualism does not provide a universal, or even communal, foundation. Organizations are increasingly seen as lacking of integrity, any kind of public spirit and generally morally disturbing. While some suggest this may be due to the actions of immoral individuals, Snell points out that this may be a consequence of a lack of moral ethos, due to the spread of liberal individualism which denounces the superiority or even helpfulness of collective or public moral values. It is based on individual reasoning and abstract considerations. In contrast, moral ethos does not comprise moral reasoning but is a 'complex mixture of embedded assumptions, implied norms, perceived pressures and expectations and expressed values impinging upon members' everyday moral reasoning in use, and may seethe with competing and conflicting forces and perceptions' (ibid., p. 276).

Bogdan Costea, Norman Crump and John Holm (2005) present two different organizational ethoses: of play and of management which some organizations aspire to bring together. The authors propose that it is possible that Western civilization has entered a phase in which a new 'managerial Dionysus' is emerging in certain organizations. Traditional management is characterized by a desire to order and to control. By contrast,

> [p]lay always connects value spheres and mediates important boundaries in social activities and personal existence in all human societies; it is the occasion of collective and individual eruptions of passion, of exuberance and anger, of resistance and agitation, of effervescence and candour.
>
> *(Ibid., p. 140)*

Play undermines and subverts simple dualities such as alienation/exploitation and transcends political rationalities. However, used in managerial contexts, it becomes a tool for control. Ethos implies normative control and this is achieved through play, by such ideas as 'self-work' and wellness, especially the contemporary idea of the 'duty to be happy'. The authors claim that at the level of managerial ethos, it has become possible to incorporate play in recent decades as an integral part of productive organizational life. This is also congruent with the recent changes in work ethos, putting the self in the centre of (moral) attention. The irrational, transgressive and chaotic Dionysian mode has taken a more prominent place in contemporary culture (replacing the rational and ordered Apollonian mode of the twentieth century), together with a consumption culture.

> [T]he 'turn to the self' has generated a reconstitution of the managerial field and of its objects in the wider context of the contemporary ethos. The vocabularies of soft capitalism – which draw on the entire range of therapeutic and spiritual technologies of the last two decades – form the matrix in which self-work becomes the central imperative of managerial action.
>
> *(Ibid., p. 148)*

Play is the form that unites self-work with contemporary main concerns of management. Managerialism became a fashionable way of life and at the epitome of its controlling and ordering drives, it strove to incorporate the paradoxes of present-day life, being drawn into the chaotic and irrational streams of culture, producing an ethos of self-improvement and self-celebration.

> The combination of work and play as legitimate facets of organisational life always contains a promise for the modern 'self-asserting self'; that finitude as shortage of enjoyment might not be a danger anymore, that organisations which promote opportunities to be 'perpetually happy' and 'perpetually young' are contiguous with the pursuit of 'total fun'. When happiness, wellness and fun are not sufficient only after office hours, their 'sourcing' and consumption spill over into all social spheres. In fact, it is their very logic to expand. So, the central historical-cultural question remains: are work organisations and managerial ideologies appropriating 'fun', or is 'fun' colonising management and organisations?
>
> *(Ibid., p. 150)*

Not just the temporal but also the spatial dimension of the organizational and managerial ethos have been recently discussed and researched. Göran Svensson, Greg Wood, Jang Singh and Michael Callaghan (2009) studied corporate codes of ethics in three different cultures: Sweden, Australia and Canada, in order to check whether there is evidence of an emerging shared ethos of such codes, their existence and contents. The authors assume that such an ethos would work as a collective imperative framework against which important decisions, such as strategic planning, would be measured in corporations. Such codes would be used to communicate a broader ethos to the employees. Some items have been found to be shared across the cultural boundaries: surveillance and training, guidance, internal communication, external communication and sustainability. These elements are areas of interest rather than norms and community standards so I propose to regard them as a contemporary international business ethos of ethical codes rather than a managerial ethos.

Much more prevailing than self-control via organizational or managerial ethoses is the trust in a professional ethos, which has long and well founded traditions (Schorske, 1968). Their roots reach at least the medieval societies, where the clerical order has a strong communal sense of duty outside of the political order. Even though the Enlightenment integrated the orders into one civic ethos, the sense of duty and loyalty of organized professions has not been diminished. It has for a long time been represented in such communities as the academic profession. Professional ethos is not only about knowledge but relationships with other members of the profession and the historically embedded norms of excellence, manifesting itself through individual and collective judgements and crystallizing itself through hierarchies and systems of prestige (Zarca, 2009).

The professional ethos is understood as a set of dispositions acquired by experience and relative towards what is regarded as more or less at the overall dimension (epistemological, esthetic, social etc.) which is important for the practice of the profession.[8]

(Ibid., p. 352)

Karin Jonnergård (2008) portrays this rather unique and strong communal engagement of professionals using the characters of the witches from Terry Pratchett's *Discworld* series of books. The witches are strongly independent, with a formidable communal integrity, and they possess a knowledge which no outsider has access to. Their work is dependent upon the trust of the clients, whereas much of the rules of how it should be carried out rely on the canons adopted by the professionals themselves: the technical core and the professional ethos. Even though much effort has been dedicated to subordinate professions to managerial control and turn professionals into 'knowledgeable workers', many have an astounding ability to persist in the face of adversities, even as overpowering as the New Public Management which has succeeded in doing away with most of the ethos of the public servant (to which we will return in Reflection 2). The outsets and the context transformed

professional knowledge from a personal capacity developed over the lifespan to a property possible for an organization to organize and utilize in manifold ways. The hero we remember from modernity is exchanged for the heroic organization to which we connect both knowledge and status.

(Ibid., p. 188)

Professionals are stripped of their knowledge and their status is no longer clear. However, there is one thing that remained – professional conduct or, in the terms of this chapter, professional ethos. The professional is subject to discipline like all employees, but the strongest disciplining force still comes from within the professional community, not from management or the organization.

Professional conduct implies the application of a behaviour that retains trust in the professionals' superior expertise and the appropriateness of professional autonomy. To achieve such trust, the profession is forced to exert discipline.

(Ibid., p. 189)

10.3 Sounds, images, dreams

I saw Ivan Meštrović's masterpiece sculpture, Grgur Ninski, or Gregory of Nin, for the first time when I was driving through the Croatian city of Varaždin in 2012. I did not expect to find it there; I knew nothing about its creator or of Grgur himself; and I did not plan to visit Varaždin. A number of serendipities led me to the place where the imposing statue is standing on one of the city's squares, in a pedestrian area, sheltered from the street by a neighbouring church. The figure of Grgur, at the same time commanding, rapt and somehow self-less, moved me so much that I spent a long time looking at him from different angles and I consequently went to see the other two copies of the sculpture: in Nin and Split, where there is also a museum dedicated to Ivan Meštrović's work (Meštrović Gallery, 2013). Grgur was the bishop of Nin in the years 900–929. He was a defender of the local customs and language, proposing to use Slavic language in the liturgy of the local Catholic church, instead of the then obligatory Latin, thus being a forerunner of similar ideas brought forward several hundred years later during the Reformation. He became a symbol of the ethos of self-determination and respect for local culture, yet without the separatist drive that often accompanies such ideas. The sculptor Ivan Meštrović can be seen as a figurehead of a similar ethos. He was a Croatian and Yugoslav artist, possibly the greatest modern sculptor of religious themes. He did not limit himself to sculptures of saints and biblical themes, but created a great number of artworks based on Slavic folklore, symbolic figures such as the Monument to the Unknown Soldier in Belgrade or the Bowman and the Spearman, dedicated to the Indians, standing in Chicago, as well as statues of real persons such as Nicola Tesla in Zagreb, or the Slovak writer Martin Kukučín in Bratislava. His preferred material was marble, bronze and wood. He was also a painter, architect, writer and a scholar, teaching at several Yugoslav and American universities. Critics speak of the unique power of expression characteristic of his sculptures, uniting sensuality of the human body and a sublime soulfulness, often tinged by melancholic harmony (Stipančić and Elias-Bursać, 1990). All of his work is highly spiritual, as if the characters were caught in a poetic moment, tapping into a wider ethos of religion, culture, solidarity; entranced and bearing witness to a wider context that the place where they are positioned can be felt to emanate. Standing close to the statue of Grgur in Nin, the only location where there was almost nobody around, I was able to experience a strong connection to the land and people inhabiting it, reverence for the local culture, even without a deeper understanding of it, or, indeed, without feeling compelled to follow its currents. The clear blue sky above the horizon delineated by the faintly shimmering mountains, an intense, almost epiphanic sunshine, the air soft with the warmth and smells of the late Mediterranean afternoon, and a humming, warm silence surrounded me, communicating, together with Grgur, the power of difference and solidarity.

Think of red wine, blue sky, green hills and a slice of bread. A most fundamental experience, rooted in the land as well as in the heritage of art, history and religion. Tricollis wine invokes a pre-ethical ethos, free of norms, values and judgements, yet having the power to unite and to move, providing a pathway to powerful archetypes, through a most sensual experience of taste.

The August day was beautiful and the weather was radiant. I had taken the cheerfully rundown regional bus from the city of Győr to Pannonhálma, a village in Northern Hungary famous for its winemaking traditions. It turned out to be almost Arcadian in its oblivion of modernity: only local shops, no advertisements of international brands, quiet streets and unpretentious whitewashed houses revived childhood memories in an eruption of sounds and smells of carefree summertime. A longish march up the hill adjacent to the village, described in my guide as the Sacred Hill of Pannonia, led me to a slightly more touristic reception area, miraculously completely empty at the time of my visit, save for the lethargic cashier, who sold me entrance tickets and provided me with a map. A further climb along an asphalt road bordered by a lush green woodland led me to the old Benedictine monastery, surrounded by a leafy garden and a vineyard. On the slope there was a modest looking wine bar, where I sat down on a plain wooden bench and ordered a glass of red wine. It came with a glass of water, and a slice of plain bread. I sat reading, drinking wine and water, and eating bread, almost all alone but for an unhurried gardener working nearby, as the waitress had retreated right after having served me.

A collaborative product of wine-giving soil since ancient times, the labour of Benedictine monks from the local monastery and the inventive genius of a legendary winemaker, Tibor Gál, the red blend called Tricollis is the archetypical red wine. The taste is perfectly straight, a plain gulp of sunshine merging with an earthly sensation, invoking the generative power of the Earth. It all fuses on the palate, providing a feeling of pure connectedness with Nature, as well as with the human labour and traditions associated with wine production, in this place reaching as far back as the Roman times.

> At the time of building their church and monastery, the Benedictine monks having settled on the Sacred Hill of Pannonia in 996 also revived the ancient viticulture of the region.... Grapes and wine closely belonged to the everyday life of the monks for many hundreds of years.
>
> *(Abbey Winery Pannonhálma, 2013)*

The Second World War and the subsequent economic changes put a temporary stop to the work of the vinery, but some years ago a second major revival has taken place and an intensive planting and reconstruction programme was put into operation. Pannonhálma has been added to the UNESCO World Heritage List (UNESCO, 2013b), and, with the help and advice of Tibor Gál, once again put on the map of the world's viticulture. The intention of this legendary winemaker was to tap into the traditions of the region, make the best use of the natural conditions, which he judged to be comparable to those of the Upper Loire Valley or Alsace, and add the best of what new technologies have to offer (Abbey Winery Pannonhálma, 2013). To this he contributed with a taste composition: the poetics suffusing it all and making the taster part of it, too.

10.4 Reflections 2

Mihály Csíkszentmihályi (1990) speaks of the state of mind called flow, which I presented in more detail in Chapter 2, Section 2, pointing out that one of the necessary conditions to achieve it and, at the same time, one of its consequences is self-control of the worker. It is especially important in the work of professionals, highly educated groups with complex work tasks demanding judgement and dedication. This professional self-control is exerted through the ethos, or internalized collective ethics and good character (Eklöf, 1999). Swedish doctors regard formal education only as a part of the qualifications for the profession. They define themselves and their professional identity in terms of a long moral tradition, with roots reaching a long gone past, perhaps even antiquity and they strive for a legitimacy that transcends legal and technical matters. A part of their ethos is directed at the setting of boundaries, defining who is not part of the profession (ibid.). Sharyn Wise (2012) presents a study of how information professionals (librarians) construct a professional identity and ethos. In a situation where many tensions arise, deriving from growing managerialism and the primacy of enterprise in their work, they dedicate much effort to resist domination and sustain a space for professional self-control. They do this by practicing their collective truths, 'ensuring that their life practice (bios) and their principles (logos) are in harmony (ethos)' (ibid., p. 173). All these actions depend on the way they enact their professional and social roles through everyday work and interactions with others.

> [P]rofessional ethos, or ethics, is not a 'grand gesture', but a matter of integrity in the everyday practice through which reflective and critical practitioners craft their professional identity.
>
> *(Ibid., p. 183)*

Together with a co-author (Kostera and Postuła, 2011) I explore the mechanisms of resistance adopted by IT professionals in their struggle to maintain a professional autonomy. During an ethnographic study of different Polish IT professionals we observed how they created an aura of 'terrible impossibility' around themselves, using references to mathematics and coding, a highly obscure jargon, a dress style visibly different to corporate dress codes (which they often justified by invoking special and disagreeable characteristics of their jobs, such as the necessity of sometimes staying overnight and 'sleeping with the head on the keyboard'), etc. We call these practices the construction of a professional Aegis. Aegis was the awe inspiring shield of Athena, decorated with the head of Medusa that had the ability of turning whoever looked at her into stone. A similar effect of petrification is often achieved by the IT professionals we studied and it seemed to be an especially effective tactic against managers who seemed repulsed and alarmed by much of the symbolism used by the professionals, especially involving code and math.

> Aegis is an effective shield because it protects the user, hiding him or her from the gaze of the antagonist, but at the same time making the gazing very dangerous for the gazer. Similarly, the jargon the IT professionals used can terrorize audiences who might be tempted, for whatever reason, to look at them too closely. The Aegis can be an effective weapon against the managerialist Panopticon. The labels the IT people prefer wearing speak of knowledge that

is not necessarily easy to grasp, reminding non-technical audiences of the horrors that mathematics and technical subjects imposed at school. They may be dazzled by the reflections in their own minds, the memories of which might almost petrify them and stop them in their tracks.... By insisting on the use of professional categories, the IT professionals turn the societal gaze against itself, the effect of which is more space for autonomous definitions of their social roles which is what they are after. Aegis is powerful shield and an accurate weapon.

(Ibid., p. 90)

It is not just the IT and librarian professions in recent years that are undergoing attempts at colonization by a managerial ideology. This is the fate of a multitude of traditional professions (Jonnergård, 2008), including the academic (Elliott, 2011). A realignment of higher education institutions, to be concerned primarily with economic goals and eschew traditional values in favour of entrepreneurial and corporate ones, makes academics vulnerable as a professional group, devoid of the institutional support they once could take for granted.

To the extent that American universities have recast themselves on the model of what might be called a market-oriented bureaucracy, employment relations on campus will also shift to reflect norms appropriate to this type of organizational structure. Students thereby become consumers, professors line managers. Although faculty are nominally hired for their subject-matter expertise, there is also a clear, and clearly articulated, chain of command to be followed by all those who wish to 'rise in the company'. Where tenure protection has been eroded, employment mobility restricted, and the discipline deprived of consistent external funding, deference to institutional control becomes a prerequisite for professional success.

(Ibid., p. 166)

As a response to these pressures, some academics may try to use existing institutions, such as lawsuits in the US. However, the recent interpretation of academic freedom only from the point of view of institutional deference and the abandonment of academic ethos as an important frame of reference in American legal practices (ibid.) and a general disappointment in the support of official and democratic institutions towards academic communities (Collini, 2012) have recently prompted academics toward professional self-organization initiatives such as the British Council for the Defence of British Universities (CDBU, 2013).

Not only professions, but also a whole sector of the contemporary economy, the public sector, is undergoing similar tendencies of colonization by actors and control tools imported from the world of business. New Public Management has had an enormous impact on the public service ethos, reframing it from an orientation process towards a concern with outputs and subjecting it to the control of markets (Brereton and Temple, 1999). The traditional public service ethos contained such ideas as altruistic work towards a public good. The simultaneous erosion of public trust and the conquest of managerial and business values of most areas of contemporary society have contributed to a gradual wearing down of this ethos. Some of its defenders engage in uncritical nostalgia and many critics in unbridled triumphalism. A synthesis of values, stressing the quality of service and discipline of the marketplace, may be a practical solution to the problem (ibid.). Other authors are not so optimistic, pointing to how NPM is undermining not only the public sector ethos but occupational professionalism in general, subjecting the employees to external (market related) control (Bezes *et al.*, 2012) and having a number of well documented detrimental effects not only on public service ethos but on the value of the areas taken over as well, resulting in more, rather than less, bureaucratization, centralization and formalization (Diefenbach, 2009). It is not only government policies such as NPM that can pose a threat to professional ethos but other factors as well, including individual shortcomings and the cultural context. For example Suzanne Goopy (2005) shows how the local culture may undermine certain professional ideals of nursing, such as the imperative of always being available.

Even though ethos has been strongly undermined in recent decades by dominant economic and political forces in Western societies, its importance and value is not diminishing. Professional and occupational ethoses have been successfully used in production systems based on self-management, such as at the Volvo plant in Kalmar, Sweden, traditional kibbutzes or the former Yugoslavia in manufacturing and education. Self-managed work teams are democratic organizational structures, independent and based on the members' responsibility for the organization and the control of work (Sexton, 1994). The self-managed team continuously corrects deviations from the assumed norm and motivates itself. That is why, in order for self-management to function people must be morally mature and be guided by an ethos. The teams should have appropriate education and training, a common vision, shared values and beliefs and trust from the side of management as well as the clients. Heterarchy (see Chapter 4, Section 2), promoting cooperation of diversity, is a suitable kind of structure for self-managed teams to develop self-governance in contemporary organizations. Introduction of autonomy in the workplace has, apart from being a powerful natural control mechanism, the consequence of enabling accumulation of genuine knowledge (Hepsø, 2008).

However, professional ethos also has a dark side in the shape of elitism and insensitivity to the needs of outsiders, including the clients. Marie Haug and Marvin Sussman (1969) address such a problem in an old, but sadly not outdated, article. Professional autonomy includes determining work activity on the basis of professional judgement. This may occur without much consideration to the clients who may want to question the authority of such isolated professions. The authors mention such groups as students, people from poor and socially disadvantaged background, people who have been subjected to discrimination, such as racism. A sense of superiority due to the possession of a rare and specialized knowledge may make some professionals insensitive towards the special needs and situations of these, and other, groups of clients. All groups with a strong ethos may develop elitism: a tendency to value some social actors higher than others, not necessarily because of their performance but on the basis of conformance to the rules of group identity. Robert Jackall (2009) shows how corporate managers construct an elitist in-culture, limiting the scope of input based on other criteria, such as genuine moral consideration, talent or hard work, if it falls outside of their rule-in-use.

10.5 Stories from organizations

The collective of people who founded and now run Emma Hostel are passionate about their cooperative ethos. They are a group of friends who once were the driving force behind the anarcho-art squat Elba, famous throughout Poland for their poetry evenings and concerts, also hosting a number of other initiatives such as: freeshop, bike workshop, screenprinting workshop, climbing wall, skatepark, cafeteria and much, much, more (Elba, 2013). The squat is still active, even if the location has been changed: the original one was evicted after a sudden, and for many people unjustified, decision by local authorities. Finally, as a result of protests, many of which were supported by well known cultural personalities, the authorities declared that they were willing to find another location for the collective, which indeed recently happened. Some of the organizers, however, decided to go their own way in the meantime and so the cooperative Emma was born in 2011. After some discussion about what they wanted to do (they played with ideas; they considered a cultural centre, a club), they decided they would run a hostel. After obtaining the lease of a part of a beautiful old building in the centre of Warsaw, in bad need of renovation, they began their work. They refurbished the first floor and opened up to guests, presenting themselves as 'an ecological, cooperative initiative in Warsaw' (Emma, 2013).

As I enter the premises,[9] my first impression is of a welcoming old building, with high ceilings and a faint smell of old stone. The day is very warm and the cool shady breeze makes me feel like I am entering a museum. My next impression is of a kitchen where people are mingling in a kindly but somewhat reserved way; my interlocutor, Gosia, coming in from an adjacent room. It is chaotic and lively, the informality emphasized by the colourful decorations on the walls and the cheerful notices pasted on the wall, a bit too jolly for my taste, inviting the guests to various cultural events. There are books in the kitchen, which, I can see that now, doubles as common room, and a computer, currently in use by a bearded man in a corduroy jacket. None of the people, except my hostess, looks at me. We briefly consider the big shapeless sofa taking up much of the space in the kitchen but then Gosia leads me to one of the rooms for the interview. It is small and quiet, with old fashioned, carefully renovated furniture. I learn that all of their furniture has been either restored or made by members of the cooperative. The design of the rooms is their own, too, and each of them has a theme associated with the cooperative and human rights movement. After the interview I ask Gosia to show me around, which she does. The rooms are all clean, colourful and decorated with portraits of famous activists: Maria Orsetti, the Polish pre-war pedagogue and social campaigner, Jan Wolski, an anarcho-cooperative organizer of the post war Poland, Rosa Parks, the black American human rights fighter, and many others. There are no explanations or stories of these people or their ideas provided in situ, only a decor that can be associated with their times and dreams, but it is possible to read about them on the hostel's website (Emma, 2013). I am shown the upmost floor, recently restored. There is still a faint smell of wood and fresh paint. Sunshine is flooding in through the windows and we can hear the birds chirp in the trees outside. One side of the hostel faces the inner yard of the building which is surprisingly quiet and green, as quite often is the case in the older parts of Warsaw. (Until the 1950s or maybe as late as the 1960s the architects left huge spaces between the houses and trees were planted or just left standing. If you ever come to Warsaw, look beyond the facades, pass through lobbies of the entrance gates in older buildings – they are often not closed – and you will find yourself in an urban garden, so unlike the streets nearby that you may think you have been teleported away.)

The website emphasizes that the hostel is not just a place but also an idea. The idea: togetherness, is one they are happy to share with their guests.

> It is crucial for us that the place is available for everybody, also for those who are travelling with their pets. *Our hostel is a peaceful, family-like place.* In particular we invite activists from informal groups or collectives, workers and volunteers of non-governmental organizations (ask us for a discount). The elderly and people who organize festivals will find special offers tailor-made for them.
>
> *(Emma, 2013)*

Togetherness is such a dream for many of us, especially in a world that seems to run faster and faster towards utter egotism and alienation; we may like to imagine ourselves in a better time, a younger world where, like in Lukas Moodysson's (2000) film *Together*, life would be more complicated but so much more rewarding. The people of Emma realize this dream; it is their reality, their broad perspective on life: including bonds between humans, their organizations, and the ecosystem.

> *We are eco-friendly* and segregate rubbish. We are doing our best to make sure sanitary products and detergents are *biodegradable and not produced by large corporations.*
>
> *(Emma, 2013)*

Their ethos forms an important part of the management of the hostel; they decide everything together or on consensus based principles and there is no general manager or leader. According to Łukasz, they become their own bosses, have power over themselves and what they do; it may turn out better or worse, but they are a community. Gosia explains:

> We act as a collective with horizontal management, with group work, and that is really important to us.... This is all horizontal work, there is no

leader, it happens, you know, that in the process someone stands out more, someone is more energetic than another, but the system, the foundation is that everything is horizontal, no single person rules, everyone has the same voice and power, and this is all a consequence of our being non-hierarchical and self-managing.

(Gosia)

They have exactly the same salaries and all the profits are directed into the company, or put aside into a membership fund. The bottom line in monetary regards, as in all others, is provided by the cooperative ethos: respect and dignity for all the employees, democratic decision making, shared responsibility, togetherness and cooperation. Emma went through a number of crises, but as a result the collective became wiser, they worked out solutions to their problems. The 'job fair' is one of the latest, and they are quite happy with it. It means that if somebody comes up with an idea about what needs to be done he or she announces it on the cooperative's regular meeting and ask if anyone is interested in carrying it out. Then people volunteer: 'I'll do it for 500 złotych.' The lowest bidder gets the job but people with a predilection for vetoing proposals have no say; vetoes are not considered constructive. This has made work much more effective. But of course not everything can be solved this way, sometimes things, such as an inquisitive researcher, turn up and they have no system to deal with them. It takes time to react, maybe someone volunteers individually, maybe nothing at all happens for a long time.

Gosia points out that Emma is a social and cultural initiative: they engage in causes such as campaigns for peace, for the environment, against racism; they co-organize concerts and literary events. But it is also a business, trying to sell a product. They provide work and a source of income for themselves and a place to stay for their guests. They also offer courses about the theory and practice of cooperative organizing and they have more ideas for the future, involving the hosting of cultural events and publishing. Emma is quite young as I write this story, but rapidly started to bring in income; the founders succeeded in avoiding bank loans, instead, they collected the money for investments from the profits. Łukasz explains that it all takes time, it has to take time: everything that happens needs compassionate communication. Corporations do not do that, because it is a cost and what counts for them foremost is money. Emma is different, 'profit' for them is not only the money. They can use the tools and techniques of management such as market research, structures and so on, but the organizing principle is different.

The principle is based on the cooperative ethos, fundamental for all the members. It does not mean that they have to all have identical ethical beliefs. Indeed, they do not have a shared code of ethics. For example, Gosia is a feminist and Łukasz an environmentalist. They respect each other's ideals and standards but they do not have to care about them as much as for their own, and they do not have to live another's life. It happens that they do not agree; it happens that they complain about the endless time everything takes (I have overheard such a conversation during my visits more than once); it has happened that they fell into a collective drift – dejection is a state of mind that easily gets contagious. Group work does not necessarily mean that they are there for each other all the time. Everyday work means taking individual shifts at the hostel. Togetherness is intense and energetic; sometimes it feels good to be alone. Nothing of this, however, is an obstacle in their collective work; Emma is a living, bustling, resourceful place where something new happens every month. This is possible because of their strong ethos.

10.6 Questions to reflect on

1. Think of an organization with a strong ethos – what kind of ethos is it? Is it related to the place? To its history? To the profession of the people taking part in it? In what way do these aspects play a role in the shaping of ethos? Do you feel attracted by it?
2. Pay a visit to an architectonic landmark of the city or region where you live. Take in all the impressions of the place and the structure. What are the dominating colours? Shapes? What is the mood? Observe the decorations and details, what do they make you think of and feel? Now take in the surroundings. What are your feelings and ideas of the place, based only on this landmark? Take photos. Write an essay.
3. Is there an ethos that you feel particularly drawn to? Why, why not? Describe it, think of ways you could share it with others and promote it.

Notes

1 c.750–650 BC, Ancient Greece.
2 1864–1920, Prussia.
3 1910–2003, USA.
4 1896–1974, Poland.
5 1926–1984, France.
6 1930–2002, France.
7 'Un ensemble objectivement systématique de dispositions à dimension éthique, de principes pratiques' (Bourdieu, 1980, p. 133).
8 Par ethos professionnel, on entend un ensemble de dispositions acquises par expérience et relatives à ce qui vaut plus ou moins sur toute dimension (épistémique, esthétique, sociale, etc.) pertinente dans l'exercice d'un megier [I also provide the original French wording because some of the notions have more than one meaning in the English language and can be translated in several ways].
9 Material from my observations and interviews (2012).

11
ETHICS

Jugoslavija
The walls bearing marks
of when brother killed brother
Such stark loneliness

Ethics offers a reflection on moral actions and the notions of right and wrong, and systems of ethics proscribe courses of action that result in the increase of good and diminution of evil. There are several main bases of this fundamental distinction. One invokes deities and their rulings, such as, for example, the ancient Romans believed that Jupiter was the ultimate law maker and that his rulings regarding human beings and societies were being made known through myths and stories, but also by the way of signs and oracles. According to Jews and Christians, the laws of God were communicated to Moses on that fateful day on the mountain in the Sinai desert. People follow these commandments because they want to avoid punishment, failure, and because they want to be successful, repaid on the spiritual plane or saved from evil. They also do so because they trust that the divinities know what is good for them, and mean to protect them, like parents protect their small children.

Another ethical system refers primarily to nature and the principles embedded in the biological makeup of organisms, including the human race. The genes tell us what is good for us as a species and we are compelled to follow Nature's laws because of the way we are made, or because we believe that it will contribute to a greater good in the longer term, such as the survival of the species.

Ethics may, alternatively, invoke an idea, neither natural nor divine in itself, but important as such for human beings, or leading them into higher and better levels of existence, or organization. For example, humanism is based on the conviction that being human is a value in itself and that human beings should cooperate with each other and avoid harming each other; but also, that they should develop what is most uniquely human in them: knowledge, civility and enlightenment. People are treated as ends, never as means, and justice is a central idea for this type of ethical perspective. Following ethical norms is a matter of choice, the more informed and conscious the better.

Furthermore, there are ethical standpoints that focus on the values of a group and its cohesion, such as patriotism or collectivism. The participation and belonging to a group are considered the most important goal that all actions and ideas of the members should be subordinated to. For example, sports teams sometimes adhere to such an ethics, embracing consensus and cooperation and renouncing individualistic behaviours. They use rivalry as motivation for the members to perform better and to develop a loyalty to their own group and sense of collective pride. Participants that do not reflect the group norm are ostracized and finally rejected. Seen from the inside, such systems are absolutist and based on rules that appear objective to the members, who follow them because they value participation, or are afraid to be cast out, or because they believe that their own group is indeed better than others. Regarded from the outside, together with other, similar groups, the values appear relative and based on internal social standards. Persons, aware of this diversity and relativity, who consider joining a group and are willing to embrace its norms may do so out of respect for its cultural system, out of a conviction of a better fit between its and the individual's aims, or for pragmatic reasons.

Some systems of ethics put the consequences of the actions as their main core, whether they are useful to individuals and groups and bring them more happiness, wealth or wellbeing in general. If the consequences of actions are good, then the action itself must be valued positively. People follow ethical systems out of sheer self-interest, because they can be persuaded to, or they are able to see the greater good.

Finally, some ethical perspectives stress the importance of morality, an inherent human faculty, which precedes all ethical codes. People should be encouraged to develop such qualities that make them more morally sensitive, that will cause them to choose good rather than evil out of their spontaneous integrity.

11.1 A short history of ethics

According to the Biblical narrative, Moses[1] was summoned by God to Mount Sinai, where he stayed for 40 days. He received there directly from God the teachings that from then on formed the ethical foundation for the covenant of Yahweh and his chosen people. According to some accounts, Moses received the *torah* in the form of a scroll; in other stories the teaching was passed on orally and Moses committed it to writing later (Armstrong, 2007). Apart from the famous ten commandments, summarizing the main rules of conduct towards God and fellow humans, the *torah* contained a number of symbolic and historical stories as well as an ethical code of conduct, which each of the children of Israel should follow. It is not limited to one people or community, however, but today forms much of the ethical core of the so called Abrahamic religions: Judaism, Christianity and Islam (ibid.).

Socrates[2] regarded knowledge as the supreme virtue and self-knowledge was, to him, a fundamental moral obligation of human beings (Armstrong, 2007). This can be achieved through a systematic questioning of taken for granted truths, unearthing the ignorance that lies at the heart of all received knowledge. The commitment to such a perpetual awareness can be summarized in an aphorism attributed to Socrates: 'The life that is unexamined is not worth living' (ibid., p. 309). He also believed in a cultivation of the soul, not responding with violence or retaliation, even if a wrong has been committed. This was not presented as a dogma but as a path towards illuminating discovery of authentic knowledge within.

The philosopher Epicurus[3] regarded pleasure, if correctly understood, as a root of real virtue. It does not imply indulgence or hedonism, but a simple life leading to the achievement of a state of tranquillity, *ataraxia*, which together with the freedom from fear, constitutes real happiness. Epicurus also believed in justice, as a kind of social agreement, of which the basis is not harming others.

> The justice of nature is a pledge of reciprocal usefulness, [i.e.] neither to harm one another nor be harmed.
>
> *(Epicurus, 1994, p. 35)*

Immanuel Kant[4] famously formulated the categorical imperative, or principle, that is valid intrinsically and has to be obeyed by all people in all contexts (Timmermann, 2007). It is from the Categorical Imperative that all other moral obligations are derived and pursuing it is an end and means in itself, i.e. it does not serve any other need or purpose. It is a kind of moral compass, which would enable to decide whether an action is right or wrong. It commands action that is good and it is a duty that must be met. The best known part of the imperative can be summarized in the following way: 'Act in such a way that you treat humanity in your own person, as in the person of any other, never merely as a means' (ibid., p. 97).

Zygmunt Bauman[5] (1993) speaks of morality as responsibility to the Other rather than obedience to rules. Such a morality is grounded in the moral impulse, which precedes reason. Responsible action does not merely mean the following of rules, but often implies the breaking of rules.

> Saints are saints because they don't hide behind the Law's broad shoulders. They know, or they feel, or they act as if they felt, that no law how generous or humane, may exhaust the moral duty, trace the consequence of 'being for' to the radical end, to the ultimate choice of life and death.
>
> *(Ibid., p. 81)*

11.2 Reflection 1

The development of business ethics as an applied discipline in the 1970s occurred as a response to the ethical problems that were identified as plaguing business organizations (Arnold *et al.*, 2010). One of the major influences in several of the extant approaches such as ethical intuitionism, holding that each thoughtful person intuitively knows what is ethical, or approaches focusing on human rights, is Immanuel Kant (ibid.). For example, Kantian moral philosophy has been used to present the situation of workers employed in sweatshops (Arnold and Bowie, 2003). The authors use the Formula of Humanity to argue that MNC managers have duties not to accept that workers are paid wages under subsistence level, even if they are congruent with local market wages. In particular, managers should not tolerate instances of coercion, such as requiring employees to work overtime by sweatshops. MNE managers hold a responsibility for what practices with respect to human rights their subcontractors engage in. Treating human beings as ends in themselves requires that managers are 'concerned with the physical welfare of people and their moral well-being' (ibid., p. 223). Thus they should be offered a wage that allows them to satisfy basic needs. It is a moral duty of the managers of MNEs to ensure that the human rights of their business cooperators are respected. Kant also argued that rich people have moral obligations towards the poor and this is an obligation that also concerns MNEs. As rich communities with identities and responsibilities businesses can be regarded as moral agents. Businesses are to be seen as ends not means, because seeing them in the latter way would undermine the employees' personhood.

If not equipped with a Kantian ethical universal foundation, we may be called to react morally to what comes our way, led by an inner compass that is referred to as conscience. In Zygmunt Bauman's (1993) view, the foundation of all moral reasoning is derived from the relationship with the other. Whereas ethics is about rules, morality is about experience and choices made in difficult and complex conditions. This is not a stance widespread in today's organizational cultures, indeed, there seems to be a tendency to circumvent morality and conscience in business. Mihaela Kelemen and Tuomo Peltonen (2001) draw the attention to the link between the desire to get rid of moral anxiety, as embodied in ethical codes, and hierarchical bureaucratic structures, aimed at a rationalizing away of conscience and moral dilemmas. Indeed, 'bureaucracy helps people escape from moral evaluation, but in return they are requested to obey the rules' (ibid., p. 158). Business is additionally putting efficiency on a pedestal, as it is concerned about the management of resources. Structural procedures and the imperative of effectiveness are used as substitutes for but cannot replace moral choices, which are about the responsibility of the Other. And yet, as the authors remind, the encounter with the Other is where morality begins. Such an approach calls for strong ongoing dialogue between the individuals in their workplaces and points to the harm following from upholding a rigid identity of individuals and organizations, as this tends to falsely alleviate moral anxieties and dilemmas. Neither individuals nor organizations can, by a set of ethical rules, or by own choices, make good moral decisions. Instead, they need to come together and collectively and within a given context, paying attention to the tensions and discrepancies of perspectives and position, make a responsible choice, albeit without a guarantee for automatic 'rightness'. Only an embodied engagement in moral relationships can help people to be ethically attuned to the situation.

Kant and Bauman can be brought together as modes of moral praxis. Stewart Clegg, Martin Kornberger and Carl Rhodes (2007) consider business ethics as practice, as a means of going beyond being prescriptive or morally relative. They regard this practice from the point of view of the construction of ethical subjectivity in and of organizations. The position of the authors is close to ethical pluralism, where choices are made in complex circumstances and with bounded rationality. They place themselves close to Zygmunt Bauman's perspective on ethics, as a moral practice undertaken in a context of high uncertainty, and to the method of the categorical imperative of Immanuel Kant, adopted in order to make sure if an action is ethical. Most of today's ethical orientations of businesses tend to be constructed around ethical codes of some kind. Such rule based mentality is one way to approach the issue of morality but not the only one. The authors take the view that knowing the rules of action, being able to tell good from bad, is not what being moral is all about. Instead, 'ethics will be enacted in situations of ambiguity where dilemmas and problems will be dealt with without the comfort of consensus or certitude' (ibid., p. 109). Indeed, it involves both reflection and anxiety to make a moral choice and no shortcuts are really available in the form of simple rules and measures to apply to each moral dilemma. Ethics needs to take into account real complex organizational situations and lived experience. Certainty is impossible and an illusion that it can be achieved does not derive from ethics but rather from the hope of avoiding anxiety. The authors invoke Bauman's (1993) proclamation that anxiety is in fact the substance of morality. It is always the subject of contestation and there is not one final set of rules that can help us avoid this; but there is a method to help check on the process of ethical choice offered by the categorical imperative: would we turn this particular rule-in-use into a universal law? The interest of the authors, then, addresses the experiences of people making organizational decisions; what they actually do when they engage with ethics.

> In that way, an 'ethics as practice' approach directs attention not towards models that define, predict or judge ethics in and of themselves, but rather towards an examination of how ethics are differentially embedded in practices that operate in an active and contextualized manner.
>
> *(Clegg et al., 2007, p. 111)*

Structure is an important part of the context within which the ethical choice is being made, so in the case of organizations, that choice cannot be solely considered on the level of the individual. Moral subjects can realize different futures through their choices and in the case of organizations, the consequences almost always concern other people and subjects. Ethics is the 'social organization of morality' (ibid., p. 111), a process whereby some futures win over other possible ones, making morality rooted in cultural patterns of action.

> Ethics is a practice of choice and evaluation circumscribed by socially established ethical models that never fully guide moral conduct; the reasons are threefold. First, where a person's actions are fully determined by predefined external criteria then moral agency is denied to that person, even if that agency is only directed towards the choice of one model over another. Second, in practice people encounter a plurality of ethical models for conduct that are not necessarily consistent with each other, such that to follow one model might always be a means of disregarding another. Third, amidst the volatility of practice, novel situations can never entirely be predicted or captured by the model: some interpretation is always required in order to make decisions about moral conduct. Together this suggests that in practice there will always be (at least) a residue of moral agency.
>
> *(Ibid., p. 111)*

This perspective presupposes a strong link between action and narrative. Ethics is also the way people narrate their dilemmas and choices, what socially defined language they use for the account and how they make sense of these narratives.

Carl Rhodes, Alison Pullen and Stewart Clegg (2010) draw upon Paul Ricoeur's (1992) theories of narrative and ethics to present the power of dominant legitimizing and normalizing narratives of organizational change to limit the ethical dimension of what is happening. Ethics requires openness for questioning, deliberation and choice. Dominant legitimizing narratives have the potential to achieve closure and thus they prevent openness for ethical questioning. Telling stories makes the world comprehensible by making connections between experience and interpretation. This is often achieved by the use of strong plots (Czarniawska and Rhodes, 2006), or plots repeated so often that they seem obvious and fully acceptable. Furthermore, Rhodes *et al.* (2010) use Ricoeur's (1992) idea that narratives are strongly linked to ethics because they offer a means to evaluate and make ethical sense of human action. They focus attention on the actions that are to be evaluated, and may open up the space for deliberation and interpretation or, if strong plots and dominant narratives are being used, they may close it. The authors conclude that they agree with the critical literature upholding that ethics cannot be limited to rules and codes but to these they add the 'tacit rules embedded in narrative' (Rhodes *et al.*, 2010, p. 546), turning into prescriptions, 'namely the way that institutionally normalized and accepted narratives contain within them ethical models that provide social means for evaluating the relative goodness of particular actions and the delimitation of which areas are open to ethical scrutiny' (ibid., p. 547). That way, organizations are sheltered from moral responsibility by means of an ethical code.

11.3 Sounds, images, dreams

Jan Drda's (1978) comedy *The forgotten devil* in the genial adaptation by Tadeusz Lis (1985) is a story of an ethical village and a moral devil. The village, Longcoat, is a cause of serious concern for the rulers of Hell. Not one soul from the village has been sentenced to eternal damnation for decades and recently its old parish priest, a humane but far from saintly character, has been taken up to heaven. The infernal bosses both marvel and rage: how is it possible that a small unimportant hamlet is so consequently evading the tarnish of sin? They consider a number of reasons: nobody in the village is particularly rich or ambitious, people are friendly and enjoy work, they do not refrain from earthly pleasures but never with the intention to harm one another, and so on. They wonder whatever happened to the old devil Trepiphaixel who has been sent to Longcoat to tempt and frighten the villagers some centuries ago but no one seems to have knowledge of his current whereabouts. They consider sending someone up to check. A thoroughly modern devil, the learned Ichthuriel is listening to the discussion with a sense of superiority: Hell is managed in such an outdated, unscientific way, small wonder it is losing ground to the humans, who, at least, have succeeded in achieving some progress. What the situation demands, he explains to his superiors, is a sound use of the science of motivation. Frightening peasants is outdated and utterly ineffective, instead, people should be stimulated to sin. The bosses light up, not because they are impressed by his speech; the reason is more practical and direct: here is someone to be sent up to Longcoat, a tedious assignment nobody is eager to take upon himself. Ichthuriel is not happy but resigns himself to the task. He will prove the superiority of scientific methods of Hell-management and a fast promotion shall, of course, follow. He takes on the post as Longcoat's new parish priest and immediately begins to introduce changes. Old figures of patron saints are to be thrown out, together with other frivolities such as flowers and decorations; the parish housekeeper, the cheerful widow Pleisner, is to move out from the parish house and her place is taken by a glum verger, whose ambitions and budding envy are encouraged by the new vicar. Finally and significantly, bars are installed in the windows. When people wonder why it is necessary to spoil a lovely view of the garden, the priest answers with a sermon on the sanctity of private ownership. Meanwhile, Marianne Pleisner is looking for a place to stay and comes across an abandoned cottage, which she rapidly turns into a cosy abode. She does not know that Trepiphaixel, the abandoned devil, has taken up his residence there, unsuccessful in his hellish endeavours, and so just idling the centuries away. To cut a long story short, the situation runs completely out of control for Ichthuriel. Trepiphaixel, now calling himself Matt, falls for Marianne head over heels. Despite his sluggishness she has been good to him, offered him food and talked with him like with a fellow human being. He decides to give up his immortality for her, dons a human appearance and starts learning a trade. All the other machinations of the new vicar also miserably fail: the sound peasant ethics and cheerful disposition of the inhabitants of Longcoat make them quite unmanageable; except for the gloomy verger, who, driven by envy, becomes the priest's sole confidant. Matt reveals the vicar's true identity to the villagers and they send him back to Hell, where he is received quite without the fanfare he was expecting.

The author of the play, Jan Drda, was a Czech writer and journalist, member of the Communist Party of Czechoslovakia. In 1968 he joined the Prague Spring movement led by Alexander Dubček, hoping to create a socialist state independent from the Soviet domination in the region. When the uprising was brutally smothered by the invading Soviet army, Drda lost his job and, soon afterwards, died while working on a new book.

In *Things fall apart* (2010) Chinua Achebe tells the story of Okonkwo, a well respected inhabitant of Umuofia, a Nigerian village inhabited by the Igbo people. Beginning in the pre-colonial times, the tale shows a fierce and uncompromising man, who at times can be cruel, and who fears weakness most of all things, always holds on to his principles and defers to the customs of his people. He is working to gain a respectable place in the community and he is, indeed, held in great esteem despite his young age, which bodes well for his future prospects. The clan is patriarchal and democratic – hardworking and ethical men have a chance to become its leaders when they reach a certain age and standing. A number of circumstances, some accidental and some brought about by his own obstinacy and ferocity, make it necessary for him to move away from his village for seven years. Meanwhile, white men arrive, proclaiming a new religion. The first missionary, Mr Brown, is a goodhearted person, of a firm but profoundly charitable Christian faith, which he proclaims to the locals in a peaceful way. Many villagers are drawn to the new religion, which seems to them strange but alluring, and the elders do not see a reason why they should offer forceful resistance. Okonkwo observes what he regards as the fall of old mores with dismay and defiance, and, not willing to change, he regrets not being able, due to his exile, to wage war on the intruders. His own son coverts to Christianity, but that far from changes his mind about the new ideas; he disowns his son and refuses any dealings with him. When he finally returns home, things have already gone too far. The kind old missionary has been replaced by a new, militant one, and the white men have seized control of the administration and jurisdiction of the region. Nothing seems to have endured of the solidity and steadiness of the old tribal ways and, what in his eyes is even worse, his fellow villagers do not seem eager to forcefully resist the foreign imposition. Nonetheless, he persuades some men to attempt an act of defiance. The white men respond harshly: they not only hold the power of armed force, but they use intimidation and humiliation as a way of dealing with the native people. Okonkwo refuses to be humiliated, he acts on his beliefs one last time to save his honour, but at the same time he violates the principles of his tribe that he believes in so much, and to the defence of which he had dedicated his life.

Chinua Achebe was the most internationally recognized African writer, for all his life working to create an awareness of and respect for African culture in the world. He believed in encounters of cultures based on mutual respect and in continuous cultural change, rooted in tradition, kindness and a regard for human dignity.

11.4 Reflection 2

Several authors take up civility and kindness as moral attitudes at work, which can be regarded as ways of ensuring ritual (self-)control. Tae Wan Kim and Alan Strudler (2012) argue that a Confucian approach focused on civility can be more useful in many organizational settings than a Kantian one. To respect a person means to value him or her as sacred, and by practicing rituals of kindness and civility, as Confucius prescribed, this sacredness is honoured and celebrated. Managers are obliged to preserve and cultivate such rituals in the workplace. According to Confucius not only direct incivility is disrespectful to the other, but a lack of civility, a failure to acknowledge the person. This approach is only in part similar to Kant's categorical imperative – it goes beyond it. To Kant a simple lack of civility may insult a person but it does not limit his or her autonomy. According to the categorical imperative a person must refrain from coercion and treat the other as an end, not as a means. To Confucius, civility is just as important as the categorical imperative is to Kant. It is an ethical system regarding civility as a way of expressing and achieving mutual respect. Through performing the right actions people make greater virtues happen: 'through participation in ritual people become sacred and worthy of respect' (ibid., p. 562). There his approach differs from Kant's: to Kant the intention is crucial and primal, to Confucius the intention may emerge from performed ritual. It is so because the characteristics of a person such as his or her autonomy are not sufficient reasons to experience respect. Civility creates a bond enabling respect.

> Ritual is a collaborative endeavor; each person involved in a ritual plays a role that accommodates others who are involved, and depends on their participation. Collaboration of such complexity requires communication,

acknowledgement from all participants about the nature and value of the roles of others.

(Ibid., p. 567)

Sue Clegg and Stephen Rowland (2010) praise kindness in pedagogical and academic life. They hold that not only is it a virtue helping to transform the organization into an ethically sound setting, but it also contributes to the abandonment of the rationalistic dichotomy between reason and emotion prevailing in so many workplaces of today. Kindness transcends and evades performance and business oriented approaches. It also subverts the commonly used economic metaphors, as kindness in itself is useless and lacks any economic value, but, nonetheless, is as much of a persistent domestic as public virtue in practice, even if it is not acknowledged in dominating discourses. Kindness is paradoxical: it involves not just intention, feeling, but it needs acts in order to be realized.

Ethics is a way of enacting freedom and moral choice. Richard Weiskopf and Hugh Wilmott (2013) conceive of ethics as a 'critical practice of questioning and problematizing moral orders and the moral rules-in-use in organizational contexts' (ibid., p. 3). They are concerned with ethical moments which occur when the normative structure of reality and the subject's position are questioned, which define the ethical dimension of social relationships. Ethics upsets power structures by questioning the established moral order, 'shared understandings' and actions. It does not necessarily mean evaluating and judging organizations and their participants or a development of criteria for such judgements.

> Instead of associating ethics with compliant enactment of a particular, privileged morality, the challenge is to engage in critical work within such mundane settings. When conceived as critical practice, ethics is an ongoing *agonistic* struggle played out in relation to established moralities embedded within relations of power and domination.
>
> *(Ibid., p. 19)*

Organizations can replace traditional means of control with existing ethical heterotopias (Cairns *et al.*, 2003), or 'unrecognized feature of organizational space, and are a response to the imperfect nature of organizational control' (ibid., p. 135). Such heterotopias are repositories of knowledge and power, providing space and moral codes for people who engage with them. They emerge as spontaneous ephemeral cultural creations, such as, for example, autonomous workgroups or project teams. Not unlike in the classic experiment of Elton Mayo (Wright, 1994), management can cooperate with them, using them as centres of self-control.

> Heterotopian workplaces are both enabling and controlling, open yet closed off, fixed and transient, and contracting yet expanding to become all-encompassing.
>
> *(Cairns et al., 2003, p. 135)*

Heterotopias are paradoxical, and embrace at the same time freedom and control, ritual inclusiveness and wariness, expansion and closure. Many contemporary workplaces include heterotopias or some of their characteristics at certain levels. New technologies and flexible working make it possible for local heterotopias to emerge whenever they are needed by the concerned participants, thus breaking out of the stability of time and space, typical of the traditional workplace. Such heterotopias do not limit the ephemeral and transient processes of acquisition and sharing of knowledge. However, contemporary management often fails to recognize the usefulness of heterotopias, as it strives to control the organization top-down in the traditional corporate mode. Instead, it often sets out to eradicate all spaces where it is not in control, fearing free space as a source of moral subversion more than anything else.

To reclaim space means, for the organizational participants, to regain ethical agency. Ronald Purser and Steven Cabana (1998) speak of the self-managing organization as one based on a new paradigm. Instead of bureaucratic impersonal rules and hierarchical structure, it is founded on democratic norms, which increase variety increasing behaviour or a transience of roles. It is the task and the ethical standards of the group that define who enacts what role, and not a stable set of regulations. On one occasion a person may act as leader and on another, as follower. Such a shift requires a new metaphor of work coordination, where norms are not external but internal and fluid, relational. Here the jazz metaphor is ideal: jazz is a collective art and jazz groups have a high degree of task independence. When something unforeseen occurs, jazz groups and self-managed teams need to improvise.

But ethics also has a dark side: as a means of control it breeds dogmatism or the over-reliance on rules rather than conscience, the tendency to adhere to closed systems of ideas and beliefs (Rokeach, 1954). Przemysław Piątkowski (2007) tells the story of a religious organization that acts on the basis of very strict ethical rules, intervening the private and professional life of the participants. The organization offers a complete set of norms, values and beliefs, making moral choices for them and freeing them from ethical dilemmas. The norms are present in all the spheres of the social life of the organization's participants, organizational as well as private. They divide the world in two: us and them. Following Michael Pratt (2000), Piątkowski adopts the metaphor of the fortress in reference to the organization. The fortress is an organization harnessing the energy of people's lives, by means of ethical norms, to realize the goals of management. The employees' private lives are not separate from their organizational lives and the moral rules adopted by management are transferred to the participants. Organizations-fortresses strive to define all the roles played by the participants and to bridge and streamline all value systems that people encounter in their lives. All incoherencies are explained by references to the organization's ethical code, thus fully encompassing the person, offering a complete set of norms, values and beliefs for every occasion, eliminating the necessity of making decisions and, in a way, letting the organization act as their conscience.

Another limitation of ethics in the practice of organizational self-control is the prevailing ethical reactiveness rather than ethical assertiveness of managers: instead of following their own moral standards, they often base their decisions on organizational codes and priorities (Jackall, 2009; Watson, 2003). Robert Jackall (2009) has shown how managers become morally muted, bracketing their own conscience and standards at work and instead follow what they see as the prevailing corporate morality. Tony Watson (2003) emphasizes that even though this may be a common contemporary trend, there still is a choice and it is, strategically, up to the managers to make the moral choices and to set the ethical tone for the whole organization. Some managers consciously and actively seek ethical awareness and go beyond the tendency to follow corporate morality.

11.5 Stories from organizations

Vegetarian cooking is our passion, Robert explained[6] in an answer to my question why he and Beata, his wife, had created VegeMiasto, one of the most popular vegetarian restaurants in Warsaw, with what a customer I talked to called 'amazing food and decent prices'. He and Beata had always liked doing it, since they were teenagers, and soon it turned out that cooking and experimenting for themselves was not enough, so they also cooked for friends, were asked to cook at weddings and parties. They did that for free, just because they loved it, and they loved hearing from people how much they enjoyed eating the food that had been prepared for them – they still do, hearing how people loved their food really inspires them. In the mid-1990s, Beata was asked by a vegetarian restaurant if she would come and work for them, she said, sure. She stayed with them for a long time and became their main chef. But that was not enough for her: the restaurant had a rather limited formula and she and her husband had lots of ideas, too many to deal with in their free time. They explored catering, cooking and actually selling the food on order. The response of customers, old and new, was almost overwhelming. Finally, Beata decided to quit her job and they founded their own firm. They continue to have very good relations with her old employer; she is composing their menu, and they sometimes lend them their premises if they have something bigger to prepare: VegeMiasto has a huge space for customers, a lovely old, multi-storey building in the very centre of Warsaw, but the kitchen is not very big. My interviewee-customer said, about this building, that it was quite amazing too; he never associated vegetarian places with something that big and so much fun. They share the building with a club which takes over in the evenings. That is why the place is so full of colours and alternative art. But they would have preferred to work on their own, to have opening times that they themselves would be able to adjust to what their customers wanted. And the clubbers are not very careful with things, the employees of VegeMiasto have to put away all of their food, plates, glasses and lock the counters every day, before they leave. The building itself is, however, a dream. It stands in a silent green yard between low, neoclassical houses of the perhaps most iconic district of Warsaw – the area around Nowy Świat,[7] built as a parade street for the king in the seventeenth century, the name meaning 'new world', a symbol of modernity, optimism and the growing city's go-ahead spirit. I visited the restaurant when they organized their now monthly giant lunch buffet for the second time and was struck by the way everything seemed to be composed, the tables, presenting a cornucopia of colourful food, around which the people, chairs and walls, seem to flow in a dynamic rhythm that made me think of a painting by Vasily Kandinsky, *The Swan* (1912), a kind of a fractal that unfolds in several dimensions and sensual spaces, carrying smells, sounds, moving images. Both the painting and the buffet itself appear to be a condensed centre, an eye of a storm of sensations, into which it is impossible not to become drawn. The walls of the building, the staircases and all of the people mingling, audibly admiring the food, picking up some on their plates, look as if they were a necessary extension of the decorated tables, part of a moving sculpture. I was also struck by the almost emphatic cooperation of the customers. They are not like any buffet lunch crowd; during my observation, lasting about two hours, when a constant crowd of people mills by, almost nobody acts out of rhythm, only some of the children try to squeeze in, to jump the queue, which it is all but an orderly line, reminding me of Kandinsky's swirling flights, of a pulsating dance rather than of a file. The room bustles and spins; I notice many people smiling: at each other, at the food, or just under their noses. Kindness is in the flow, it seems so obvious, as if one of the streams, an organizing principle of the dance. It is perhaps not surprising to learn that the owners do not regard their restaurant as a business. Many restaurant owners nowadays think that vegetarian cuisine is fashionable, something cool that people want, and try to make money out of it; they may have a business plan, a marketing by far superior to VegeMiasto's quite straightforward promotion based on social media and friend-to-friend recommendations; but they have no real mission. Beata and Robert do not think much of such an approach, it strikes them as a waste of time, something they would not want to do at all.

> If we were [determined] to make money on this place, after one year, we would not be here any longer.
>
> *(Beata)*

Instead, they see it as a kind of materialized proposition, living proof of what they believe in. Good vegetarian food is, to them, a way of life, something that extends beyond nutrition and certainly beyond business. It is a way of realizing their ethics. Preaching it would not be a good way of reaching others, some do not want to listen, others like arguing and that is not really what the entrepreneurs want. Beata recalled how happy she was when she organized a party for her family, when family members without any earlier connections to vegetarianism approached her afterwards to tell her how amazing and life-changing it had been, how they now appreciate how it is to be a vegetarian, some wanted to become one, others reported a joy and also an instant understanding. Cooking is Beata's and Robert's way of sharing both; belief and passion are for them one and the same thing. They recall how they cooked for their own wedding party, because they wanted this kind of food for the occasion, and no other, and because that was their way of experiencing it. There was also some more ordinary food at the dinner, provided by a mainstream catering service, but, to the newlyweds' joy, everyone wanted to eat the food they had prepared, vegetarians and non-vegetarians alike. In the end, they almost did not eat it themselves.

> For us, everything we do, is connected with the idea, it is good to show it to people, it is good to share it. It is something that can change their lives in a positive way.
>
> *(Robert)*

Much of the food available in supermarkets is not healthy, it contains substances that can cause serious problems, immediately or cumulatively. And quite often, it is produced in a way that lacks empathy, is out of synch with the natural environment. Beata and Robert have a message for others which they express not in words but in what they cook: there is an alternative way of eating, based on genuinely natural foodstuffs, made to minimize the suffering of animals and people, one that can make the consumer feel good. As well as the cook. They told me how they enjoyed every minute of it, how Beata could wake up in the middle of the night, because of a dream she had about a new cake, a beetroot and chocolate cake, and she would rapidly note down the recipe. (I have tasted this cake, it was lovely, not too sweet; smooth and lavish, but with a rather surprising edge; a fitting synecdoche of all their food.)

But VegeMiasto is a business, too, and a successful one. It makes its ends meet, even if all surplus means are directed into new ideas: the entrepreneurs have started a lunch catering service, the lunch buffet is a regular monthly event, and will perhaps be organized even more often, all the time new things appear on the menu, some destined to be popular, such as spinach pancakes with various delicious stuffings, some rather experimental and non-obvious, such as beetroot rice. The firm is a way of making a living for the owners and it offers a decent wage to the employees. They do not want to grow, conquer markets, and they have no need of formalized procedures, structures or codes of ethics. All of their employees work there because they believe in what they are doing. All, except one, are vegetarians. All like food and believe it should be healthy and tasty.

> There is an energy ... they all care very much for the people here being able to eat good food, they want them to like it here, to see that this is great.... Not like this: coming to work, sitting there for eight hours, and okay, now home. They really live through thus place, sometimes even we are amazed, for example, it's after work and they meet here, talk, they come in on their free time to fix something, or look after something, they really care about this place. This makes us happy ... that they somehow have a need to do what they are doing.
>
> *(Beata)*

Yeah, because ... we cannot be here all the time. So they have to do things themselves. It's *their* workplace.

(Robert)

Roman Batko (2013) argues that ethics is a primarily a venture located within the realm of the spirit; it may, through structure and rules, influence people's behaviour, but its power springs from the Anima, the soul. If it does not, it fails to make a difference.

11.6 Questions to reflect on

1. Make a list of what you consider to be the seven main sins of organizations, and another of the seven main organizational virtues. Think of fitting examples of each, from your own experience or from literature.
2. Which are your most important ethical values? Which values are characteristic of your workplace, or, if you are a student, university? Are these two systems compatible? What kind of relationship is there between them – one based on synergy, conflict, peaceful coexistence, or something else? Does that make you feel stronger or the opposite?
3. Describe an organization you admire for its ethical stance. Get as much information as you can, use internet and other media resources, visit them, try to get an interview with a participant. How do they make a difference in the economy and in society?

Notes

1 *c.*1391–1271 BC, Ancient Egypt and Moab.
2 469 BC–399 BC, Ancient Greece.
3 341 BC–270 BC, Athens, Ancient Greece.
4 1724–1804, Prussia.
5 1925–, Poland and the UK.
6 Story based on interviews with VegeMiasto's owners, 2013, the restaurant's website, and my field observations 2012 and 2013.
7 The restaurant has since moved to an independent location, also in the centre of Warsaw, but in its modern part, in Aleja Solidarnosci.

12
ECOLOGY

This world was created
by Kronos, vomiting
stones and gods into being,
rivers, fields, and clouds,
the rainbow,
finally,
himself.
Inside out.
The insides of Kronos
became the blue womb.
The blue skies
around us

Ecology is a new term and new science, but as a philosophy it has a long history, reaching Antiquity, when it was observed that nature is amazingly complex and able to cooperate in intelligent ways.

The first level of ecology is an acknowledgement of this clever complexity. Organisms work together to help each other to survive, as much as they compete and use each other as nourishment. Environments respond to the climatic and geographical conditions as a whole, and each population of organisms has a role to play within that whole.

The second level is an awareness of the synergy and unity of ecological environments. They are more than climatic and geographical niches – they are systems, where the individual parts work together and the links between them produce something more than the sum of the parts. An ecosystem can be seen as a giant living organism, and the whole planet can indeed be viewed that way.

The third level is an ecological consciousness, a respect for and sensitivity to the needs and demands of that huge living system which provides the conditions of life, perhaps as the only planet in the known Universe, certainly as one of the very few. The Earth has been developing for millions of years to reach the level of diversity it has today and the human race has been part of it during a relatively short period of time. Even though there is a place for us on this planet, we cannot act as if we were the masters, because we are neither the only species, nor the most important; and we are not in control. Through an irresponsible and careless approach to the environment the human race has already destroyed and diminished the ecological diversity and wealth of life-forms. There are many signs that we are on the way to even more irreparable and catastrophic destruction, because of our greed, recklessness and limited perspective. Ecology of the third level, a planetary consciousness, is an approach to the world aimed at changing that perspective and preventing the imminent global catastrophe of our own doing. To be able to save our planet, and our own future as a species, much more is needed than a science helping us to understand how organisms work together – an awareness offered by ecology of the first two levels. Ecology of the third level, implying a change of attitude towards not only technology and waste, but life, its meaning and the aims worth pursuing, is, many believe, a necessary condition to making it possible for life on Earth to go on. Life has a capacity for self-organization, where whole systems emerge and work in ways that are not reducible to their parts. In that sense the global ecosystem also has a power of self-healing and survival. It is possible for humans to cooperate with these forces, rather than act without a consideration for the environment.

On the third level ecology, a state of mind and an approach to life, science and work, is compatible with environmentalism, a social movement for a respectful approach to the environment, including principles of sustainability – the ability to survive in the longer term. The elimination of harmful human impact is one of the central issues for this movement, by the reconciliation of demands of economy, equity and environmental requirements.

Ecology is interdisciplinary, as a science and as a life philosophy, it demands a holistic view and an ability to communicate across scientific and cultural boundaries.

An ability to understand processes and to be able to focus on dynamics rather than on static entities is another important precondition. No ecological understanding is possible without these two central capabilities.

12.1 A short history of ecology

According to Hesiod's[1] *Theogony* (1914a), Gaia, the mother Earth, together with Chaos, the primeval emptiness and Eros, the embodiment of the attraction between beings were the *Prôtogenoi*, the first beings in the history. They gave birth to all other creatures, including giants, gods and humans. Gaia is portrayed as powerful and motherly. She loves all her children equally, regardless of their virtues or vices: sublime gods as well as terrible monsters. She shows little mercy if her sense of balance is disturbed. Sometimes her love manifests itself as cruelty.

Herodotus[2] famously described the marvels of nature he encountered during his travels in his *Histories* (2008). His interest in not just the curiosities but also how the elements worked together mark him out as one of the early pioneers of ecology (Silver *et al.*, 2001). Among others, his is one of the earliest depictions of mutualism in nature: how Nile crocodiles happily endured sandpipers pulling leeches out of their teeth. Thus the birds got food and the crocodiles hygiene.

> The crocodile enjoys this, and never, in consequence, hurts the bird.
>
> *(Herodotus, 2008, p. 123)*

Carl von Linné, known internationally as Linnaeus,[3] established the first universally embraced convention for the classification and naming of species of organisms, the Linnaean taxonomy, which is still widely used in biology. The system was based on a hierarchy, consisting of several levels, based on shared physical characteristics. Linnaeus' work sprang from his sense of awe before nature, his belief that all the species and creatures were part of a larger whole where even the smallest flower played an important and unique role. His sensitivity and respect for nature make him a precursor of modern ecology (Broberg, 2006).

Gregory Bateson[4] (1972) proposed a broad view on ecology that included human beings, their civilizations and cultures. According to him, ecology is a unity described by patterns of information which form the foundation for biological and human realms. We live in a world of flows and relationships that can only be understood in their context. If human activity degenerates and turns destructive, the whole informational pattern, the ecology of the mind, has to be understood in order to prevent an eco-crisis.

James Lovelock's[5] famous Gaia hypothesis (2000) moves beyond a materialistic approach that predominated in the previous century. The Earth is a complex living system that consists of several spheres, actively searching for optimal living conditions, and striving for balance through homeostasis. It is the context for all life, controlling vital parameters such as the temperature of the surface, the structure of the atmosphere and the salinity of the oceans. The mechanisms of self-regulation have currently been disrupted as a result of destructive human activities (Lovelock, 2007). Only humans can undo this damage through environmentally sound policies and the application of eco-friendly technologies.

12.2 Reflection 1

Environmentalism has a history from at least the Enlightenment and has had some vital moments during recent history, such as the late 1960s, but it was the 1990s that became known as the decade of the environment. Among the pioneers of organizational environmentalism were Paul Shrivastava and Stuart Hart (1992) who saw the rise of

> a broad and ever expanding set of concerns dealing with environmental pollution, public protection from technological and health hazards, worker and consumer safety, and, most recently, ecological sustainability.
>
> *(Ibid., p. 185)*

They advocate for a broad, systemic approach to ecological issues among managers and saw the necessity to overcome organizational resistance to such a change of fundamental mindset. The change is necessary, they argue, but organizational practice and theory seems to be ill prepared to take it on. Elisabeth Ryland (2000) also notices a lack of understanding and talks of a gap between the awareness: individual and organizational, and ecology. This gap, she proposes, can be bridged with the help of the Gaia archetype. It makes us aware of the danger to the natural environment and to the life on Earth that we humans pose through our industrial organizations. Alas, it seems infinitely more difficult to remedy the destruction than it is to allow it to continue. This poses a challenge that demands a change of a systemic magnitude: ecologically aware individuals have now an almost negligible amount of power as compared to the global corporations that are responsible for most of the pollution and destruction of the environment. Quite understandably, people are worried about survival, the future of humanity and the whole planet. Humans experience nowadays a collective sense of guilt. Contemporary culture is at the same time suffused with this sense of guilt and actively pursuing denial of the extent of the destruction. It gives rise to seemingly bizarre collective fits of depression, frustration and panic. We have to wake up to the realization that our planet is a living system that needs our help in the restoration of balance that will enable it to heal herself and provide conditions for the continuation of all life, including our own species. When we make the effort Gaia will help us with providing us the balance we humans so desperately need, and currently lack. It is a profound and reciprocal relationship. Ryland argues that sustainable growth organizations can be a link in the forging of such relationships. They can form the foundations for a new system, based on the principles of ecological balance. Being located between the individual and the environment, they may acquire the power needed for change. An ecologically oriented organization can more effectively cooperate with the ecosystem in search for symbiosis than individuals can. We can thus actively invoke the power of Gaia to lead us towards an eco-revolution that will be a powerful move toward the restoring of a broader perspective to management. Sustainable management means respect and attention to the wellbeing of the whole planet. For such organizations, the ecosystem itself in a sense provides, symbiotically support-ing their survival.

> Leading proponents of the environmental value system advocate a new and sustainable industrial revolution. The sustainable approach is intended to counteract the widespread poverty, social crises, global instability, and general habitat destruction resulting from the untenable assumption of current economic principles.
>
> The goal for sustainable business activity is one of stable global biosystems rather than unlimited material prosperity of the few.
>
> *(Ibid., p. 397)*

One of the most interesting and practical ways of making sustainable management happen is ecopreneurship. It is an entrepreneurial activity that combines ecological and business purposes and where the entrepreneur's value system is oriented towards ecology (Bennett, 1991). Michael Schaper (2005) portrays the green entrepreneur as someone viewing the ecosystem as a window of opportunity, making possible an innovative action that is symbiotically beneficial to both the organization and its environment.

> The adoption of environmentally-responsible business practices can conceivably open up an additional range of opportunities for entrepreneurs. The move to a sustainable business framework provides numerous niches which enterprising individuals and firms can successfully identify and service. These include the development of new products and services; improving the efficiency of existing firms; new methods of marketing; reconfiguring existing business models and practices; and so forth.
>
> *(Ibid., p. 6)*

Ecopreneurship is not just another form of entrepreneurship, a space for creative people and organizations, but it represents a new business model, where the organ-ization is not seen as separate from its environment and the focus of the activity is on the larger whole (ibid., 2005). Eco-organizations make active use of manage-ment ideas but its aims are not associated only with its individual wellbeing and growth. In fact, growth may be forsaken, if it does not benefit the particular eco-system that the organization exists in. There are many possible forms that such an organization can take, from unselfish social entrepreneurial organizations to firms that in the first place offer a livelihood for the entrepreneur and the employees. A combination of these aims is usually the reason for setting up a business in the first place. The dream of working for a green and ethical employer and perhaps even further ecological causes is, for some people, a compelling force to become involved in business (Dixon and Clifford, 2007). Some mainstream observers may regard their activities as chaotic and a balancing between not incoherent aims. But the ecopreneurs themselves see this as an extra source of energy to develop their ideas. Ecopreneurs are both idealists and businesspeople at the same time, and they are often true visionaries. Sustainable business starts in new innovative eco-companies. Astad Pastakia (1998) believes ecopreneurs to be change agents for the entire society. They do not trust their businesses to market forces but instead they strive to actively shape the environment to be more sensitive towards *ecosystemic* forces. Some strive at a reduction of negative effects on the environment but the most visionary ones go further.

> Eco-friendliness in the absolute sense would refer to a product or process that is not only benign towards ecosystems but which actually generates positive externalities for the environment.
>
> *(Ibid., p. 158)*

All ecopreneurs blur the boundaries between the social and the business dimensions of their organizations. They do not see these spheres as separate and they act as if they were indivisible. Alistair Anderson (1998) argues that through actions of such kind, ecopreneurs give actual substance to environmentalism, they create and fix real change in society. They do so by the shifting, sometimes ever so subtle, of the meanings of terms such as value and growth, which they use as including environmentalist ideas. Value creation is for them a much broader notion than when it is seen from a mainstream economic perspective. Indeed, such a concept of what value is has been systematically increasing since the early 1990s. This trend is to a large degree due to the activity of ecopreneurs who take it for granted. Being embedded in the social context, they develop links and actively use relationships to spread their ideas through enculturation. Ecological issues have become an important part of the moral dimension and as such they suffuse the cultural context of organizing.

> The emergence of environmental concern can be understood as social change; one which we can comprehend in terms of value changes.
>
> *(Ibid., p. 142)*

Not all environmentally oriented organizations are ecopreneurial and not all have equal impact on the shaping of the future context of organizing. Stefan Schaltegger (2002) proposes a framework for ecopreneurship as the ultimate and most radical form of environmental management. The other four, ranked with respect to the degree of environmental orientation and the market are: environmental administrators, environmental managers, alternative activists and bioneers. Environmental administrators only concentrate on following regulations and try to adhere to the rules that regulate environmental issues. Environmental managers consider ecological problems an auxiliary sphere of their businesses and show interest in them mainly to achieve other ends such as cost reduction and eco-efficiency. Alternative activists are strongly concerned about ecological issues but keep mainly to their own company, their activity being limited to a niche of the alternative scene. Bioneers are small and medium-sized organizations operating in an eco-niche, focused on creating innovation that would further ecological causes and attract eco-conscious consumers. Ecopreneurs aim at large and expanding markets and have an ambition of making a significant contribution to their development as well as making a difference in respect to eco-conscious business solutions.

> The entrepreneurial challenge is thus to be economically successful with the supply of products and services that change – on a purely voluntary basis – consumption patterns and market structures, leading to an absolute reduction of environmental impact.
>
> *(Ibid., p. 51)*

Ecopreneurs do not have to be innovators in the traditional sense, i.e. they do not always invent new products or ideas. However, they introduce whole new ways of making business and aim at institutionalizing environmental concerns as part and parcel of market structures (ibid.). The ideal type of an ecopreneur is depicted by Robert Isaak (2002) as one who creates 'green-green' business with an explicit aim of transforming the context they operate in.

> [A] 'green-green business' is one that is designed to be green in its processes and products from scratch, as a start-up, and, furthermore, is intended to transform socially the industrial sector in which it is located towards a model of sustainable development.
>
> *(Ibid., p. 82)*

Ecopreneurs often set up their businesses to feel in control of their lives and to be able to engage in something they believe in. Quite often, however, they also explicitly wish to make a contribution beyond their own private sphere and help to change the world. They are value-driven and they create their own values. The 'green theme' is deeply entwined with everything they do, including marketing, networking and motivation strategies. The author expresses his hope that green-green businesses will be one day brought 'to a critical mass and thereby assure global sustainable development' (ibid., p. 90).

12.3 Sounds, images, dreams

John Slavin's paintings (John Slavin, 2013) present Nature as she is when there is no one watching. The artist is an expressionist painter, inspired by Van Gogh, portraying landscapes from the Island of Skye, the Pyrenees Orientales and Languedoc. He believes that it is possible to express the spirit of nature in painting, by discovering the poetics of a place. He explains his work on his website:

For three decades I have been making pen drawings from nature; river waters and rocks, trees of all sorts and mountainscapes which include the cloud of dawn, dusk and moonrise. I have made upwards of fifty canvases in thick expressionistic oil paint from my detailed pen studies.

(John Slavin, 2013)

When I met him last winter, John told me his story of finding the right landscape to paint. He is intuitively drawn towards a type of scenery and stays in it for some time to paint it. As it happened, the journey is leading him to the south, perhaps because of the light and shadow. In his view, light and shadow belong together, they are intertwined and cannot be separated. To see it and to paint it is for him more than enough, he does not long for any cultural references or echoes of human civilization. Shadows and light can best be enjoyed in nature, and recently it is the deeper tones and sharper contrasts he is interested in, rather than the greys of North Scotland, which fascinated him a few years ago. His paintings of the Isle of Skye depict cliffs and mountains, the colours are foggy, dark, the greyscale dominating over some accents of green and blue, the lines firm but rounded. *Moving Mists* shows the primordial power of the Earth, where the mountain protruding from the sea is still in movement, among the water and the black forest in the foreground, it is the moment of the birth of a mountain. We see the moment from the point of view of the Earth: millions of years, measured by the clock of the movement of tectonic plates, a rhythm beyond human imagination. *Loch na Beiste* shows the rivalry of three elements: rock, air and water, locked in a battle for dominance, entangled in a brotherly but lethal embrace. They are, perhaps, fighting for Gaia's attention, at heart not all that much concerned about power for and by itself, but they know that the mightiest of them will win her interest. The *North Atlantic Island Skies* shows a scene where the mountains and the water are seemingly at peace, but this is just a moment of dreaming, the cliffs look as if they were purring, caressed by the white clouds, leaning over them from a blue sky. Upmost there is a suggestion of menace, a presentiment of the violent awakening that is awaiting the sleeping landscape. John Slavin's southern landscapes show another face of Gaia. Here she is more of an indulgent mother, she seems to be smiling at her offspring playing in the sun. The colours are lively and bright, vibrant yellows, reds and oranges springing out from the frames, entwined with deep greens and blues, with very active contrasts and intense lines. *The Road to Montsegur* has a mountain as its main protagonist as well, but it is not violent or engaged in a display of power; it is quite serene, happily allowing trees and moss to play in its lap. Only the way it holds its back against the sky shows how powerful it really is, an old giant secure in its skin. *Bugarach from the Devil's Armchair* is about chestnut trees, with the mount Bugarach visible in the distance, through their entangled branches. Their pulse is so much more rapid than the mountain's, they must appear to it as a bunch of rowdy children. There is, however, an aura of infinite patience emanating from the wizened cliff. Not that it in any way is able to mitigate the mischievous trees: they are losing themselves in the game they are playing, one excluding everyone else outside.

Autumn Rain River Saltz portrays a vibrant river, cascading through a hilly land-scape, among trees and bushes that seem to be longing to get in tune with her. Out of the shadows there radiates a desire, maybe to fuse with her, maybe just to grasp and hold her. In the distance a mountain lives in its own pace, it could not care less for the tomfoolery of the young ones.

The paintings convey an understanding of Nature, her energies, rhythms and moods more than any other artworks I have encountered, they seem to spring from a profound link between the Earth and the artist.

> I feel I am open enough to channel the harmonious universality of nature through brush work.... [M]y surname 'Slavin' is probably of Old Irish origin denoting 'sliabh', a mountain. Without a doubt, the splendid stature and magnificent bearing of the Scottish Highlands, home of my ancestors, finds heartfelt expression in the core of my work.
>
> *(John Slavin, 2013)*

The song *Gaia* by the Swedish metal band Tiamat presents a dark face of the Earth, the omnipotent, elemental mother. The song begins on a solemn tone, sublime and grave. The rain is falling, rivers overflow, a majestic garb of clouds encircle the landscape. The music now becomes darker, as the singer narrates the tale of the flood, all creation being engulfed in a raging elemental elegy. The water satisfies her thirst, awakens the energy hidden since long in the parched soil but it has no mercy for the individual creatures: 'when Nature calls we all shall drown' (Tiamat, 1994). The tune turns more serene with the almost playful guitar solo, raindrops, whirl-winds and maelstroms performing a musical gig together, improvising towards each other, in the honour of Gaia, whose presence can be felt in the background, a powerful if solitary audience. The song was recorded in 1994 as part of the album *Wildhoney*, which can be described as belonging to the genre of gothic metal inspired by psychedelic rock. The songs on the album are linked together by sounds such as bird music and tones calling into mind the sounds of nature. A review praises its 'ethereal quality' due to intertwining keyboard and guitar lines, as well as the song performance. *Gaia* is described as spun of 'a bevy of contrasting elements, ranging between heavy and light' (Allmusic, 2013).

12.4 Reflection 2

Jonathan Gosling and Peter Case (2013) consider dreaming a collective way of imag-ining the future of the whole ecosystem, with an ability to send out messages and visions by shamanic dreams warning of the disastrous consequences of climate change and pollution. The authors propose to concentrate on the dream, not on the person dreaming it, and they suggest a way of connecting the individual dream with a wider context by applying a broader moral perspective, focusing on the ecosystem as a whole. In this way, ecological thinking needs an eco-centric ethics (ibid.) but also a different approach to time from what is common in our societies.

Hans Rämö (2004) places ecological thinking into an epistemological context of how we view time and space. The current dominating understanding of time, chronological time (see Chapter 6, Section 2), encourages a linear approach to the world, where the environment can be bracketed out and taken out of managerial thinking. Likewise, abstract geometric space or *chora* (see Chapter 6, Section 2) which is the common contemporary view on the nature of space, depersonalizes the environment and helps to see it as a domain open to human action. Such an approach to time and space results in a way of thinking in organizations that focuses only on costs and benefits and organizations of this kind can be persuaded to include environmental goals only if they produce effects that they can regard as economically rational. Organizations that adopt a different view on time and space, the *kairotopic* notion, represented by the idea of concrete place (*topos*) and timely moments (*kairos*) (see Chapter 6, Section 2) are more likely to embrace environmental aims as an integral part of their functioning, although they are also more prone to falling to delusions and responding to fads. They are based on a holistic ethical idea of a fundamental unity of the organization and its environment. At the same time, however, they are less likely to distance themselves from the discourses they adopt and rationally re-evaluate them.

Another important issue to consider with regard to green organizing is leadership. Do greener business needs a different model of leadership or is it just a matter of learning new ways of thinking and embracing of new sensitivities? Donald Fisher (2010) believes that such a leadership can and needs to be learned. He presents sustainability as one of the major challenges of the future, which all organizations need to take into consideration. It is a new philosophy, embracing both environmental awareness and protection and profitability, ideas of growth as well as social justice. In order to implement this philosophy a new set of tools and instruments for measurement and planning is needed, on the one hand, and on the other, a knowledge of and proficiency in all the available resources that enable a successful linking of environmental and economic goals.

Oliver Boiral, Mario Cayer and Charles Baron (2008) take a different view on environmentally sound leadership, arguing that it must embrace consciousness development and an approach to leadership that presupposes a re-evaluation of existing conventions and taken for granted truths and an awareness of the complexity and interrelatedness of problems. The challenges presented today are complex and wide-ranging, encompassing not only environmental issues but profound changes within the organization and mobilization of employees. Management needs to be directly responsible for these changes and for the attunement to ecological values. Environmental leadership includes both a personal commitment to these values and an ability to organize employees and make them sensitive towards these values. Some of the environmentalist values that managers must consider if they want to commit their organizations toward a greener way of functioning, may seem at odds with mainstream managerial values which emphasize growth, free markets and technological progress. Environmental issues have traditionally been treated instrumentally and taken into consideration only if they carried any economic values. The new set of values challenges these taken for granted ideas and are primarily concerned with ecosystemic balance, limitations to growth and a symbiosis with nature. The new set of values may be incorporated and merged with the old one, as profits do not necessarily exclude environmental concerns and vice versa. The management style that is needed to propagate these values may vary from person to person, but it definitely needs to be original and it demands skills that some managers may have and some not. The individuals may be more or less in step with the demands of such a redefinition of leadership and more or less willing to embrace the new ideas and learn the new skills, among them empathy and emotional sensitivity. This is, ultimately, a question of an altered consciousness. Personal development plays an important part in how environmental issues are approached by organizations. Managers on all levels are instrumental for the reorientation of organizations towards a greener policy. They need to embrace a more systemic and holistic view, as the environmental challenges facing today's organizations are complex and interdisciplinary. Managers have to take all these problems into account and not be limited in their thinking towards a single discipline (such as economics). They have to be able and willing to adapt and to take into consideration the daily managerial work of environmental issues. This may require global and radical changes in the organization's structures and policies, from strategic planning to everyday rules for recycling and prevention of pollution. Another collective effort that is needed is a commitment to permanent learning of ways of cooperation with rather than exploitation of the environment. The mobilization of these activities is the responsibility of the manager, as is the incorporation of more participative management practices. Only genuinely empowered employees are able to become dedicated to environmental values and able to react swiftly in response to emerging challenges. The agenda for the development of such greener leadership is a long term one: it may include the development of new promotion and selection schemes, the setting up of training programmes to promote environmental thinking, introduction of accounting systems that advance ecological issues and the support of organizational citizenship attitudes. Hierarchical cultures breed irresponsibility and this may be lethal to any change agenda of this magnitude and kind.

Greener organizations rely not only on the epistemological foundations of their internal cultures or the models of leadership practiced within them, but also on the consumers' attitudes. Andreas Chatzidakis, Pauline Maclaran and Alan Bradshaw (2012) present Exarcheia, an Athenian neighbourhood renowned for its anticapitalist ethos. They argue that it forms a heterotopia (see Section 5.1 and Section 11.4), where utopian cultures are developed and practiced, in particular related to green and ethical marketplace behaviours. It can be seen as a pioneering place for the birth and advance of ecological thinking and consumer lifestyles and from which they are able to spread to other places, open to embrace them. Such heterotopias may act as key agents in the process of transformation of the contemporary consumer society by facilitating the emergence of a particular kind of social capital, in a way not dissimilar to that which lies at the heart of the development of modern urban cultures. A similar point is made by Marius de Geus (2002) who observes that ecotopias, utopias imagined by humans but not always realized as is the case with Exarcheia, can be regarded as 'navigational compasses' by other communities and so, in time, influence the emergence of a more sustainable society. They can help to monitor ecological problems and solutions and perhaps also serve as an inspiration for those who are concerned about the current state of the environment, economy and human civilization. First and foremost, they help to develop an ecological imagination, by monitoring, or looking at the world through 'greener' glasses, inspiring politicians and practitioners with green ideas, and the providing of a kind of virtual reality where green ideas can be tested without serious social and economic consequences.

> Certainly, utopia as an 'enforceable and realizable blueprint' has been dead for a long time, but long live the critical, imaginative, and inspiring ecotopian visions in the history of political thought.
>
> *(Ibid., p. 199)*

Ecology can also be used as yet another management fad, or a tool used in dishonest marketing. Vinícius Brei and Steffen Böhm (2011) show a marketing campaign which was extensively using ecological slogans to attract clients. The recent growth of sales of bottled water has caused many detrimental environmental problems, some of them serious, such as the drying up of certain areas. The companies that sell water, however, try to convince consumers that, by buying bottled water, they contribute to the protection of the environment. Some campaigns are based on actual facts, such as the providing of water by some companies to the parts of Africa that suffer severe droughts. The companies may have made substantial efforts to help these areas by financing the building of wells and developing infrastructure. However, this was but one side of their actions, the other remaining ecologically harmful – they, too, contributed to the depletion of the reservoirs of such water. The associations with environmentalist values are only meant to attract clients who regard themselves as adhering to green lifestyles. Such campaigns are more like strategies for seduction than actual examples of corporate greening.

Ecology is also being used by the capitalist system to pursue the ends that are so characteristic of it – economic gain, even though it is exactly this activity that lies at the very roots of the current environmental problems. It also employs it for gaining legitimacy. Robert Fletcher (2012) argues that capitalism actually uses the climate crises it produces as a means to gain a more solid footing and a source for future expansion. The trade in carbon markets is growing exponentially and contributing to the perseverance of the system and thus the ecological degradation it causes. The system actually exploits the problems for gain through disaster capitalism (Klein, 2008). Fletcher (2012) observes that carbon markets not only commodify natural resources but financialize them. The problem is turned into gain and at the same time redefined as something entirely different, thus making any real attempts at its solution less likely and deactivating yet another, dramatic alarm signal for change. The perfidy of the whole story is that it does so by invoking an eco-logical ethos: the cuts, drastic saving and other austerity measures are motivated by the politicians as a 'response to the environmental problems' and as an enactment of ecological value systems.

12.5 Stories from organizations

Entering BioBazar,[6] one finds oneself in the midst of one of Rebecca Campbell's paintings, perhaps *Abundance* (Campbell, 2013), depicting a vegetable garden with rows of cabbages, carrots, gigantic leeks and many other kinds of greens, where some small animals eye the crops and each other hungrily, fearfully or maybe just curiously? Or maybe *The Pantry*, a methodical cornucopia: shelves full of tempting fruit, vegetables, meats, pastry and preserves. The market is located on the premises of Norblin factory in Warsaw, a silverware plant from the early nineteenth century. Since the 1980s the factory has been hosting a museum and a theatre, and recently also BioBazar. Every Saturday, the old buildings once again buzz with people, and, alas, cars (upon entering I wonder irritably, how do they belong in this eco-sanctuary?). Big posters show the way to the different halls: certified eco-products, producers awaiting certification, soups. . . . Most of the stalls are indoors, except two of the soup kitchens, tempting the frozen passersby with gorgeous smells and steam-ing pots. They look genuine, like those I remember from my grandmother's kitchen, and they probably really are old. The stoves, too, look old, with used, blackened surfaces, and the unmistakable smell of burning coal transports me into another world. When I was small, I often accompanied my grandmother to War-saw's markets where she was selling apples from her garden. There were always marketplace kitchens, selling soup, hot sausage and baked beans. And the fruit and vegetable stalls emanated a powerful smell of greens, melting sweetness and fresh earth. When I enter the halls, I cannot help smiling: this is it, the smell, and the colourful chaos of these old bazaars. The vegetables are happily unpolished, they come in various shapes and shades, they cascade down from the tables, as if falling into the hands of the customers, who swarm the stalls. The sellers talk incessantly, not only praising their produce, but chatting, I can hear one complaining about the weather and how it makes her angry about everything, especially the government. In the fish hall there are fewer people and the smell of fresh and smoked fish is sharp but not entirely unpleasant, toned down by the ice it is displayed in, and the cold day. A lady selling small fresh fish explains that everything is local, the fish comes from rivers and lakes, but some of the smoked fish comes from the sea. She tempts me with homemade herring salad and I am unable to resist. This, too, is a madeleine, it is just like my grandmother used to make it: salty, with a strong taste of onion and oil, and a bitter hint of the sea. People stand around the tables reflectively, carrying bags full of produce in their hands, contemplating the food. The cheese hall is joy-fully chaotic as well, pyramids of wooden cases unabashedly sliding down, cus-tomers tasting cheeses and sellers singing the praises of their products.

'Our cows run around in the pastures like gazelles, they are happy cows, and you can taste it in the cheese for yourselves', I hear a man explaining to a group of buyers. I grab a piece too, it is delightfully creamy.

In this unusual place: a tribute to old local industry; art, embodied by the theatre whose presence is strongly marked on the premises, by posters, photographs and by the ticket office manned by an older man whom everyone has to pass by while entering the bazaar; encircled by shining high rises. But it also has a strong connection to the terrain. I can feel the smell of the sandy Warsaw earth; there are trees in the yard and the grass is bursting through the concrete. The whole place is an urban ecosystem, an essence of Warsaw. As I climb the stairs leading up to the office of the founders, Joanna and Agnieszka, I have another flash of recollection: the space has the same honesty, grey sobriety and straightforward geometry that I remember from the factory where my grandfather used to work as a grinder. Joanna and Agnieszka invite me to sit down, we have tea together and they explain how it all hangs together.

> BioBazar exists from 2008. We have earlier been, that is, we still do it, distributing ecological produce under our own brandname.... Farmers do not really know where to sell these products, selling to shops is difficult because you have to deliver to several shops in town, go and get the returns, prepare accounts, for example, reclaim your own money: there is a multitude of problems, and in big cities it's difficult to reach the clients directly. And then, it has always been our chagrin, how do you explain to someone what difference there is between the ketchup that stands beside, and is unecological, not always made just of tomatoes, and the one made of real tomatoes? It *has to be* more expensive. So that they understand the difference and what they are paying for.
>
> *(Joanna)*

The bazaar was an answer to both these problems. On the one hand, it was to provide ecological farms with an outlet to sell their produce, a place to meet clients face to face. It also is a space where the founders could put up big signs saying 'this is ecological', distribute material saying where the products come from, how they are made. Agnieszka and Joanna hoped for people to be interested in this kind of place but the response overwhelmed them and surpassed anything they have anticipated. Obviously, lots of people do care if the ketchup is made from tomatoes, if the hens are allowed to run free, if the fish has been caught ecologically. The founders' former experiences with educating shop owners and discussing ecology with chain store managers were not encouraging; business plans and market studies always seemed to say that this was not a profitable way to go. But ensuring a direct contact between producer and buyer turned out to be a colossal success. It is important to be able to tell clients: these products are ecological, and address the increasing number of people who 'think about ecology – and then it goes on, it becomes a way of life' (Agnieszka).

It was difficult at first to convince the farmers; they asked how many people would come, and the founders did not know, they could only share their hopes. But they managed to persuade them to come and see if it would work. The ensuring of suppliers and getting all the formal licences and permissions from local authorities took them eight weeks. But from day one the bazaar filled with crowds of people, as if it has always been there, one of the marketplaces of old times, having floated in from another dimension. The crowds attracted the media, and all the TV stations hurried in to get the event into their main news of the day, it went on air even on the national news: this was really something extraordinary, an ecological bazaar meeting such a demand! ('This was a catastrophe of abundance', Joanna laughs, 'it just happened, we did not organize this, we did not even have such contacts.') The farmers stayed with BioBazar, of course, and many others stand in line to be able to be considered ecological and ethical, in order to cooperate with them. It is already the biggest eco-event in Poland. The entrepreneurs constantly come up with new ideas, they test some of them, such as a moving eco-shop, selling produce from a van in different locations of Warsaw; selling sustainable trees for Christmas; film projections about ecological concerns; and establishing a network of ecologically aware organizations and consumers in the neighbourhoods where they operate.

> In our firm it is so that the way from idea to realization is short, it means that if the idea is good and we feel that it will succeed, then we just do it. Sometimes it works, sometimes not, because of course not every idea is a stroke of genius, but we are a small organization and we trust each other, so when we have an idea, we say: okay, let's try it. This is impossible in a corporation.
>
> *(Joanna)*

The main reason for doing all this is, for them, to help people to live in harmony with the environment; everything we do should be done with respect for the wider context, not just when we eat, but the whole way of life. A bazaar is a place of contact, it has always been, people mingle and meet face to face. This is the magic moment: it is not an accident that it was in countries big on trade that the most dynamic and open minded cultures developed, people of different walks of life, nationalities and religions were able to meet, sometimes got married as a result, there was no other place where this could happen. So, to Agnieszka and Joanna, the market is not just a place where supply and demand meet, but a place of possible enlightenment, of exchange of ideas, stories, emotions, views of life, and much, much more.

> I think, this [ecology] is something that if someone is engaging in it, they really have to be dedicated, the economical situation is not easy today, and you really have to like it, believe in it, if you want to engage in it. Because this is not a straightforward business.
>
> *(Joanna)*

But they do make money on the marketplace in the end, and they immediately invest it in new ideas and initiatives. They like to see their bazaar develop, organically grow, thrive, and they enjoy thinking of how it will continue to flourish in the future.

12.6 Questions to reflect on

1. Go to the seaside, the bank of a river, or a lake and look into the water, as intensely as you can, for at least seven minutes. Think: where do we come from? What are we? Where are we going?
2. Look out of the window, at the clouds. Watch them pass by. What do they look like? What do their shapes remind you of? If they were animals – what kind of animals would they be? Write a poem, compose a song, or paint them.
3. Find a rock, take a picture of it, touch it, listen to it. Find out about it in a geology encyclopedia: how old is it? What does it consist of? How did it materialize?
4. Eat a slice of organic bread very slowly, with no spread, just plain bread. Think, while eating, of where it comes from, what it contains, how the crops grew from seeds in the earth, how the seasons changed, the sun, the rains, the harvest. Consider the work of the farmers, the bakers, the drivers transporting the produce to the shop. Finally, the person who sold it to you; you, buying and slicing it.

Notes

1 *c.*750–650 BC, Ancient Greece.
2 *c.*484–425 BC, Caria, Ancient Greece.
3 1707–1778, Sweden.
4 1904–1980, UK and USA.
5 1919–, UK.
6 Material from field study: interview (2012) and observations (2012–2013).

13
A CODA

Cinderella lived in an old stone building by the central square together with her father, his second wife and her two half-sisters, his father's daughters from the second marriage. Every day she took care of the cleaning, did the laundry, cooked and brought home the grocery, while her sisters went on shopping sprees, visited hairdressers or gyms during the days and went dancing in the evenings. Nobody said thank you to Cinderella, everyone seemed to assume that she was there to do all that work and that was that.

As you well know, one day the prince threw a grand ball to which all the eligible young ladies in the duchy were invited. The sisters busied themselves with making themselves pretty for the occasion several months in advance, shopping, visiting spas, working out in the gym and trying out new, stupendous diets. On the day of the ball they went to the ducal palace with her parents in their beautiful new car, while Cinderella stayed at home to prepare pea soup. Suddenly a woman, dressed in a vibrant ragged dress and feathers, knocked on the door. She was singing an old tune and smoking a pipe and Cinderella thought she was very cute, she invited her for tea. The woman handed a pair of blue jeans and a lovely colourful shirt to her host, urging her to go to the ball.

'That's a present! But please be home by midnight, it's very important that you do', she said and went on her way.

The ball was indeed fantastic and Cinderella had a great time. She looked stunning and danced astoundingly well, and so she attracted the prince's attention, and not just his. Everybody wanted to dance and talk with her. But then suddenly the clock struck 12 and she remembered what she had promised the woman. Not wanting to go against her wish, however peculiar it might seem, she darted out from the ballroom, stumbled on the velvety carpet and lost one of her boots, that unbeknownst to her must have come unlaced. She did not want to halt, fearing that someone might want to try to stop her, and just continued running. Jogging on the cold and slippery paving stones in only one shoe was terribly uncomfortable, so, after a while, she had to slow down. How surprised she was when she suddenly felt a large hand on her shoulder. Alarmed, she turned around.

'I'm sorry, my daughter', it was her father, gasping for breath from the run, 'I'm so sorry … I didn't know … I didn't understand … I thought you didn't care for dancing, clothes, and suchlike vanities … All days long, you were cooking and cleaning, I thought … And today I saw you changed in this way, I realized how much like me you were.'

The hugged, both very moved. A nasty light rain started to drizzle, the ground felt chilly and soggy. Cinderella pointed down and said: 'Dad, my feet. I'm freezing. Let's go now.' Without hesitation, the father took off his own shoes and handed them to his daughter. They started to walk slowly down the street. To a passerby they must have presented a hilarious couple: a young woman in huge male shoes and a well dressed older man only in his socks. But there were no humorously predisposed passersby around, everyone and his uncle was attending the ball or else sleeping. Even stray dogs deserted the streets, discouraged from nightly doggy frolic by the rain. The father and the daughter were not interested in how they looked, their attention was elsewhere: they talked, as they had not done for years, as they, in fact, never had. The father tried to explain his horrendous misunderstanding of his daughter, he told her about his failing marriage, his lack of contact with his vacuous daughters, who barely knew how to put together a shopping list and never read even a short silly book, and about the problems he was having with his business, the dishonest co-workers, who took every opportunity to appropriate his funds but could not be counted upon to put in real effort into the work. The daughter listened attentively and, when he was describing the business problems, she started shooting in advice how to solve them. After one of such comments, the father stopped in his tracks and caught his head with his both hands.

'What a fool I am! Look, you're right, you know exactly what to do! Your advice is very sound, my daughter! And I, the sorry old fool, have been worrying all this time that I have no son to pass my business on to! Come and work with me, my daughter. How about joining me at the shop tomorrow early morning?'

And so she did. Indeed, she turned out to be very much like her father in that she had a talent for business, they were both brilliant merchants and so the company thrived. However, she was different from him in one regard – she had a good intuition about people. They fired the dishonest co-workers and, in their place, found some trustworthy and scrupulous craftsmen and -women who helped them to develop the firm which they turned into a cooperative. Father and daughter came up with ever new ideas and tried new contacts, learned from each other and inspired one another.

Meanwhile, as is well known, the prince began looking for the owner of the lost boot. He stopped by at Cinderella's home, too, but she was not there, being busy with the firm. The sisters, who were really intent on the prince choosing one of them, did everything to look as if the abandoned Doc Marten was their natural footwear. One of them was smart enough to secretly buy herself a pair in advance, to throw away one, and to show it to the prince, who was convinced, even though the boots did not really match and the girl was not really like that other one, but then, he was not very observant. He proposed to her and was accepted. The other one was very sad for a few days, but then, when it transpired that she was invited to join her sister at the court, she was instantly consoled. This is, however, a peripheral story: nothing much interesting happened. It was not a very interesting prince after all, nor a very interesting duchy. They did not achieve anything special, nor were there any particular misfortunes to recount. A duchy like many others.

However, the cooperative was extraordinary. You can read about it in history books and textbooks in economics alike. They do of course, not reveal that the father from time to time brought home some new candidate for Cinderella's husband, explaining to her discreetly behind a closed door: 'Look, daughter, a perfectly good man. Look, this one really looks honest.' But Cinderella, who had a good intuition about people, knew better and politely refused. Until she herself met the man who became her husband. And what a great husband he was! They all lived happily ever after, the firm and the city prospered, and the members of the Cinderella Cooperative, as it came be known, all said: 'This is a lovely place to work!'

And so it was.

REFERENCES

Abbey Winery Pannonhálma (2013) Accessed 10.05.2013 at www.pannonhalmibor.com/.

Achebe, Chinua (2010) *Things Fall Apart.* London: Penguin.

Adam, Barbara, Richard Whipp and Ida Sabelis (2002) 'Choreographing Time and Management: Traditions, developments and opportunities', in: Richard Whipp, Barbara Adam and Ida Sabelis (eds) *Making Time: Time and management in modern organizations.* Oxford: Oxford University Press, pp. 1–30.

Afnan, Soheil, M. (1958) *Avicenna: His life and works.* London: George Allen & Unwin.

Agar, Michael (1996) *The Professional Stranger: An informal introduction to ethnography.* New York: Academic Press.

Akinci, Cinla and Eugene Sadler-Smith (2012) 'Intuition in Management Research: A historical review', *International Journal of Management Reviews*, 14, pp. 104–122.

Allmusic (2013) *Tiamat, Wildhoney: Review.* Accessed 26.04.2013 at www.allmusic.com/album/wildhoney-mw0000940313.

Altman, Matthew C. (2007) 'The Decomposition of the Corporate Body: What Kant cannot contribute to business ethics', *Journal of Business Ethics*, 74/3, pp. 253–266.

Anderson, Alistair R. (1998) 'Cultivating the Garden of Eden: Environmental entrepreneuring', *Journal of Organizational Change Management*, 11/2, pp. 135–144.

Aquinas, Thomas (1949) *De Regno: On kingship, to the king of Cyprus.* Toronto: The Pontifical Institute of Mediaeval Studies. Accessed 22.02.2013 at http://dhspriory.org/thomas/DeRegno.htm#1.

Arendt, Hannah (1999) *The Human Condition.* Chicago: University of Chicago Press.

Argyris, Chris and Donald Schön (1978) *Organizational Learning: A theory of action perspective*, Reading, MA: Addison Wesley.

Aristotle (1987) *De Anima.* London: Penguin.

Aristotle (1991) *The Art of Rhetoric.* Transl. Hugh Lawson-Tancred. London: Penguin.

Armstrong, Karen (2007) *The Great Transformation: The beginnings of our religious traditions.* New York: Anchor Books.

Arnold, Denis G. and Norman E. Bowie (2003) 'Sweatshops and Respect for Persons', *Business Ethics Quarterly*, 23/13, pp. 221–242.

Arnold, Denis G., Robert Audi and Matt Zwolinski (2010) 'Recent Work in Ethical Theory and its Implications for Business Ethics', *Business Ethics Quarterly*, 20/4, pp. 559–581.

Atkins, Paul W.B. and Sharon K. Parker (2012) 'Understanding Individual Compassion in Organizations: The role of appraisals and psychological flexibility', *Academy of Management Review*, 37/4, pp. 524–546.

Augustine (1940) *Confessions*. Transl. Albert C. Outler. Accessed 10.03.2013 at www.ourladyswarriors.org/saints/augconf.htm.

Babiak, Paul and Robert D. Hare (2006) *Snakes in Suits: When psychopaths go to work*. New York: Harper Collins.

Barnard, Chester Irving (1966) *The Functions of the Executive*. Cambridge, MA: Harvard University Press.

Bateson, Gregory (1972) *Steps to an Ecology of Mind*. New York: Ballantine Books.

Bateson, Gregory (1979) *Mind and Nature: A necessary unity*. Toronto: Bantam Books.

Batko, Roman (2013) *Golem, Awatar, Midas, Złoty Cielec: Płynna organizacja publiczna*. Warszawa: Sedno.

Bauman, Zygmunt (1991) *Modernity and the Holocaust*. Cambridge: Polity Press.

Bauman, Zygmunt (1993) *Postmodern Ethics*. Cambridge: Basil Blackwell.

Bauman, Zygmunt (2000) *Liquid Modernity*. Cambridge: Polity.

Bauman, Zygmunt (2011) *Collateral Damage: Social inequalities in a global age*. Cambridge; Malden, MA: Polity Press.

Bauman, Zygmunt (2012) 'Times of Interregnum', *Ethics and Global Politics*, 5/1, pp. 49–56.

Bauman, Zygmunt and Leonidas Donskis (2013) *Moral Blindness: The loss of sensitivity in liquid modernity*. Cambridge: Polity Press.

Bennett, Steven J. (1991) *Ecopreneuring*. New York: John Wiley & Sons.

Bergson, Henri (2002) *The Creative Mind: An introduction to metaphysics*. New York: Kensington.

Beyes, Timon and Chris Steyaert (2012) 'Spacing Organization: non-representational theory and performing organizational space', *Organization*, 19/1, pp. 45–61.

Bezes, Philippe, Didier Demaziere, Thomas le Bianic, Catherine Paradeise, Romuald Normand, Daniel Benamouzing, Frédéric Pierru and Julia Evetts (2012) 'New Public Management and Professionals in the Public Sector', *Sociologie du Travail*, 54/S1, pp. e1–e52.

Boddy, Clive R. (2006) 'The Vices of Management Decisions: Organizational psychopaths', *Management Decision*, 44/10, pp. 1461–1475.

Boddy, Clive R. (2010) 'Corporate Psychopaths and Organizational Type', *Journal of Public Affairs*, 10/4, pp. 300–312.

Boddy, Clive R. (2011) *Corporate Psychopaths: Organisational destroyers*. London: Palgrave Macmillan.

Boiral, Oliver, Mario Cayer and Charles Baron (2008) 'The Action Logics of Environmental Leadership', *Journal of Business Ethics*, 85/4, pp. 479–499.

Boulding, Kenneth E. (1981) *Ecodynamics: A new theory of societal evolution*. London: Sage.

Bourdieu, Pierre (1980) *Questions de sociologie*. Paris: Minuit.

Brei, Vinícius and Steffen Böhm (2011) 'Corporate Social Responsibility as Cultural Meaning Management: A critique of the marketing of "ethical" bottled water', *Business Ethics: A European Review*, 20/3, pp. 233–252.

Brereton, Michael and Michael Temple (1999) 'The New Public Service Ethos: An ethical environment of governance', *Public Administration*, 77/3, pp. 455–474.

Broad, William J. (2007) *The Oracle: Ancient Delphi and the science behind its lost secrets*. London: Penguin.

Broberg, Gunnar (2006) *Carl von Linné*. Stockholm: Svenska institutet.

Brook, Peter (1995) *The Empty Space*. New York: Touchstone.

Brother Anthony of Taizé (2010) 'Ko Ŭn's "Maninbo": History as poem, poem as history', *World Literature Today*, 84/1, pp. 43–46.

Bryggeriet (2010) Accessed 19.04.2013 at www.bryggeriet.org/.

Buczek, Katarzyna (2007) *Hugo Kołłątaj i edukacja*. Warszawa: Wydawnictwa UW.

Burrell, Gibson (1997) *Pandemonium: Towards a retro-organization theory*. London: Sage.

Butler, Stephen A. (2010) 'Solving Business Problems Using a Lateral Thinking Approach', *Management Decision*, 48/1, pp. 58–64.

Cairns, George, Peter McInnes and Phil Roberts (2003) 'Organizational Space/Time: From imperfect panoptical to heterotopian understanding', *Ephemera*, 3/2, pp. 126–139.

Campbell, Joseph (1993) *The Hero with a Thousand Faces*. Princeton: Princeton University Press.

Campbell, Joseph with Bill Moyers (1988) *The Power of Myth*, ed. B.S. Flowers. New York: Doubleday.

Campbell, Rebecca (2013) *Murals, Panels, Paintings, Illustration, Design*. Accessed 24.04.2013 at www.rebeccacampbell.co.uk/pages/home.htm.

CBOS (2013) *Civil partnerships (public opinion poll)*. Warszawa: CBOS.

CDBU (2013) *Council for the Defense of British Universities*. Accessed 16.03.2012 at http://cdbu.org.uk/.

Chang, Ha-Joon (2008) *Bad Samaritans: The guilty secrets of rich nations and the threat to global prosperity*. London: Random House.

Chatzidakis, Andreas, Pauline Maclaran and Alan Bradshaw (2012) 'Heterotopian Space and the Utopics of Ethical and Green Consumption', *Journal of Marketing Management*, 28/3–4, pp. 494–515.

Check-Teck, Foo (2011) 'Beyond Jungian Synchronicity, Decision Making via Poetical Imagery: The case of *Kuan Yin*, Avalokitesvara and *Ling Qian*', *Chinese Management Studies*, 5/2, pp. 131–145.

Chomsky, Noam (2011) 'Noam Chomsky', *Targeted Individuals Canada*. Accessed 18.06.2013 at http://targetedindividualscanada.wordpress.com/2011/05/24/noam-chomsky/.

Cicero (2004) *Selected Works*. Transl. Michael Grant. London: Penguin.

Clegg, Stewart, Martin Kornberger and Carl Rhodes (2007) 'Business Ethics as Practice', *British Journal of Management*, 18/2, pp. 107–122.

Clegg, Sue and Stephen Rowland (2010) 'Kindness in Pedagogical Practice and Academic Life', *British Journal of Sociology of Education*, 31/6, pp. 719–735.

Coelho, Nuno, M.M.S. (2013) 'Controversy and Practical Reason in Aristotle', in: Liesberh Huppes-Clutsenaer and Nuno M.M.S. Coelho (eds) *Aristotle and the Philosophy of Law: Theory, practice and justice*. Dordrecht: Springer, pp. 87–108.

Collini, Stefan (2012) *What are Universities for?* London: Penguin.

Corvellec, Hervé (2009) 'The Practice of Risk Management: Silence is not absence', *Risk Management*, 11/3–4, pp. 285–304.

Coser, Lewis (1974) *Greedy Institutions: Patterns of undivided commitment*. New York: The Free Press.

Costea, Bogdan, Norman Crump and John Holm (2005) 'Dionysus at Work? The ethos of play and the ethos of management', *Culture and Organization*, 11/2, pp. 139–151.

Csaszar, Felipe A. (2012) 'Organizational Structure as a Determinant of Performance: Evidence from mutual funds', *Strategic Management Journal*, 33/6, pp. 611–632.

Csíkszentmihályi, Mihaly (1990) *Flow: The psychology of optimal experience*. New York: Harper and Row.

Csíkszentmihályi, Mihaly (2003) *Good Business: Leadership, flow, and the making of meaning*. New York: Penguin.

CSW (1998) *James Turrell, Space Division Wedgework: Instalacje świetlne*. Accessed 2.05.2013 at http://csw.art.pl/new/98/turrell.html.

Cunliffe, Ann (2013) *Self and Scholarship: Alterity, poetics and passion*. Inaugural lecture, Leeds: The University of Leeds.

Cunliffe, Ann and Matthew Eriksen (2011) 'Relational Leadership', *Human Relations*, 64/11, pp. 1425–1449.

Czarniawska, Barbara (1997) *Narrating the Organization: Dramas of institutional identity*, Chicago: Chicago University Press.

Czarniawska, B. (2000) *A City Reframed: Managing Warsaw in the 1990s*. Reading: Harwood.

Czarniawska, Barbara (2008) 'Humiliation: A standard organizational product?' *Critical Perspectives on Accounting*, 19, pp. 1034–1053.

Czarniawska, Barbara and Carl Rhodes (2006) 'Strong Plots: The relationship between popular culture and management theory and practice', in Pasquale Gagliardi and Barbara Czarniawska (eds) *Management and Humanities*. London: Edward Elgar, pp. 195–218.

Czarniawska-Joerges, Barbara (1993) *The Three-dimensional Organization: A constructionist view*. Lund: Studentlitteratur.

Czarniawska-Joerges, Barbara and Rolf Wolff (1991) 'Leaders, Managers, Entrepreneurs On and Off the Organizational Stage', *Organization Studies*, 12/4, pp. 529–546.

Dane, Erik and Michael G. Pratt (2007) 'Exploring Intuition and its Role in Managerial Decision Making', *Academy of Management Review*, 32/1, pp. 33–54.

Danneels, Erwin (2003) 'Tight-Loose Coupling with Customers: The enactment of customer orientation', *Strategic Management Journal*, 24/6, pp. 559–576.

de Certeau, Michel (1984) *The Practice of Everyday Life*. Berkeley: University of California Press.

de Geus, Marius (2002) 'Ecotopia, Sustainability and Vision', *Organization Environment*, 15/2, pp. 187–201.

de Troyes, Chrétien (1988) *Arthurian Romances*. New York: Everyman's Library.

Dees, J. Gregory (2001) *The Meaning of Social Entrepreneurship*. Accessed 07.11.2005 at www.caseatduke.org/documents/dees_sedef.pdf.

Deleuze, Gilles and Félix Guattari (1996) *What is Philosophy?* New York: Columbia University Press.

Denhardt, Robert B. (1981) *In the Shadow of Organization*. Lawrence: University Press of Kansas.

Dew, Nicholas (2009) 'Serendipity in Entrepreneurship', *Organization Studies*, 30/7, pp. 735–753.

Diefenbach, Thomas (2009) 'New Public Management in Public Sector Organizations: The dark sides of managerialistic "enlightenment"', *Public Administration*, 87/4, pp. 892–909.

Dionysius the Areopagite (1899) *The Celestial Hierarchy (Works, Vol. 2)*. Accessed 05.03.2013 at www.tertullian.org/fathers/areopagite_13_heavenly_hierarchy.htm#c3.

Dixon, Sarah E.A. and Anne Clifford (2007) 'Ecopreneurship – a New Approach to Managing the Triple Bottom Line', *Journal of Organizational Change Management*, 20/3, pp. 326–345.

Dörfler, Viktor and Fran Ackerman (2012) 'Understanding Intuition: The case for two forms of intuition', *Management Learning*, 43/5, pp. 545–564.

Drda, Jan (1978) *Bajki czeskie*. Katowice: Śląsk.

Durant, Rita (2002) 'Synchronicity: A post-structuralist guide to creativity and change', *Journal of Organizational Change Management*, 15/5, pp. 490–501.

Dutton, Jane E., Monica C. Worline, Peter J. Frost and Jacoba Lilius (2006) 'Explaining Compassion Organizing', *Administrative Science Quarterly*, 51/1, pp. 59–96.

Edenius, Mats and Ali Yakhlef (2007) 'Space, Vision and Organizational Learning: The interplay of incorporating and inscribing practices', *Management Learning*, 38/2, pp. 193–210.

Eklöf, Motzi (1999) *The Ethos of the Doctor: Studies in the identities, interests and ideals of the Swedish medical profession, 1890–1960*. Doctoral dissertation, Linköping: Linköping University.

Eko Przedszkole Mały Krokodyl (2013) Accessed 11.04.2013 at www.przedszkolezabki.pl.

Elba (2013) *Elba skłot*. Accessed 23.04.2013 at http://elba.bzzz.net.

Elliott, J.E. (2011) 'Managing Academic Freedom: Recent cross-Atlantic developments', *Prometheus*, 29/2, pp. 163–176.

Emerson, Ralph Waldo (2012) *The Essential Writings of Ralph Waldo Emerson*. New York: Random House.

Emma (2013) *Emma Hostel*. Accessed 23.04.2013 at www.emmahostel.pl.

Epicurus (1994) *The Epicurus Reader: Selected writings and testimonia*. Transl. and edited by Brad Inwood and L.P. Gerson. Indianapolis: Hackett.

Ericsson, Daniel (2004) 'Entreprenörskapsfetischism: Noter om entreifiering och entrepomorfisering', in: Daniel Ericsson (ed.) *Det o(av)sedda entreprenörskapet*. Lund: Academia Adacta.

Fayol, Henri (1949) *General and Industrial Management*. London: Pitman.

Feldman, Martha S., Ruth Nicole Brown and Debra Horner (2003) *Change and Changing: How change processes give meaning to change plans*. Washington: National Public Management Conference.

Fisher, Donald (2010) 'Leading a Sustainable Organization', *Journal for Quality & Participation*, 32/4, pp. 29–31.

Fletcher, Robert (2012) 'Capitalizing on Chaos: Climate change and disaster capitalism', *Ephemera*, 12/1–2, pp. 97–112.

Flusty, Steven (2004) *De-Coca-Colonization: Making the globe from the inside out*. London: Routledge.

Foucault, Michel (1984) 'Des espaces autres', *Architecture, Mouvement, Continuité*, 5/10, pp. 46–49.

Foucault, Michel (1991) *Discipline and Punish: The birth of the prison*. London: Tavistock.

Foucault, Michel (1997) 'The Ethics of the Concern of the Self as Practice of Freedom', in: Paul Rabinow (ed.) *Ethics: Subjectivity and truth*. New York: The New Press.

Fromm, Erich (1994) *Escape from Freedom*. New York: Henry Holt.

Frost, Peter J. (2011) 'Why Compassion Counts!', *Journal of Management Inquiry*, 20/4, pp. 395–401.

Fuchs, Christian (2003) 'Structuration Theory and Self-Organization', *Systemic Practice and Action Research*, 16/2, pp. 133–167.

Gabriel, Yiannis (2000) *Storytelling in Organizations: Facts, fictions, and fantasies*. Oxford: Oxford University Press.

GfK (2009) *Jak Polacy widzą związki gejów?* Warszawa: GfK Polonia.

Giddens, Anthony (1979) *Central Problems in Social Theory: Action, structure, and contradiction in social analysis*. Los Angeles: University of California Press.

Glinka, Beata and Svetlana Gudkova (2011) *Przedsiębiorczość*. Warszawa: Wolters Kluwer.

Goopy, Suzanne E. (2005) 'Taking Account of Local Culture: Limits to the development of a professional ethos', *Nursing Inquiry*, 12/2, pp. 144–154.

Gosling, Jonathan and Peter Case (2013) 'Social Dreaming and Ecocentric Ethics: Sources of non-rational insight in the face of climate change catastrophe', *Organization*, 20/5, pp. 705–721.

Grabher, Gernot (2002) 'The Project Ecology of Advertising: Tasks, talents and teams', *Regional Studies*, 36/3, pp. 245–262.

Grześczak, Inga (2012) *Alfabet antyczny*. Warszawa: Sedno.

Guillet de Monthoux, P. (1993) *Det sublimas konstnärliga ledning: Estetik, konst och företag*. Stockholm: Nerenius & Santerus.

Guillet de Monthoux, Pierre (2004) *The Art Firm: Aesthetic management and metaphysical marketing from Wagner to Wilson*. Stanford: Stanford Business Books.

Gustavsson, Bengt (2001) 'Towards a Transcendent Epistemology of Organizations: New foundations for organizational change.' *Journal of Organizational Change Management*, 14/4, pp. 352–378.

Harris, Howard (2002) 'Is Love a Management Virtue?', *Business & Professional Ethics Journal*, 21/3–4, pp. 173–184.

Hatch, Mary Jo (1993) 'The Dynamics of Organizational Culture', *Academy of Management Review*, 18/4, pp. 657–663.

Hatch, Mary Jo and Majken Schultz (2002) 'The Dynamics of Organizational Identity', *Human Relations*, 55/8, pp. 989–1018.

Hatch, Mary Jo and Majken Schultz (2008) *Taking Brand Initiative: How to align strategy, culture and identity through corporate branding*. San Francisco: Jossey-Bass/Wiley.

Hatch, Mary Jo, Monika Kostera and Andrzej K. Koźmiński (2005) *Three Faces of Leadership: Manager, artist, priest*. London: Blackwell.

Haug, Marie and Marvin Sussman (1969) 'Professional Autonomy and the Revolt of the Client', *Social Problems*, 17/2, pp. 153–161.

Hawker, Philippa (2005) 'Break with the Past', *The Age*. Accessed 30.04.2013 at www.theage.com.au/news/film/break-with-the-past/2005/09/08/1125772639995.html.

Hedlund, Gunnar (1994) 'A Model of Knowledge Management and the N-Form Corporation', *Strategic Management Journal*, 15, pp. 73–90.

Hepsø, Vidar (2008) ' "Boundary-spanning" Practices and Paradoxes Related to Trust among People and Machines in High-tech Oil and Gas Environment', in: Dariusz Jemielniak and Jerzy Kociatkiewicz (eds) *Management Practices in High-tech Environments*. Hershe; New York: Information Science Reference, pp. 1–17.

Hernes, Tor (2004) *The Spatial Construction of Organization*. Amsterdam: John Benjamin.

Herodotus (2008) *The Histories*. London: Penguin.

Hersey, P., K.H. Blanchard and D.E. Johnson (2007) *Management of Organizational Behavior: Leading human resources*. Upper Saddle River, NJ: Pearson Education.

Herzog, Werner (1972) *Aguirre, the Wrath of God*. Werner Herzog Filmproduktion – Hessischter Runtfunk.

Hesiod (1914a) *Theogony*. Transl. Hugh G. Evelyn-White. Accessed 12.02.2013 at www.sacred-texts.com/cla/hesiod/theogony.htm.

Hesiod (1914b) *Works and Days*. Trans. Hugh G. Evelyn-Whyte. Accessed 14.03.2013 at www.sacred-texts.com/cla/hesiod/works.htm.

Hesse, Hermann (2008) *Siddhartha: An Indian modern poem*. New York: Modern Library.

Heyd, Milly and David Heyd (2003) 'Perception as Missing: On Bill Viola's "Going Forth by Say" ', *Notes in the History of Art*, 22/4, pp. 30–38.

Hill, Ronald Paul and Debra Lynn Stephens (2003) 'The Compassionate Organization in the 21st Century', *Organizational Dynamics*, 32/4, pp. 331–341.

Hjorth, Daniel (2005) 'Organizational Entrepreneurship: With de Certeau on creating heterotopias (or spaces for play)', *Journal of Management Inquiry*, 14/4, pp. 386–398.

Hjorth, Daniel and Bengt Johannisson (2009) 'Learning as Entrepreneurial Process', *Revue de l'Entrepreneuriat*, 8/2, pp. 57–78.

Hobbes, Thomas (1651) *Leviathan*. The Project Gutenberg. Accessed 05.03.2013 at www.gutenberg.org/files/3207/3207-h/3207-h.htm.

Hochschild, Arlie (1983) *The Managed Heart: Commercialization of human feeling*. Berkeley: University of California Press.

Hodgkinson, Gerard P., Eugene Sadler-Smith, Lisa A. Burke, Guy Claxton and Paul R. Sparrow (2009) 'Intuition in Organizations: Implications for strategic management', *Long Range Planning*, 42, pp. 277–297.

Höpfl, Heather (1992) 'The Making of the Corporate Acolyte: Some thoughts on charismatic leadership and the reality of organizational commitment', *Journal of Management Studies*, 29/1, pp. 23–33.

Howard, Harris (2013) 'Is Love a Management Virtue?', *Business and Professional Ethics Journal*, 21/3–4, pp. 173–184.

Hyde, Michael J. (2004) *The Ethos of Rhetoric*. Columbia: University of South Carolina Press.

Isaack, Thomas S. (1978) 'Intuition: An ignored dimension of management', *Academy of Management Review*, 3/4, pp. 917–922.

Isaak, Robert (2002) 'The Making of the Ecopreneur', *Greener Management International: The Journal of Corporate Environmental Strategy and Practice*, 38, pp. 81–92.

Iser, Wolfgang (1970) *Die Appellstruktur der Texte: Unbestimmtheit als Wirkungsbedingung literarischer Prosa*. Konstanzer Universitätsreden, 28, Constance: Universitätsverlag.

Isidorus of Seville (2006) *The Etymologies*. Transl. and introduction Stephen A. Barney, W.J. Lewis, J.A. Baech and Oliver Berghof. Cambridge: Cambridge University Press.

IT Dragon [pseudonym] (2013) Accessed 18.04.2013 at www.tiger.com.pl/.

Jackall, Robert (2009) *Moral Mazes: The world of corporate managers*. Oxford; New York: Oxford University Press.

Jarmusch, Jim (1995) *Dead Man*. Miramax Films.

Johannisson, Bengt (2005) *Entreprenörskapets väsen – en personlig bild*. Lund: Studentlitteratur.

Johannisson, Bengt (2008) 'Towards a Practice Theory of Entrepreneuring', award lecture, *Global Award for Entrepreneurship Research*. Swedish Entrepreneurship Forum, the Research Institute of Industrial Economics and VINNOVA.

John Slavin (2013) *John Slavin: Artist Painter*. Accessed 26.04.2013 at www.john-slavin.co.uk/.

Jones, Geoff, Christine McLean and Paolo Quattrone (2004) 'Spacing and Timing', *Organization*, 11/5, pp. 723–741.

Jones, John (1993) *High-Speed Management: Time-based strategies for managers and organizations*. San Francisco: Jossey-Bass.

Jonnergård, Karin (2008) 'The Witchcraft of Professionalism: The attractiveness of ideal types of professions', in: Monika Kostera (ed.) *Organizational Olympians: Heroes and heroines of organizational myths*. London: Palgrave Macmillan, pp. 184–194.

Jung, Carl G. (1990) *The Archetypes and the Collective Unconscious* (Collected Works, Vol. 9). Princeton: Princeton University Press.

Jung, Carl G. (1992) *Psychological Types*. Princeton: Princeton University Press.

Jung, Carl G. (1993) *Synchronicity: An acausal connecting principle*. Bollingen, Switzerland: Bollingen Foundation.

Kafka, Franz (2012) *The Castle*. Ware: Wordsworth Editions.

Kallendorf, Craig and Carol Kallendorf (1985) 'The Figures of Speech, *Ethos* and Aristotle: Notes toward a rhetoric of business communication', *Journal of Business Communication*, 22/1, pp. 35–50.

Kandinsky, Vasily (1912) *Improvisation No. 29: The Swan*.

Kanjilal, Debjani, Azam M. Bejou and David Bejou (2012) 'Compassion: The missing link in economics and management', *Journal of Relationship Marketing*, 11/1, pp. 15–20.

Kant, Immanuel (2008) *The Critique of Pure Reason*. Project Gutenberg. Accessed 15.02.2013 at www.gutenberg.org/files/4280/4280-h/4280-h.htm.

Kelemen, Mihaela and Tuomo Peltonen (2001) 'Ethics, Morality and the Subject: The contribution of Zygmunt Bauman and Michel Foucault to "postmodern" business ethics', *Scandinavian Journal of Management*, 17/2, pp. 151–166.

Kelemen, Mihaela and Monika Kostera (2002) (eds) *Critical Management Research in Eastern Europe: Managing the transition*. London: Palgrave Macmillan.

Kempiński, Andrzej M. (2001) *Encyklopedia mitologii ludów indoeuropejskich*, Warszawa: Iskry.

Kernochan, Richard A., Donald W. McCormick and Judith A. White (2007) 'Spirituality and the Management Teacher: Reflections of three Buddhists on compassion, mindfulness, and selflessness in the classroom', *Journal of Management Inquiry*, 16/1, pp. 61–75.

Kets de Vries, Manfred (1998) 'Charisma in Action: The transformational abilities of Virgin's Richard Branson and ABB's Percy Barnevik', *Organizational Dynamics*, 4, pp. 7–21.

Kets de Vries, Manfred (2003a) ' "Doing an Alexander": Lessons on leadership by a master conqueror', *European Management Journal*, 21/3, pp. 370–376.

Kets de Vries, Manfred (2003b) 'The Dark Side of Leadership', *Business Strategy Review*, 14/3, pp. 25–28.

Kets de Vries, Manfred (2006) 'The Spirit of Despotism: Understanding the tyrant within', *Human Relations*, 59/2, pp. 195–220.

Kets de Vries, Manfred (2009) *Reflections on Character and Leadership: On the couch with Manfred Kets de Vries*, San Francisco: Jossey-Bass.

Kim, Tae Wan and Alan Strudler (2012) 'Workplace Civility: A Confucian approach', *Business Ethics Quarterly*, 22/3, pp. 557–577.

Klein, Gary and Karl E. Weick (2000) 'Decisions: Making the right ones, learning from the wrong ones', *Across the Board*, 37/6, pp. 16–22.

Klein, Naomi (2000) *No Logo: Taking aim at the brand bullies*. New York: Picador.

Klein, Naomi (2008) *The Shock Doctrine: The rise of disaster capitalism*. London: Penguin.

Ko Ŭn (2005) *Ten Thousand Lives*. Los Angeles: Green Integer.

Kociatkiewicz, Jerzy (2000) 'Dreams of Time, Times of Dreams', *Culture & Organization*, 6/1, pp. 71–86.

Kociatkiewicz, Jerzy (2004) *The Social Construction of Space in a Computerized Environment*. Doctoral dissertation, Warsaw: Polish Academy of Sciences, Accessed 21.02.2009 at www.kociak.org/files/drweb.pdf.

Kociatkiewicz, Jerzy and Monika Kostera (1999) 'The Anthropology of Empty Spaces', *Qualitative Sociology*, 22/1, pp. 37–50.

Kociatkiewicz, Jerzy and Monika Kostera (2012a) 'Sherlock Holmes and the Adventure of the Rational Manager: Organizational reason and its discontents', *Scandinavian Journal of Management*, 28/2, pp. 162–172.

Kociatkiewicz, Jerzy and Monika Kostera (2012b) 'The Good Manager: An archetypical quest for morally sustainable leadership', *Organization Studies*, 33/7, pp. 861–878.

Korczak, Janusz (2011a) *Król Maciuś Pierwszy*. Warszawa: WAB.

Korczak, Janusz (2011b) *Król Maciuś na bezludnej wyspie*. Warszawa: WAB.

Korthagen, Fred A.J. (2005) 'The Organization in Balance: Reflection and intuition as complementary processes', *Management Learning*, 36/3, pp. 371–387.

Kostera, Monika (1996) *Postmodernizm w zarządzaniu*. Warszawa: PWE.

Kostera, Monika (2006) 'The Narrative Collage as Research Method', *Storytelling, Self, Society*, 2/2, pp. 5–27.

Kostera, Monika (2012) *Organizations and Archetypes*. London: Edward Elgar.

Kostera, Monika (2013) *Fast Poetry*. Accessed 13.05.2013 at www.kostera.pl/English.htm.

Kostera, Monika and Agnieszka Postuła (2011) 'Holding up the Aegis: On the construction of social roles by polish IT-professionals and the change in agency', *Tamara Journal for Critical Organization Inquiry*, 9/1–2, pp. 83–92.

Koźmiński, Andrzej K. (1982) *Po wielkim szoku*. Warszawa: PWE.

Koźmiński, Andrzej K. (2005) 'Flexibility-Based Competition: Skills and competencies in the New Europe', *Human Factors and Ergonomics in Manufacturing*, 15/1, pp. 35–47.

La Pira, Frank (2011) 'Entrepreneurial Intuition: An empirical approach', *Journal of Management and Marketing Research*, 6, pp. 1–22.

Law, John (1994) *Organizing Modernity*. Oxford; Cambridge, MA: Routledge.

Lefebvre, Henri (1991) *The Production of Space*. Oxford: Basil Blackwell.

Lévinas, Emanuel (1999) *Totality and Infinity: An essay on exteriority*. Pittsburgh, PA: Duquesne University Press.

Lewin, Kurt, Ron Lippitt and Robert White (1939) 'Patterns of Aggressive Behavior in Experimentally Created Social Climates', *Journal of Social Psychology*, 10/2, pp. 271–301.

Leybourne, Stephen and Eugene Sadler-Smith (2006) 'The Role of Intuition and Improvisation in Project Management', *International Journal of Project Management*, 24/6, pp. 483–492.

Linsley, Philip M. and Philip J. Shrives (2009) 'Mary Douglas, Risk and Accounting Failures', *Critical Perspectives on Accounting*, 20/4, pp. 492–508.

Lis, Tadeusz (1985) 'Zapomniany Diabeł', *Teatr Telewizji TVP*. Accessed 13.05.2013 at www.teatrtelewizji.tvp.pl/spektakle/artykul/zapomniany-diabel_591780/.

Lovelock, James (2000) *Gaia: A new look at life on Earth*. Oxford; New York: Oxford University Press.

Lovelock, James (2007) *The Revenge of Gaia*. London: Penguin.

Lubit, Roy (2002) 'The Long-Term Organizational Impact of Destructively Narcissistic Managers', *Academy of Management Executive*, 16/1, pp. 127–138.

Lucretius (2007) *The Nature of Things*. London: Penguin.

Magala, Sławomir (2009) *The Management of Meaning in Organizations*. London: Palgrave Macmillan.

Mahmoudsalehi, Mehdi, Roya Moradkhannejad and Khalil Safari (2012) 'How Knowledge Management is Affected by Organizational Structure', *The Learning Organization*, 19/6, pp. 518–528.

March, James G. (1971) 'The Technology of Foolishness', *Civilokonomen*, 18/4, pp. 4–12.

March, James G. (1991) 'Exploration and Exploitation in Organizational Learning', *Organization Science*, 2/1, pp. 71–87.

Marriott, Neil, Howard Mellett and Louise Macniven (2011) 'Loose Coupling in Asset Management Systems in the NHS', *Management Accounting Research*, 22/3, pp. 198–208.

Martin, Randy (2002) *Financialization of Daily Life*. Philadelphia: Temple University Press.

Maturana, Humberto R. and Francisco J. Varela (1980) *Autopoiesis and Cognition: The realization of the living*. Holland: Reidel.

Mendell, Henry (1987) 'Topoi on Topos: The development of Aristotle's concept of place', *Phronesis*, 32/2, pp. 206–231.

Merton, Robert K. (1968) *Social Theory and Social Structure*. New York: The Free Press.

Merton, Robert K. and Elinor Barber (2004) *The Travels and Adventures of Serendipity: A study in sociological semantics and the sociology of science*. Princeton: Princeton University Press.

Meštrović Gallery (2013) *Meštrović Gallery, Split*. Accessed 10.05.2013 at www.mdc.hr/mestrovic/galerija/index-en.htm.

Mills, C. Wright (1959) *The Sociological Imagination*. London: Oxford University Press.

Minton, Ann (2009) *Ground Control: Fear and happiness in the twenty-first century city*. London: Penguin.

Mintzberg, Henry (1976) 'Planning on the Left Side and Managing on the Right', *Harvard Business Review*, 54/4, pp. 49–58.

Mintzberg, Henry (1983) *Structures in Fives: Designing effective organizations*. Englewood Cliffs, NJ: Prentice Hall.

Mintzberg, Henry (1999) 'Managing Quietly', *Leader to Leader*, 12/1, pp. 24–30.

Mir, Raz and Ali Mir (2002) 'The Organizational Imagination: From paradigm wars to praxis', *Organizational Research Methods*, 5/1, pp. 105–125.

MoMa (2013) *Pablo Picasso: Three Musicians*. Accessed 1.05.2013 at www.moma.org/collection/object.php?object_id=78630.

Monks, Claire P., Peter K. Smith, Paul Naylor, Christine Barter, Jane L. Ireland and Iain Coyne (2009) 'Bullying in Different Contexts: Commonalities, differences and the role of theory', *Aggression and Violent Behavior*, 14/2, pp. 146–156.

Moodysson, Lukas (2000) *Together (Tillsammans)*. Sonet Film.

Moore, Rowan (2011) 'Sagrada Familia: Gaudí's cathedral is nearly done, but would he have liked it?', *Guardian*. Accessed 8.05.2013 at www.guardian.co.uk/artanddesign/2011/apr/24/gaudi-sagrada-familia-rowan-moore.

Morgan, Gareth (1993) *Imaginization: New mindsets for seeing, organizing and managing*. Thousand Oaks, CA: Sage.

Morgan, Gareth (2006) *Images of Organization*. Thousand Oaks, CA: Sage.

Morgenstern, Janusz (1960) *Do widzenia, do jutra! (Goodbye, See You Tomorrow)*. Warszawa: Studio Filmowe Kadr.

Mourier, Pierre (2001) 'Velocity Management: Creating organizational instinct', *Strategy & Leadership*, 29/2, pp. 24–28.

Moxnes, Paul (2013) 'The Hero's Dream and Other Primordial Patterns of Imagery: Archetypal influences on organisational fantasies and ideations', *Journal of Organizational Change Management*, 26/4, pp. 638–653.

Museums Sheffield (2013) *Ruskin Collection*. Accessed 27.04.2013 at www.museumssheffield.org.uk/collections/ruskin-collection.

Nilson, Henrietta (2009) *Henriettas collage: Kreativa kvinnor i familjeföretag*. Vaxjö: Drivkraft.

Northrop, F.S.C. (1946) 'Leibniz's Theory of Space', *Journal of the History of Ideas*, 7/4, Leibniz Tercentenary Issue, pp. 422–446.

O'Mahony, John (2002) 'The Enigma of Werner H.', *Guardian*. Accessed 7.05.2013 at www.guardian.co.uk/film/2002/mar/30/books.guardianreview.

Obłój, Krzysztof (1986) *Zarządzanie: Ujęcie praktyczne*. Warszawa: PWE.

Obłój, Krzysztof (2010) *Pasja and dyscyplina strategii*. Warszawa: Poltext.

Olczak-Ronikier, J. (2011) *Korczak: Próba biografii*. Warszawa: WAB.

Opdebeeck, Hendrik and André Habisch (2011) 'Compassion: Chinese and western perspectives on practical wisdom in management', *Journal of Management Development*, 30/7–8, pp. 778–788.

Open Culture (2013) 'Jimmy Page Tells the Story of *Kashmir*'. Accessed 29.04.2013 at www.openculture.com/2011/09/jimmy_page_tells_the_story_of_kashmir.html.

Orton, J. Douglas and Karl E. Weick (1990) 'Loosely Coupled Systems: A reconceptualization', *Academy of Management Review*, 15/2, pp. 203–223.

Ossowska, Maria (2000) *Etos rycerski i jego odmiany*. Warszawa: PWN.

Pastakia, Astad (1998) 'Grassroot Entrepreneurs: Change agents for a sustainable society', *Journal of Organizational Change Management*, 11/2, pp. 157–173.

PBS (2008) *Homoseksualiści dyskryminowani?* Warszawa: PBS DGA.

Pelzer, Peter (2001) 'Dead Man – the encounter with an unknown past', *Journal of Organizational Change Management*, 15/1, pp. 48–62.

Pfeffer, Jeffrey (2013) 'Does it Matter if B-schools Produce Narcissists?', *Bloomberg Businessweek*. Accessed 11.02.2013 www.businessweek.com/articles/2013–01–15/does-it-matter-if-b-schools-produce-narcissists.

Piątkowski, Przemysław (2007) 'The Spiritual Status of Work in Opus Dei', *Journal of Management, Spirituality & Religion*, 4/4, pp. 418–431.

Plato (1999) *The Apology*. Transl. Benjamin Jowett, Project Gutenberg. Accessed 15.03.2010 at www.gutenberg.org/etext/1656.

Plato (2007) *The Republic*. Transl. H.D.P. Lee and Desmond Lee. London: Penguin.

Plato (2008) *Symposium*. Transl. Benjamin Jowett, Project Gutenberg. Accessed 25.02.2013 at www.gutenberg.org/files/1600/1600-h/1600-h.htm.

Pratt, Michael (2000) 'Building an Ideological Fortress: The role of spirituality, encapsulation and sensemaking', *Studies in Cultures, Organizations and Societies*, 6/1, pp. 35–69.

Purser, Ronald E. and Steven Cabana (1998) *The Self-Managing Organization: How leading companies are transforming the work of teams for real impact*. New York: The Free Press.

Rämö, Hans (1999) 'An Aristotelian Human Time-Space Manifold: From *chronochora* to *kairotopos*', *Time & Society*, 8/2, pp. 309–328.

Rämö, Hans (2002) 'Doing Right Things and Doing the Right Things', *International Journal of Project Management*, 20/7, pp. 569–574.

Rämö, Hans (2004) 'Spatio-temporal Notions and Organized Environmental Issues: An axiology of action', *Organization*, 11/6, pp. 849–872.

Rhodes, Carl, Alison Pullen and Stewart R. Clegg (2010) '"If I Should Fall from Grace...": Stories of change and organizational ethics', *Journal of Business Ethics*, 91/4, pp. 535–551.

Ricoeur, Paul (1992) *Oneself as Another*. Chicago: University of Chicago Press.

Ritzer, George (1996) *The MacDonaldization of Society*. London: Pine Forge Press.

Roark, Tony (2011) *Aristotle on Time: A study of the* Physics. Cambridge: Cambridge University Press.

Rogiński, Szymon (2009) *Projekt UFO (The UFO Project)*. Accessed 30.04.2013 at www.szymonroginski.com/.

Rokeach, Milton (1954) 'The Nature and Meaning of Dogmatism', *Psychological Review*, 61/3, pp. 194–201.

Ronny Hallberg (2010) Accessed 19.04.2010 at www.bryggeriet.org/2010/05/minnesstund-for-ronny-hallberg/.

Rousseau, Jean Jacques (2007) *Emile*. Teddington: The Echo Library.

Rumi (2000) *A Spiritual Journey*, ed. Juliet Mabey. Oxford: Oneworld.

Ruskin, John (2012) *Unto this Last: Four essays on the first principles of political economy*. Hong Kong: Forgotten Books.

Ryland, Elisabeth (2000) 'Gaia Rising: A Jungian view at environmental consciousness and sustainable organization', *Organization & Environment*, 13/4, pp. 381–402.

Rynes, Sara L., Jean M. Bartunek, Jane E. Dutton and Joshua D. Margolis (2012) 'Care and Compassion Through an Organizational Lens: Opening up new possibilities: Introduction to Special Topic Forum', *Academy of Management Review*, 37/4, pp. 503–523.

Sadler-Smith, Eugene and Lisa A. Burke (2007) 'Fostering Intuition in Management Education: Activities and resources', *Journal of Management Education*, 33/2, pp. 239–262.

Saint Teresa of Avila (2007) *Devotions, Prayers and Living Wisdom*, ed. Mirabai Starr. Boulder, CO: Sounds True.

Sarason, Yolanda (1995) 'A Model of Organizational Transformation: The incorporation of organizational identity into a structuration network', *Academy of Management Best Papers Proceedings*, pp. 47–51, DOI: 10.5465/AMBPP.1995.17536267.

Sarasvathy, Saras D. (2008) *Effectuation: Elements of entrepreneurial expertise*. Cheltenham; Northampton: Edward Elgar.

Schaltegger, Stefan (2002) 'A Framework for Ecopreneurship: Leading bioneers and environmental managers to ecopreneurship', *Greener Management International*, 38/2, pp. 45–58.

Schaper, Michael (2005) 'Understanding the Green Entrepreneur', in: Michael Schaper (ed.) *Making Ecopreneurs: Developing sustainable entrepreneurship*, Aldershot: Ashgate, pp. 3–12.

Schorske, Carl E. (1968) 'Professional Ethos and Public Crisis: A historian's reflections', *Modern Language Association*, 4/1, pp. 979–984.

Schwartz, Howard (1990) *Narcissistic Processes and Corporate Decay: The theory of the organizational ideal*. New York: New York University Press.

Seneca (1917–1925) *Epistles, Vol 1*. Transl. Richard M. Gummere. Cambridge, MA: Harvard University Press. Accessed 10.03.2013 at www.stoics.com/seneca_epistles_book_1.html#%E2%80%98I1.

Senge, Peter (2006) *The Fifth Discipline: The art and practice of the learning organization*. London: Random House.

Sennett, Richard (1998) *The Corrosion of Character: The personal consequences of work in the new capitalism*. New York: Norton.

Sennett, Richard (2006) *The Culture of the New Capitalism*. New Haven, CT: Yale University.

Sennett, Richard (2012) *Together: The rituals, pleasures, and politics of cooperation*. New Haven, CT: Yale University Press.

Sexton, Carol (1994) 'Self-Managed Work Teams: TQM technology at the employee level', *Journal of Organizational Change Management*, 7/2, pp. 45–52.

Shrivastava, Paul and Stuart Hart (1992) 'Greening organizations 2000', *International Journal of Public Administration*, 17/3–4, pp. 607–635.

Sievers, Burkard (2000) 'Competition as War: Towards a socio-analysis of war in and among corporations', *Socio-Analysis*, 2/1, pp. 1–27.

Sikka, Prem (2010) 'Smoke and Mirrors: Corporate social responsibility and tax avoidance', *Accounting Forum*, 34/3–4, pp. 153–168.

Silver, Whendee L., Sandra Brown, Fred N. Scatena and John J. Ewel (2001) 'A History of the Ecological Sciences: Early Greek origins', *Bulletin of the Ecological Society of America*, 82/1, pp. 93–97.

Simon, Herbert (1987) 'Making Management Decisions: The role of intuition and emotion', *Academy of Management Executive*, 1/1, pp. 57–64.

Singer, Victoria (1999) *Entrepreneurial Training for the Unemployed: Lessons from the field*. New York: Garland.

Skystone Foundation (2010) *James Turrell: Roden Crater*. Accessed 2.05.2013 at http://roden-crater.com/james.

Smith, Adam (1799) *Essays on Philosophical Subjects*. Basildon: James Decker.

Smith, Adam (2010) *The Theory of Moral Sentiments*. London: Penguin.

Smith, Edwin (2003) 'Ethos, Habitus and Situation for Learning: An ecology', *British Journal of Sociology of Education*, 24/4, pp. 463–470.

Snell, Robin S. (2000) 'Studying Moral Ethos Using and Adapted Kolbergian Model', *Organization Studies*, 21/1, pp. 267–295.

Sonenshein, Scott (2007) 'The Role of Construction, Intuition, and Justification in Responding to Ethical Issues at Work: The sensemaking-intuition model', *Academy of Management Review*, 32/4, pp. 1022–1040.

Spelthann, Volker and Axel Haunschild (2011) 'Organizational Creativity in Heterarchies: The case of VFX production', *Creativity and Innovation Management*, 20/2, pp. 100–107.

Srinivasan, M.S. (2012) 'Igniting Innovation: A holistic approach', *XIMB Journal of Management*, 9/1, pp. 135–144.

Stipančić, Branka and Ellen Elias-Bursać (1990) 'Ivan Meštrović's Melancholic Art Deco', *The Journal of Decorative and Propaganda Arts*, 17, pp. 54–59.

Stogdill, R.M. (1974) *Handbook of Leadership: A survey of the literature*. New York: Free Press.

Sun-Tzu (2008) *The Art of War*. London: Penguin.

Svensson, Göran, Greg Wood, Jang Singh and Michael Callaghan (2009) 'A Cross-cultural Construct of the Ethos of the Corporate Code of Ethics: Australia, Canada and Sweden', *Business Ethics: A European Review*, 18/3, pp. 253–267.

Szpilman, Władysław (2000) *Pianista*. Kraków: Znak.

Taylor, Frederick (1911) *Principles of Scientific Management*. Accessed 12.03.2013 at www.marxists.org/reference/subject/economics/taylor/principles/ch01.htm.

Taylor, Kathleen (2002) 'Is Imagination More Important than Knowledge? Einstein', *Times Higher Education*. Accessed 11.02.2013 at www.timeshighereducation.co.uk/story.asp?storycode=172613.

Tiamat (1994) *Wildhoney*. Century Media.

Timmermann, Jens (2007) *Kant's Groundwork of the Metaphysics of Morals: A commentary*. Cambridge: Cambridge University Press.

Tosey, Paul, Max Visser and Mark N.K. Saunders (2011) 'The Origins and Conceptualizations of "Triple-Loop" Learning: A critical review', *Management Learning*, 43/3, pp. 291–307.

Tranströmer, Thomas (2006) *The Great Enigma: New collected poems*. Transl. Robin Fulton. New York: New Direction Books.

Tranströmer, Thomas (2011) *Haiku Poems*. Trans. Patty Crane. Accessed 2.05.2013 at www.blackbird.vcu.edu/v10n1/poetry/crane_p/014pc_page.shtml.

Tsoukas, Haridimos and Robert Chia (2002) 'On Organizational Becoming: Rethinking organizational change', *Organization Science*, 13/5, pp. 567–582.

Tuan, Yi-Fu (1977) *Space and Place: The perspective of experience*. Minneapolis: University of Minnesota Press.

UNESCO (2013a) *Works of Antoni Gaudí*. Accessed 8.05.2013 at http://whc.unesco.org/en/list/320.

UNESCO (2013b) *Millenary Benedictine Abbey of Pannonhalma and its Natural Environment*. Accessed 10.05.2013 at http://whc.unesco.org/en/list/758.

Valli, Eric (1999) *Himalaya – l'enfance d'un chef*. Kino International.

Valli, Eric. (2001) 'Introduction', in: Debra Kellner (ed.) *Himalaya*. New York: Harry N. Abrams, pp. 8–9.

Viola, Bill (2002) *Going Forth by Day*, Deutsche Guggenheim Berlin. Accessed 7.05.2013 at http://pastexhibitions.guggenheim.org/viola/index.html.

Visser, Max (2007) 'Deutero-learning in Organizations: A review and reformulation', *Academy of Management Review*, 32/2, pp. 659–667.

Vitruvius (2009) *On Architecture*. Transl. Robert Tavernor and Richard Schofield. London: Penguin.

Vogus, Timothy J. and Kathleen M. Sutcliffe (2012) 'Organizational Mindfulness and Mindful Organizing: A reconciliation and path forward', *Academy of Management Learning & Education*, 2/4, pp. 722–735.

Wang, Long and Keith Murnighan (2011) 'On Greed', *The Academy of Management Annals*, 5/1, pp. 279–316.

Wang, Long, Deepak Malhotra and Keith Murnighan (2013) 'Economics Educations and Greed', *Academy of Management Learning and Education*, 10/4, pp. 643–660.

Watkins, Ceri (2005) 'Representations of Space, Spatial Practices and Spaces of Representation: An application of Lefebvre's spatial triad', *Culture and Organization*, 11/3, pp. 209–220.

Watson, Tony J. (2003) 'Ethical Choice in Managerial Work: The scope for moral choices in an ethically irrational world', *Human Relations*, 56/2, pp. 167–185.

Weber, Max (1992) *Economy and Society*, ed. G. Roth and C. Wittich. Berkeley: University of California Press.

Weber, Max (2012) *The Protestant Ethic and the Spirit of Capitalism*. Oxon.: Routledge.

Weick, Karl (1979) *The Social Psychology of Organizing*. Reading, MA: Addison-Wesley.

Weick, Karl E. (1989) 'Theory Construction as Disciplined Imagination', *Academy of Management Review*, 14, pp. 516–531.

Weick, Karl, E. (1995) *Sensemaking in Organizations*, Thousand Oaks, CA: Sage.

Weick, Karl E. (1998) 'Improvisation as a Mindset for Organizational Analysis', *Organization Science*, 9/5, pp. 543–555.

Weick, Karl E. (2001) *Making Sense of Organization*. Oxford: Blackwell.

Weick, Karl E. (2002) 'Puzzles in Organizational Learning: An exercise in disciplined imagination', *British Journal of Management*, 13, pp. S7–S15.

Weick, Karl E. (2003) 'Organizational Design and the Gehry Experience', *Journal of Management Inquiry*, 12/1, pp. 93–97.

Weick, Karl E. (2005) 'Organizing and Failures of Imagination', *International Public Management Journal*, 8/3, pp. 425–438.

Weick, Karl E. (2006) 'The Role of Imagination in the Organizing of Knowledge', *European Journal of Information Systems*, 15, pp. 446–452.

Weiskopf, Richard and Hugh Willmott (2013) 'Ethics as Critical Practice: The "Pentagon Papers", deciding responsibility, truth-telling, and the unsettling of organizational morality', *Organization Studies*, 34/4, pp. 469–449.

Wenders, Wim (1987) *Wings of Desire*. Road Movies Filmproduktion-Westdeutscher Runtfunk.

Whipp, Richard, Barbara Adam and Ida Sabelis (eds) *Making Time: Time and management in modern organizations*. Oxford: Oxford University Press.

Willmott, Hugh (1981) 'The Structuring of Organizational Structure: A note', *Administrative Science Quarterly*, 26/3, pp. 470–474.

Wise, Sharon (2012) 'Working to Think Otherwise: Tracing *Ethos* in information professionals' reflections on learning and practice', *Australian Academic & Research Libraries*, 43/3, pp. 169–188.

Wright, Susan (1994) 'Culture in Anthropology and Organizational Studies', in: Susan Wright (ed.) *Anthropology of Organizations*. London: Routledge, pp. 1–31.

Xinzhong, Yao (2000) *An Introduction to Confucianism*. Cambridge: Cambridge University Press.

Yanow, Dvora (1995) 'Built Space as Story: The policy stories that buildings tell', *Policy Studies Journal*, 23/3, pp. 407–422.

Zarca, Bernard (2009) 'L'ethos professionnel de mathématiciens', *Revue française de sociologie*, 50/2, pp. 251–384.

Zerbst, Rainer (2005) *Antoni Gaudí i Cornet – une vie en architecture*. Köln: Taschen.

Zimmer, Kirstin (2002) 'Supply Chain Coordination with Uncertain Just-in-time Delivery', *International Journal of Production Economics*, 77/1, pp. 1–15.

INDEX